Advance Praise for Four Days With Kenny Tedford

"Kenny is definitely a hero that everyone needs. Please have sequel! This book will change your life as it did mine."
~ **Miles Barbee**, acclaimed Broadway and screen Deaf actor and star of *The Silent Natural*

"A touching and sensitively crafted account of a differently-abled and extraordinarily gifted storyteller. This collaborative oral autobiography is a fine piece of work, and it is a pleasure to spend days in its company."
~ **Joseph Sobol, Ph.D.**, Director, George Ewart Evans Centre for Storytelling, University of South Wales

"Authentic, compelling and poignant...profound life lessons from an unlikely and extraordinary person!"
~ **Sandy Cohen**, Tennessee Director of the Library Services for the Deaf & Hard of Hearing

"You cannot help but see how a simple thing in life can be both magnifying and amusing...whenever you have a tough day, simply think about Kenny...he will nudge your conscience with a cornucopia of his personal and humorous stories."
~ **Peter Cook**, internationally renowned Deaf performing artist

"In a current society where labels seem to carry a lot of weight, it is enlightening to see how one man disregards the labels assigned to him by others (including his family and friends). On his journey to success, Kenny Tedford has triumphed by focusing on his strengths and abilities. A must read for anyone wanting to learn how to see the person (and not the label)."
~ **Libby Tipton**, certified sign language interpreter, and president, Jonesborough Storytellers Guild

FOUR DAYS WITH KENNY TEDFORD

LIFE THROUGH THE EYES OF A CHILD TRAPPED IN A PARTIALLY BLIND & DEAF MAN'S BODY

PAUL SMITH & KENNETH "KENNY" LEE TEDFORD, JR.

Behler
PUBLICATIONS
USA

Behler Publications

Four Days With Kenny Tedford
A Behler Publications Book

Library of Congress Cataloging-in-Publication Data
Names: Smith, Paul, 1967 July 3- author. | Tedford, Kenny (Kenneth Lee),
    Jr., author.
Title: Four days with Kenny Tedford : life through the eyes of a child
    trapped in a partially blind & deaf man's body / by Paul Smith and
    Kenneth "Kenny" Lee Tedford, Jr.
Description: USA : Behler Publications, [2020] | Summary: "Kenny Tedford is   a charming combination of
Helen Keller and Forrest Gump that includes   deafness, blindness, an inability to speak clearly until the age
of ten,   and mental challenges that give him the same child-like innocence that
    made Gump so lovable. Despite his cognitive impairment, Kenny is a   masterful storyteller; he is one of
only two deaf people in the world   with a master's degree in storytelling, which he earned at the age of
fifty-five, almost half a century after being told by teachers and
    psychologists that he would never complete the third grade, and never   work in any field other than menial
labor"-- Provided by publisher.
Identifiers: LCCN 2019012057 (print) | LCCN 2019980100 (ebook) | ISBN
    9781941887028 (paperback) | ISBN 1941887023 (paperback) | ISBN
    9781941887035 (ebook) | ISBN 1941887031 (ebook)
Subjects: LCSH: Tedford, Kenny (Kenneth Lee), Jr. | Deaf--United
    States--Biography. | Deafblind people--United States--Biography. |
    People with disabilities--United States--Biography. |
    Storytellers--United States--Biography.
Classification: LCC HV2534.T33 A3 2020 (print) | LCC HV2534.T33 (ebook) |
    DDC 362.4/1092 [B]--dc23
LC record available at https://lccn.loc.gov/2019012057
LC ebook record available at https://lccn.loc.gov/2019980100

FIRST PRINTING
ISBN 13: 9781941887028
e-book ISBN 9781941887035

Published by Behler Publications, LLC, USA
www.behlerpublications.com
Manufactured in the United States of America

To my wife, Lisa,
for her unwavering love and support
as I follow my dreams.
~ Paul Smith

To my mom and dad,
for treating me like a son, not a disabled son.

And to disabled people everywhere.
I hope the story of my journey helps you with yours.
~ Kenny Lee Tedford, Jr.

Table of Contents

Acknowledgments

We'd first like to thank all the wonderful people in Kenny's life who helped make him who he is today. Most of your names are already mentioned in the book, so we won't repeat them here. But you know who you are. Without you, there wouldn't be a story to tell.

Thanks to our editor at Behler Publications, Lynn Price, for seeing even more in this project than we did, and pushing us to make it happen. Thanks to our literary agent, Maryann Karinch, as well as Lisa Smith, Ben Smith, Jon Christiansen, and James Kevin for reviewing early manuscripts and providing wonderful guidance.

We'd also like to thank all the other people who contributed to the making of this book in some way, by contributing their time, talent, or even their home where we met for our interviews. That list includes David Greene, Judy Greene, Debbie Gregg, Joe Honeycutt, Valerie Menard, Carol and Paul Meyer, Jeff Meyer, Rita Needham, Sean Read, and Bryan and Danielle Upshaw.

Lastly, we'd like to extend a special thank you to the National Storytelling Network and David Hutchens for inviting us both to speak at the National Storytelling Conference in 2012, where we first met. The rest, as they say, is history.

Meeting Kenny

I was sitting in the front row waiting for the next performance to start when I saw him. He was a large man. Sixty-ish. With grey hair encircling a bald head, and glasses thick enough to start a fire on a sunny day.

He walked slowly and deliberately, with a slight list to one side. He made his way down the aisle and sat in the chair next to me.

Following quickly behind him was a twenty-something man with dark hair. The young man pulled one of the empty chairs out of the row, turned it around backwards, placed it directly in front of the older man, and sat down with his back to the stage.

I was intrigued, to say the least.

A few minutes later, the next speaker walked on stage and started her performance. The young man, who'd been staring at the older man, silent and motionless since sitting down, suddenly sprang into action. He lifted his hands in front of his chest and began a flurry of cryptic motions that identified him immediately as a sign language interpreter, and the older man as deaf.

I thought that was pretty ballsy, a deaf guy at a three-day storytelling festival. [1]

I knew immediately I wanted to meet him. So at the next break, I introduced myself. We exchanged a few pleasantries,

---

[1] June 28, 2012, at the National Storytelling Conference in Covington, Kentucky.

enough to know that he was an affable sort of guy. But we both had to go to our next set of workshops.

An hour later, I was walking with a tray of food, looking for an empty table, and that same affable fellow walked up to me and asked if I wanted to have lunch with him. I quickly accepted.

We sat at a table by ourselves, his interpreter having been given time off for lunch.

For the next hour, I listened to Kenny Tedford tell his story.

I listened while he spoke with impressive diction, but with the muted tones of a deaf person. And he read my lips, seemingly, as easily as I spoke with them.

But, underneath the telltale tone of his voice, I noticed something else telling. His vocabulary and sentence structure were both charmingly juvenile. As his story unfolded, I started to understand why. His deafness turned out to be only one of many challenges life dealt Kenny Tedford. He was almost blind in one eye, and had poor vision in the other, partially paralyzed on his left side, unable to speak well until the age of ten, and had somewhat limited cognitive abilities, all of which were a result of brain damage suffered at birth. And as if that weren't enough, in the years since, he'd endured a string of near-fatal illnesses that should have left him dead many times over.

Despite it all, the man sitting in front of me seemed to be the most delightful individual one could ever meet. His temperament and outlook on life and humanity were unquestionably positive in a way I can only describe as childlike. In fact, he struck me as a remarkable combination of Helen Keller and Forrest Gump. Keller, of course, was deaf, blind, and mute. But she was a brilliant thinker and accomplished writer. The fictional Forrest Gump, on the other hand, was a model of physical health once he shook off the leg braces. But he suffered a diminished mental capacity that gave him his childlike charm.

Kenny Tedford, however, had both sets of challenges.

So there I sat, watching this somewhat goofy-looking, old, bald, roly-poly man, smiling at me with enormously distorted bug eyes through his impossibly thick glasses, telling me almost unbelievable stories in the words of a child, but with the voice of a grown man, who'd never properly heard the sound of his own voice.

I was mesmerized.

The hour ended way too quickly. I'd only scratched the surface of Kenny's life. But it was enough to be fascinated by what I'd heard, and to be frustrated that I didn't know more.

I wondered how a man in his circumstances could have such a positive disposition. *Why isn't he bitter at life for dealing him such a crappy hand,* I wondered. I was pretty sure I would be.

I had so many questions. But it was time for the next session. My chance encounter was over. I didn't know if or when I would ever see or speak to Kenny Tedford again. But what I did know was that I felt strangely blessed having met him.

The following year turned out to be one of the most important turning points in my life, and unquestionably, the single most important in my work.

I was in my mid-forties and two decades into a successful, yet, uninspiring corporate career. I was a walking cliché of the "Decade of Greed" that was the 1980s. Not quite Gordon Gekko, but perhaps his tamer, less ambitious younger brother: business undergraduate degree, two years as a consultant, Ivy League MBA from the same school that produced junk-bond billionaire Michael Milken and real-estate mogul turned President Donald Trump, followed by a constant march up the corporate ladder at a Fortune 50 company.

Don't get me wrong. I liked my job. But I was in a place that I think most people find themselves at work. They love a small part of their job, the part that made them choose that career to begin with. They hate a small part of their job, office politics or filling out their expense report. And, in the middle, is the large swath of responsibilities they like well enough, but nothing they'd do without getting paid for. Not bad work, in other words, just nothing that makes you jump out of bed in the morning.

I wanted a career filled with only that first part, the part I loved. And after fifteen or so years, I finally figured out what that was. I loved the few days a year I got to deliver a keynote address at the division meeting, or teach a leadership class for the newly-promoted managers.

In short, I wanted to be a full-time speaker and trainer.

I loved the work.

I felt like I was better at doing that than I was my regular job.

And, as trite as it might sound, those were the days that I was convinced I was making a real difference in people's lives. After all, nobody ever stood up and applauded at the end of one of my staff meetings.

But most companies don't have full-time jobs like that. The only people who seemed to get to do that were people who'd written a bestselling book and got invited to speak and train for a different company every week.

So, that's what I'd spent the last two-and-a-half years working on, writing a book on a topic I was passionate about: the power of storytelling as a leadership tool.

And along the way I learned something important about myself. I learned that I love writing! And that's important, because it turns out there are generally two types of people in that new career I wanted: People who love being on stage, but hate writing; and people who love writing, but are terrified of public speaking. Fortunately, I found I loved both. I'd definitely found my calling.

My first book[2] was published in August of that year, two months after I met Kenny Tedford at the National Storytelling Conference.

I waited to see what would happen.

Within a few weeks, the book went into its second printing, and then a third. It even started showing up on a few bestseller lists.

I was ecstatic! But the phone wasn't ringing yet.

Then, after about six months and a couple of more print runs, I got my first request to speak at a corporate event. I took a vacation day from my company and went.

After a few more weeks, I got another request. And then another.

Within three months I'd spent all of my vacation time for the year attending speaking engagements. About the same time I'd gotten an offer from my publisher to write another book.

My plan was working! I was absolutely thrilled!

But, how long would it last? There was just no guarantee. Plus, being an author and speaker comes with no regular monthly salary. No benefits. No retirement plan.

And there I was, too young to retire, and the only breadwinner in a family with two boys to put through college.

I spent the next several weeks struggling with the decision. I eventually got to the point that quitting my cushy corporate job made sense in every logical way except for one; I just didn't have the courage to go through with it.

I figured I wasn't too old to benefit from someone older and wiser. So I decided to ask my dad for advice. But at eighty years old, he was hard of hearing. And even with his hearing aids, phone calls could be frustrating, and therefore, short. So I wrote him a letter and asked him what I should do.

---

[2] *Lead with a Story: A Guide to Crafting Business Narratives that Captivate, Convince, and Inspire*, by Paul Smith.

I assumed he'd write back and tell me one of two things. He'd either say, "You can do it, son, I've got faith in you. Follow your dreams." Or, he'd say, "Are you nuts? Just keep your head down for the next few years till you can retire comfortably. Then go play around with this writing and speaking stuff."

But he didn't tell me either of those things. In fact, he didn't really give me advice at all. He just told me a story about himself that I'd never heard before, and neither had any of my siblings.

His letter explained that when he was in the first grade, he knew exactly what he wanted to do when he grew up. He wanted to be a singer, like Frank Sinatra, Bing Crosby, or Tony Bennett.

Then, about the second or third week of school, his teacher asked the class if any of them had any special talents, like dancing or magic tricks. Well, apparently my dad raised his hand and announced that he could sing! This, despite the fact that he'd never sung in front of anyone other than his mom in the kitchen. Apparently, she listened to the radio while she cooked. And since he'd been listening and singing along with her, he fancied himself something of a crooner.

So the teacher did what any self-respecting teacher would do. She invited young Bobby Smith to stand up and sing a song.

And he did! He stood up and belted out his favorite song right there, acapella, in front of the entire class. He said, "I still remember the song. It was 'I Don't Want to Set the World on Fire' by the Ink Spots."

Well, apparently, he nailed it. He got all the words and melody just right. When he was finished, the teacher and the students stood up and applauded him. He'd gotten a standing ovation on his first public performance. And he said, "That's when I knew what I was destined to do with my life."

His letter went on to say, "Unfortunately, that turned out to not just be the first time I ever sang in front of an audience. It turned out to be the last time I ever sang in front of an audience."

Life had gotten in the way. School. Jobs. Marriage. Kids. Despite that, he admitted that the real reason was that he just never had the courage to go through with it. "One day," he said, "you'll wake up and be eighty years old like me, and it'll be too late."

And as if that weren't enough, and it certainly was, he closed the letter with these words:

"I'd love to see you pursue your dream. But that doesn't mean in *your* lifetime, son, that means in *mine*. Love, Dad"

And that's when everything stopped.

The sound of the television in the background. The squabbling conversation between my kids in the next room. The noise from cars driving by the house. The uncomfortable spot in the chair I was sitting in. The nagging thought of the lingering project I hadn't yet completed at work.

All. Gone.

The only thing I could feel or hear was my heart, which was now beating out of my chest.

Did he say what I think he just said?

Yes, he did.

My father had laid down the gauntlet in front of me and challenged me to pick it up. Not sometime in the future, years down the road. But right now!

My dream was no longer just my dream. It was now my father's dream, too. At this point, I thought, he'll never achieve his dream of being a professional singer. But through me, if I had the courage to go through with it, he could enjoy the closure he never had with his own dream.

Two days later, I walked into my boss's office and I resigned from a twenty-year career to pursue my dream.

The next morning, with a renewed sense of courage and purpose, I started the planning for my next book. But this one wouldn't be another business book. Of course, if I was going to make a successful speaking career out of this, I'd definitely need to write other business books.

But not yet.

I wanted this book to be about purpose. If making a difference in people's lives was really one of the reasons I made this change, then I should put my money, and my time, where my mouth was. Instead of capturing leadership lessons in the form of stories, I wanted this book to capture life lessons. I wanted to write an entire book filled with incredible stories of people who'd faced unusual challenges and overcome them. People who learned remarkable life lessons, probably the hard way. I wanted to produce a book that parents could use to teach their kids character traits like creativity, curiosity, kindness, integrity, self-reliance, hard work and struggles, fairness, humility, friendship, a positive mental attitude, and respect for others.[3]

I knew from experience with my first book I'd probably need to interview a hundred fascinating people to find enough to fill the book. But where to start?

It didn't take me long to decide.

The first call I made was to Kenny Tedford.

Two weeks later, Kenny and I had our interview, which we conducted over Skype so he could read my lips. It was a little awkward at first. But once I learned to keep my hands and my coffee mug away from my mouth, it worked out pretty smoothly.

---

[3] *Parenting with a Story: Real-Life Lessons in Character for Parents and Children to Share*, by Paul Smith.

I was only looking for one short, compelling story from each person to fill a page or two of the book, so I'd only need about an hour for the interview. Just enough time to hear a few stories and pick the best one. And my plan was to make a recording, so I wouldn't have to slow the flow of the conversation for my note taking to keep up.

Having had my fascinating lunchtime conversation with Kenny a year earlier, I already had a pretty good idea of the kind of questions to ask to get at the handful of stories I was most interested in hearing. And Kenny did a masterful job of telling them. They were even more compelling and engaging than I remembered. Or, maybe he just had more time to tell them properly.

Either way, at precisely 39 minutes into the conversation, I asked Kenny, "Have you ever written any of these stories down?"

He said that he'd been asked that question a lot. Apparently, people at his performances request books or transcripts or videos of his stories so they can relive them.

"But," he said, "I can't write very well."

Apparently written language is one of the more affected areas of his cognitive disability. He can carry on a fairly normal verbal conversation, as long as he can read your lips. And the stories he tells on stage are captivating. But his attempts to turn those stories, or any complex ideas, really, into the written word always seem to fail.

In fact, he told me that people often marvel at the difference between his verbal and written communication. He said, "People tell me I'm great to talk to. But then they read an email I wrote, and they say, 'I don't have a clue what you're saying. Let's just talk in person when I see you tomorrow.'"

An IQ test in his late 40s quantified that limitation. The psychologist who administered it was surprised to report

Kenny's scores were in the range of a typical 3rd to 5th grader when assessed with written answers to written questions. But in conversation, he would have put Kenny somewhat higher.

What I didn't know for sure -- and neither did Kenny -- was how much of his cognitive struggles were a result of real physiological brain damage, and how much were simply a result of the difficulties of learning when you're deaf. Apparently, it's not uncommon for deaf children to miss a lot of the regular classroom instruction that hearing children get during their formative years. And that especially impacts their verbal and language abilities. Kenny's belief has always been that he was affected by both. Not knowing how to know such a thing, I satisfied myself with that assumption as well.

And while all that certainly explained the reason why he'd never written his stories down, I still felt the same thing his audience members must have felt when he told them: Disappointment. He clearly has a lifetime of amazing stories. It seemed almost criminal that they were never written down.

I was only two weeks into my new life as an author, and I'd just signed a contract for a new book that would take up almost all of my time over the next year. But before I knew what was happening, I said something that probably surprised me as much as it surprised Kenny:

"I'll do it, Kenny. I'll write your book."

And so began our journey.

Chapter 1: Realizing I Was Different

Don't take it offensively, but you sound like a duck.

Those are the first words I remember hearing from Kenny Tedford when we started our interviews in September of 2013. The first thing we had to do was figure out how to communicate with each other. His hearing loss is in the 71 to 90 decibel range, what audiologists call "severe deafness." People with that level of hearing loss can usually benefit from hearing aids or cochlear implants, but often have to rely on lip reading and sign language.

The surprising thing about his hearing was that it wasn't simply a matter of volume. I always assumed that anyone who had some degree of deafness heard the same sounds as other people, but just quieter, or maybe not at all. But that's not the way it always works. Kenny's hearing isn't just weak. It's distorted, too, as he went on to explain . . .

Actually, you sound like a really quiet Donald Duck, talking with a mouth full of marbles. But I'm trying to pretend you're a duck that can talk.

It was a great analogy. I can imagine exactly what that would sound like. But I also found it amusing to imagine myself as a talking duck with a taste for marbles.

What that all meant was that even with his hearing aids and the amplified telephone speaker he has, it's difficult for him to understand anyone over the phone. Almost all of our conversations had to be in-person, or over a video call so he could read my lips.

And the first thing I asked him in that first meeting was to take me all the way back to the beginning.

I suppose my story started on September 17, 1953, in Memphis. That's the day my momma fell down a flight of steps in front of our house. Her name was Bessie Faye Tedford. Some people say it was raining and that's why she slipped. Other people say it was because she was drunk. Either way, she was seven months pregnant with me when it happened.

I was supposed to be born in November. But when Momma fell that day, the biblical cord got wrapped around my neck.

Did he just say, "biblical cord?" We were only thirty seconds into our first interview and I was already confused. Was I hearing him wrong because I wasn't used to listening to a deaf person talk? Was it a mispronunciation? Does he really think that's what it's called? Or maybe he's just pulling my leg and we'll both be laughing about this in another thirty seconds. I had no idea which was more likely. What I did know was that I'd completely missed the next several sentences out of his mouth trying to figure it out. If it weren't for the recording I was making, we'd have had to start over. Focus, Paul.

They say I couldn't get enough oxygen in my brain, so they had to get me out two months early. They called me a "blue baby." And they had to revive me during the delivery, twice. The doctors told my parents I'd have brain damage. And they didn't know if I would make it.

Well, obviously I lived. But I had to spend my first three months in a inkabator.

That last word prompted me to adjust my mental odds of the "biblical cord" reference slightly in favor of mispronunciation, which I found more endearing than a joke at my expense.

It was supposed to just be two months. But I was too weak, just an itty-bitty thing. I was my momma's seventh of nine children. When I grew up, I learned that seven is God's number. It's the perfect number. But I didn't know any of that yet.

While I was still in the hospital, they found out not getting oxygen also made me almost completely deaf, and legally blind in my left eye. And I had some paralysis on the left side of my body.

The doctor told my parents I would be "retarded" and probably never be able to speak. He said they should just put me away and focus on the other six children. Well, that made my daddy mad. Apparently, he was a proud man. Momma's first five kids were from another marriage. But I was only Daddy's second child, and his first son. So he wasn't about to give me away.

They say he got in the doctor's face and looked all mean and said, "I don't think I heard you right, doc. What'd you say about my boy?"

The doctor's eyes got really big like they do when you seen a ghost. Then he talked in a scaredy-cat voice. "I'm sorry. I, uh... I meant to say that you have a beautiful baby boy."

"That's what I thought you said." He knew I was gonna have a hard life. But he wanted to help me make the best of it, at least for as long as he could. My daddy's name is Kenneth Lee Tedford, and they named me after him, so my name is Kenneth Lee Tedford, Junior.

I guess that's how my story begins.

~ ~

Life is a series of short stories, one leaving off where the next one starts. But most of us don't have them named and memorized. Fortunately for me, Kenny had.

It was 10 o'clock in the morning on our first of four days of in-person interviews at my house. My wife had made a nice breakfast and we'd enjoyed a cup of tea on the patio before getting started. We spent our first few minutes deciding where to start. My eyes instantly focused on the story he called, "The Night I Lost My Manhood in the Haunted House." Of course I asked for that one first.

Wouldn't you?

My request sent Kenny into a fit of genuine laughter.

Why does everyone always want to hear *that* story? I could have twenty stories, and everyone always goes, 'We wanna hear how you lost your manhood in the haunted house!'

"Of course, they do!" I said. "Who doesn't want to hear a good sex story?"

I said that not knowing if Kenny could understand me through his own belly laughs.

It was close to Halloween. A group of deaf friends of mine, Joe, John, and Crystal, decided to get together and go to a haunted cemetery and haunted house. They asked if I could come with them, and I said, "Sure! I love haunted things." So we all met up at the place. And it was awesome! It was this huge property, like a farm. And there were monsters behind the trees and spooky things everywhere. It was really decked out. And they had hot chocolate and popcorn. It was a beautiful Fall evening.

But it was really popular, so there was a long line we had to wait in. And while we waited, it got dark. We were talking to each other, mostly in sign language: "Are you scared? . . . Yeah, you scared?"

But I said, "Not me. I can handle this." I was acting like the big tough guy. Well, eventually it was our turn, and we got to go through the cemetery. There were grave markers everywhere, covered with leaves. And my deaf friends just walked right into the middle of the place. The deaf are suckers for stuff like this, because they can't hear anything sneak up on them. But I kind of stayed back a little bit, I figured something was gonna happen.

And sure enough, about that time, a monster jumped out from one of the graves. My friends started screaming and running away. A man that worked there started yelling at them to stop running, because it wasn't safe. But that's not gonna work with deaf people, so I had to go run after them to get 'em to stop.

Then we decided to just go on to the haunted house, because they'd gotten scared enough at the cemetery. When we got close enough, you could see monsters and ghosts in the windows when the lights would flash. My friends looked at me and asked me if I was getting scared now. I just said, "No. I'm not the one who ran out of the cemetery like a baby, remember?"

We got into the house and started walking down the hallway. It was dark, and there were spider webs everywhere. Really creepy. And I started feeling a little edgy. Maybe even a little scared.

Then we went into this room, it was a funeral parlor. It had a casket with a body in it. And if you've been in haunted houses as much as I have, you knew what was gonna happen. The body was gonna rise up. So there we were, three completely deaf people and me. Two of them to my left and one to my right. And we were all waiting for this body to rise up.

And that's when I heard it. And if I can hear something, it's got to be pretty loud. But I knew what it was immediately, because I had just seen this movie called *The Texas Chainsaw Massacre*. It was a chainsaw buzzing at full speed right behind us. The hearing people behind us screamed and all ran out of the room immediately. But the three deafs just kept signing to each other, talking about the dead body in the casket, how ugly it was, and wondering if it was gonna rise up.

One of the hallmarks of a good story is that the listener loses track of time. I was so engrossed in the story that I didn't realize how long I'd been listening. And as much I was enjoying this story, I was getting a little impatient. All this detail about the goings-on in the haunted house seemed like strange foreplay. Maybe it's a deaf thing, I thought. I decided I'd just have to be patient.

So the guy buzzes his chainsaw a few more times, but none of us even turned around. Finally, he says something really loud. I imagine it was something like, "Hey, I've got a chainsaw and I'm gonna cut you in half!"

Well I figured I'd help this guy out. I turned around and told him, "These three people are deaf."

And he says, "Oh, okay." He fires up his chainsaw again. But, you have to understand. His chainsaw engine is running and it's really loud. But the chain isn't actually moving, so it doesn't hurt anyone. He walks up behind them and rakes the chainsaw blade across the back of all of their legs in one quick motion. They turned around and saw a crazy man with a bloody chainsaw blade in his hand and their legs hurt and they jumped out of their skins! They turned around to run the other way, and right then is when the dead body in the casket jumped up in their faces. They weren't even done screaming about the chainsaw. I thought they were gonna have heart attacks right there.

Well, they all ran around the casket and out of the room with me chasing after them. And it was pretty dark in there. John managed to get out of the house. Crystal was running down the hallway right in front of me. And somehow Joe got behind me. He must have gotten lost in the hallways. And they were both screaming like crazy.

Seriously? I took another mental pause. Nobody in this story seemed any closer to getting laid than they did when it started. I felt like a teenage boy desperately flipping through a stolen Playboy Magazine to find a sufficiently naked picture.

We came to the last hallway to get out of the house. And it was so dark we were staying really close together. Well, it turns out they'd taken out the floor in that hallway and replaced it with a sponge pit.

When Crystal got to the spongy part of the floor, she fell down in it. I guess that's what was supposed to happen. And then, of course, I fell on top of her. And Joe fell on top of me. I tried to get up. But every time I got a few inches up, I fell back down. Joe was too heavy. I kept trying, but I kept falling back down. So Crystal started yelling and screaming and calling me names.

I don't think she knew it was me and Joe on top of her. It must have felt like one big huge heavy man that she didn't know. And to make it worse, it probably seemed like I was humping her on her butt. And so then she started kicking like mad! And she was kicking right where my jewels are, if you know what I mean. And she started kicking harder and harder, all while she was yelling louder and louder. And I'm screaming at her to stop. But she's deaf, stone deaf!

I started to realize while she was kicking me that I may never have babies in my life! I was losing my manhood right there on the floor of that haunted house. I could feel my jewels headed to the back of my butt!

And there it was. I laughed out loud at the absurdity of the situation in all its slapstick glory. But also, with a knowing and bittersweet realization at the innocent misdirection this entire story had been. I'd assumed "losing his manhood" was Kenny's child-like and awkward way of describing losing his virginity. Perhaps a combination

*of losing virginity and gaining manhood? Regardless, the result was that
for the last ten minutes I'd been waiting, and waiting, and WAITING to
hear about him having sex in a haunted house, only to find out the whole
damn story was just about him getting kicked in the balls.*

*I could tell he had no idea how misleading his story title was. It
would have been an impressively clever ruse had it been intentional. I
found his accidental execution even more charming.*

*As he continued the story, I wondered how long I could go
without explaining what had just happened. Or, if I should at all.*

But it wasn't over yet. Because while I was going up and
down trying to get out of this mess, and in pain trying to save
my jewels, Joe was bouncing up and down humping *me* on *my*
butt. So I started yelling at him, "Get off of me!" But he's stone
deaf too, and we're all face down in the dark, so nobody can see
anyone's lips.

Then I looked up to try to get some help. And standing
there looking down on us is John. And he's just laughing his
head off. In fact, several of the people who had just run out had
turned around and were watching us and laughing. So I yelled
up at them, "Don't just stand there! Get me out of this. I can't
stand it anymore!"

Finally, somebody flipped the light switch on and helped us
up. I thought, "Thank God this is over." But I couldn't even
stand up straight I was in so much pain. I just stood there bent
over holding my jewels. And Crystal stood up and turned
around and she started to slap me across the face! I reached up
just in time to stop her.

And as soon as she recognized me, her face looked terrified.
She said, "Oh my gosh, Kenny, I didn't know it was you! I
thought you were a stranger trying to do something awful to
me." Then Joe came out of the sponges, laughing with a smile on
his face. I'd just lost my manhood and almost had my face
slapped, and everyone else is laughing and smiling. Go figure.

I was in so much pain, it took a while to get home. I could barely walk. But I got there. I went straight to the bathroom and took all my clothes off to take a shower. I looked down, and it was all purple and blue! My jewels. That kind of made me sick to my stomach. And then when I was washing myself, and I got down a little bit below my belly button, I felt something strange. It was like little bumps or ridges. I looked down. And it was hard to make out. But there on my skin were three words that look like they'd been stamped on my skin backwards, "Just Do It." That woman had kicked me so hard with the back of her Nike tennis shoe, it left a mark!

Well, that threw me into another fit of laughter. "No, no, no, no, Kenny. No way."

I'm tellin' you, Paul, her shoes left a mark!

"On your penis?"

Nooooah, it's not on my Wally. Between my belly button and there. Everything else down there was too black and blue to see much else. But there it was.

My jewels hurt for four days. I even went to my doctor to make sure everything was okay. Of course, I had to tell him what happened. And I got about halfway into the story and he started cracking up! Can you believe it? It took me a lot of years before that story was funny to me. But this was the first time he'd ever heard it, and I'm in his office to make sure my parts are still gonna work and he can't stop laughing.

Well, I guess deaf people talk loud, because one of the nurses came into the room to listen to the story. And then another one. And another one. Pretty soon half the doctors and nurses were listening to the story, and I said, "Don't you all have patients to take care of?"

They said, "Nah, there's only two other people in here right now."

So I finished telling the story and my doctor looked at me and said, "Please tell me you're gonna tell that in a show."

I said, "No way! This is too personal."

He said, "You've got to tell it. It's funny!"

"Oh yeah, Doc. Well, it wasn't your jewels."

And that was the night I lost my manhood in the haunted house.

After another good laugh, I couldn't resist the urge. I told Kenny that part of what's so entertaining about his stories is the unintentional confusion it sometimes creates. This wasn't the first time it had happened. And I hoped my explaining it wouldn't make it the last. But I was pretty sure I couldn't stop it from happening even if I wanted to.

I told him, "For example, just the title of this story, the night I lost my manhood. I assumed you made a mistake and really meant the night you lost your virginity. Or, maybe when you gained your manhood. You know, if you ask a lot of guys when they became a man, they'd tell you it was the first time they had sex. So in a sense, losing your virginity is gaining your manhood."

As those words were coming out of my mouth, a look of confusion washed over Kenny's face. It looked a lot like I imagine my face did when he was two-thirds of the way through his story and nobody had their pants off yet.

And then he said the following . . .

But I didn't think guys had 'virginity.' I thought that's just what girls have.

And that's the moment I knew for sure I wouldn't be able to stop Kenny Tedford from being Kenny Tedford even if I tried.

~ ~

I asked Kenny a question I'd wanted to ask ever since meeting him: "When did you first realize that you were different?"
Kenny thought about that for a moment, and then began . . .

Probably by the time I was four or five years old. We were living in Dallas by then. My daddy lost his job with the Tennessee Highway Patrol just a couple of months after I was born. Some people say my Uncle Larry got him fired. I don't know if that's true or not. But my mom's and dad's sides of the family didn't get along very well. He ended up getting a job at the railroad.

Anyway, by the time I was four of five, I remember being sick a lot. One time I had double pneumonia, it got so bad my parents called the whole family in to say goodbye. They said my body parts were shutting down. I was about four. I don't remember most of it. But I remember waking up at 4:30 in the morning and begging my momma for ice cream. That's when they knew I was going to make it.

And then there were the seizures.

One day Momma was out in the back yard hanging laundry. And my father was in the front mowing the yard. Daddy thought Momma was watching me. And Momma thought Daddy was watching me. I was in my bedroom playing and I started having a seizure. Somehow I swallowed my tongue and couldn't breathe. Momma told me that when she came calling for me, she found me on the ground not breathing. She ran and got Daddy. And he came running in. He was on a medical ship in the war, so he knew what to do. He yelled to Momma to run and put ice in the bathtub. So she started filling it up with ice water.

Daddy picked me up and dropped me in the tub. Somehow the ice loosened me up. Then he reached in and pulled my tongue out. That let me start breathing again. And then they took me to the hospital.

I had three or four of those before I was six.

The seizures damaged my eyes even more than they already were. Made me cross-eyed. And my left eye would look away when I didn't have my glasses on. That made me look goofy even when I wasn't tryin' to look goofy.

I smiled at that last comment. But not for the reason Kenny probably assumed. Yes, it was funny. But the condition he was talking about was one I was intimately familiar with. The medical term for it is strabismus. But it's more commonly called "wandering eye," and I suffered from it myself at the same age.

The typical treatment at the time was to exercise the eye muscles. My father tied a tennis ball to a string and attached it to the ceiling above my bed. Each night I had to lie there for fifteen minutes while one of my parents would swing the ball back and forth, first one way, and then the other. Now in a circle, then an oval. I had to follow the ball with my eyes without moving my head.

Eventually the muscles strengthened, and the condition disappeared. But what remained were the memories.

Unlike Kenny's, however, my memories weren't of how goofy I looked with one eye wandering off to the side. Although I'm sure I looked just as goofy as he did. What I recall, rather fondly, was fifteen minutes every night that I was the sole focus of my parents' attention. And in a household of seven people, that was rare.

I can still see myself, lying there in bed in my favorite pajamas, with my father or mother sitting gently beside me on the bed. The exercises themselves were surely tedious and boring by any objective measure. But I looked forward to them every night anyway. And I missed them when they became no longer necessary.

It was the first of what turned out to be many moments of self-reflection that Kenny's stories prodded me into. Sometimes I would interrupt and share those thoughts with him.

But not this time.

I kept this one to myself, which meant my smile probably lingered longer than must have seemed warranted to him. But I got the impression it was a reaction he was used to, and that he was comfortable not knowing exactly why.

I never had another seizure after that. They say that puzzled the doctors, because most people that have that many keep having them their whole life.

These are just little things I don't really tell a lot of people. But I guess if I'm gonna tell my life story I should tell it right. And these are all things that make me who I am. But they don't control me.

I remember having to wear these big, thick glasses. Everyone called them "Coca Cola" glasses or "Coke bottle" glasses because they were thick like the bottom of a Coke bottle. When you looked at me, my eyes would look really big, like bug eyes. I didn't like the way I looked in the mirror when I wore them. And other kids would call me "four eyes," and other names.

I thought about my own experience with glasses as a child. Mine weren't quite thick enough to warrant the Coca Cola moniker. But that didn't seem to stop me from getting called "four eyes," too.

In fact, I remember being so self-conscious about them that I started wearing them only when absolutely necessary, like during class to see the blackboard. During recess, lunchtime, and any social settings, they'd come off and get stuffed in a pocket.

By the time I was in middle school, I'd abandoned them completely. I opted for other coping strategies, like sitting on the front row or copying someone else's notes.

Then I thought about Kenny. Glasses weren't optional for him.

Suddenly, I felt shallow and privileged.

When we would have family get-togethers, everyone else seemed to be able to talk and hear everyone else just fine. But I couldn't.

I remember asking my momma why I couldn't see or hear very well, like everyone else. That's when she told me about being a blue baby, and being in the incubator. But she also told me it made me different in other ways, too. She said it caused some paralysis on my left side, and that I didn't have as much feeling there.

Then she said, "Have you noticed that when you cry, you don't have as many tears from your left eye?"

"Yes."

"That's the paralysis."

Then she said, "Have you noticed that sometimes when you drink something, it runs down your chin on the left side?"

And I knew that happened sometimes, especially if there was ice in the drink. But only because someone would look at me and say, "Hey Kenneth, you're leaking!" I never could feel it.

I tried using a straw a few times. But the straw would move around the glass when I put it down. And I couldn't see very well out of my left eye, so sometimes when the straw moved over to the left side before I picked it up again, it would poke me in the eye.

One time when I was a teenager and I was with a girl, the straw moved over to the left. When I bent over to take a drink, it went up my nose on the left side. But I can't feel or see anything on that side of my face, so I didn't know it was there. I came up with the straw hanging out of my nose looking like some kind of a walwus. Wal-Wus. WAL-WUS. Ugh, I can't say it. A W-A-L-R-U-S. How do you say it?

"Walrus."

That's it! Ha, ha, ha . . . I love it! I looked like a walwus. But with an R. Not the way you want to look when you're on a date with a pretty girl. She started pointing at my face and trying to tell me. Can you image how stupid I looked?

Kenny laughed out loud at himself, at the absurdity of looking longingly into the eyes of a girl while he had a straw hanging out of his nose. Plus, he was genuinely amused that he couldn't pronounce the word walrus.

His laughter gave me license to laugh with him. So I did. And it felt good. I was acutely aware of my own paranoia that at some point in these interviews I would insult him by laughing at something he didn't consider funny. This walrus story relieved that fear. I got the impression that in our future conversations the first person to laugh at Kenny Tedford was going to be Kenny Tedford.

You can put that in the book, I can't pronounce walwus. . . How do you say it again?

"Wal-Rus."

Wal-Rus.

"You got it. Wal-Rus . . . It is kind of hard to say." We both enjoyed another good-natured laugh. "Did you ever learn to drink with a straw?"

No, not really. Unless it was in one of those plastic cups with the lid that had a hole in it to keep the straw in one place. That worked pretty well. But it was usually best if I just got rid of the straw and no ice.

Anyway, as far as my brain damage, I suppose I always knew I wasn't like my brothers and sisters. But it's hard for anyone that young to grasp how different they are.

I remember not always getting to play with them because I couldn't understand the games, or because I couldn't hear well enough. My dad would have to come over and say, "Include Kenneth! Include Kenneth!"

And Daddy actually told me I was different. That's why I didn't start the first grade until I was seven years old. The school said I wasn't ready yet, on account of my brain damage.

And he told me that's why he pushed me to do things sometimes, even when I thought he was being mean.

Like this one time, Daddy took me out into the back yard and pointed to a big, tall tree. And he said, "Son, you see that tree? I want you to climb to the top of it." And to a little kid, that tree was like the Empire State Building.

"Why, Daddy?"

He said, "I want you to see what you can see from up there. See what the world looks like. Then you come down and you tell me a story."

Well, I couldn't even reach the first limb, so he picked me up and held me high enough to reach it. I grabbed on and then he let go of me gently. There I was, just hanging from the lowest branch!

"Dad!!"

"Think. Think," he said. "How are you gonna get up there?" I squirmed around a bit, and then he said, "Use your legs. See that branch there?"

So I picked one foot up and put it on a little branch and was able to lift myself up a little. And then I found another one. And another one. Pretty soon I was climbing like a monkey! I was having the time of my life!

When I got about halfway up, I started getting a little nervous. I could see the roof of my house and the whole yard. But there were a lot of leaves, so I could barely see my father. But then he walked around to where I could see him again and started pointing up to the top of the tree. So I started climbing higher.

I got all the way to the top! It was unbelievable! I saw Jim's house. Susan's house. Sharon's house. The corner store. And I could see my school and it was two blocks away! I saw people walking along the road. I started screaming 'hello' at people, but I don't think they could hear me. I looked down and saw Daddy. He had a big smile on his face and was giving me the thumbs up.

And then behind Daddy, I saw my mother running out the back door. She was waving her hands all over the place at me. I watched her run up to Daddy, and start pounding on his back. Then she pointed at me, and she was really mad about something. They were fussing back and forth, and I started cracking up, because it looked like they were playing with each other. And then Momma started running around in circles and waving her arms over her head like she was going crazy!

Well, then Daddy made that motion with his finger than means "Come here." So I started climbing down the tree. I got all the way to the last branch, but it was too far to the ground. There was no way I could get down. I looked at Daddy, and he said, "Jump!"

I looked down, and looked at him and said, "Nooooah!"

And I saw mother saying, "No, no, no, he'll get hurt!"

Daddy said, "Jump!" again.

"No!"

Then he just said, "Trust me." And it was the way that he looked at me. His eyes just said, "I'm gonna take care of you. I would never let you get hurt." So I jumped! And Daddy caught me! He put me down on the ground, and gave me a high five. And then I gave him a hug.

Then Momma came over hugging me and fussing all over me, "Oh, my baby, my baby . . ."

That's when Daddy said, "Stop. You can't baby him anymore. He's safe. He's fine." And then he turned to me and said, "Now, Kenneth. Tell your Momma what you saw."

So I told her the story about how Daddy helped me onto the first branch of the tree, and how I climbed up all by myself, and all the wonderful things I could see from the top!" And she totally changed. She looked at Daddy and gave him one of those looks that means, "I'm still mad at you but I'm not gonna talk about it right now." But then she turned to me and said, "That was a beautiful story, Kenneth. Now, I'm going inside to get dinner on the table."

After she left, I asked my father, "Daddy, what was Momma doing running around in circles waving her arms all over the place?"

He said, "Oh, don't worry about that, son. She was just doing the tree dance."

A few months later, we went to the lake for a picnic. My daddy loved picnics. Momma made homemade tuna salad, and we sat at a picnic table and ate. And this lake had a beach. I don't know if you've ever seen a lake with a beach. But it's got sand like at the ocean, only it's safe so the family can swim in it. And they had one of those ropes with bobbing balls on them to tell you where you couldn't go any farther.

Well, we were all playing in the water. But I never went into the water any deeper than up to my chest because I couldn't swim. And Daddy came up to me and said, "Come on. I'm gonna teach you how to swim."

That scared me a little, so I said, "No, no, no, no, no."

He just said, "Trust me." And he looked at me with those eyes like he did before when I climbed the tree. All this time, Momma was still cleaning up the picnic table.

So Daddy picked me up and sat me on his shoulders. Then he started walking out deeper into the water. When he got up to his chest my feet were hanging in the water. And then he tilted his head back and looked up at me and said, "Are you ready?"

I just said, "Noooooah!" because I didn't know what he was gonna do with me.

He said, "You've got to learn to swim, son."

"No, no, no!"

The he said, "I'm gonna count to three, and then I'm throwing you."

I said, "Nooooah!" again, and I grabbed his arm.

He said, "Let go."

"No."

He said, "Let go, Kenneth," and then he pulled his arm away real quick. He stood me up so I was standing on his shoulders. And now he's holding my legs and I'm holding his wrists.

He told me to let go of his wrist, and I told him, "No!" again. "Daddy, I'm gonna drown!"

He said, "Do you really think I would let you drown?" And right about the time I was saying "Yes!" he threw me into the water! And I started screaming. And that wasn't a wise thing to do. Because when you're screaming, your mouth is open. And so water started getting into my throat. And I started bobbing up and down and coughing. I saw my Daddy come up quick and he grabbed me by the hair and pulled my head out of the water. I wrapped my legs around his waist, and he gave me a big hug.

As soon as a caught my breath, I started pounding on his chest, "Why did you let me drown!"

He told me to stop. And we were eye to eye. I looked and he had those same eyes that told me that he loved me. He said, "You did good! You did good!"

I said, "But I almost drowned!" And about that time, he looked behind me at something. So I turned around and looked, and it was Momma. She was on the beach running around in circles waving her arms all over the place, like she did under the tree that time. And I said, "Daddy, what's Momma doing?"

"Oh, don't worry about that, son. She's just doing the beach dance."

The mental image made me laugh, and decided I liked Kenny's father very much. It takes courage to put your children in positions to struggle. There's always some small amount of risk. Without the struggle, there's no learning. And there's the rub for a parent.

I thought about the times I put my own children in positions to struggle: learning to jump off the diving board, staying on the baseball team until the end of the year instead of quitting mid-season, sticking with piano lessons just one more year.

But mostly what I thought about were the times I didn't make them struggle, and should have. How much stronger, smarter, braver, more talented, or well-adjusted would my children be if I had the courage of Kenny's father?

Then I thought about my role as a manager and leader for the last twenty years at work. How many times had I failed to let one of my team members struggle and just finished the project myself? How many times had I swooped in with money or resources to get something done just so I wouldn't look bad to my own management?

How much more capable, experienced, and resourceful would my direct reports be if I'd been a more courageous leader?

When we got back on the beach, Momma hugged me and kissed me and fussed all over me. When Daddy walked by, he just mumbled something like "That boy's never gonna grow up if you don't let him . . ."

And I thought, "When I grow up I want to be a man like my Daddy!" So I made Momma stop fussing all over me and put me down. I ran over to Daddy, and he said, "That's my boy!" And he hugged me. And I knew that I was loved. My momma loved me in her way. And Daddy loved me in his. That was the most important thing I learned that day.

Indeed. I was both impressed and dismayed that Kenny learned such an important lesson at the age of seven. It wasn't until my forties, reading Gary Chapman's book The Five Love Languages, *that I really understood that concept. And, thinking rather highly of myself having been gifted with normal mental faculties and university degrees, I wondered why it took me over three decades longer to learn it than it took Kenny with all of the mental and physical challenges he had to contend with.*

The answer, of course, is that just like there's more than one type of love language, there's more than one type of intelligence. It was only hubris and lack of imagination that gave me any reason to think I should be better qualified, or even as qualified, as Kenny Tedford to learn that subtle lesson of human nature.

That moment was an important reality check for me. If I was going to properly grasp the wisdom from this man's life, I'd need to think of him not as someone with disabilities and limitations, like I was a psychologist studying a patient, but as someone with a unique perspective and life experiences I didn't possess and that I wanted to learn from.

I needed to think of Kenny not as my subject. But as my teacher.

That moment shaped the direction of our interviews, and our relationship, for months to come. Until it would change again.

But I also learned to swim that day. And I eventually learned to love the water, and canoeing. And I'm so grateful that my father did what he did that day, to get me over my fear of the water. Today people probably get in trouble or get sued for doing it the way he did it. But I'm glad he did.

Chapter 2: Dealing With Bullies

I guess my first opportunity to see how I would fit in with other kids was when I went to school for the first time.

When they first met me, they would say things like, "He's a strange fella. He walks funny. He talks funny. He looks funny." And I thought I looked okay. I didn't really think much was wrong with me. I kind of thought it was the world that had the problem, not me.

On one of those first few days at school, I went home and asked my mom, "Momma, why do people out there in the world, when I go to school or play on the playground, they come up to me and they go . . ."

At that point, Kenny mumbled, bent his right hand awkwardly at the wrist, and started slapping it against his chest. I recognized it immediately as the way children (and some adults) mock people with disabilities.

I sneered as he demonstrated. Partly out of genuine disgust at the thought of someone teasing a child that way. But partly as a way of hiding the embarrassment and shame I felt, knowing I'd done the same thing in my youth. And while the adult me would never do something like that in front of a disabled person, a more honest reflection reminded me that I was well into my adult years the last time I'd done something like that in jest when someone said something I thought was silly or foolish, probably around the water cooler at work, or at a family gathering.

I desperately hoped Kenny couldn't see through the facade of my sneer.

And my mother said, "Who's pickin' on you?"

"Pickin' on me? What makes you think someone's pickin' on me?"

"Because you're crying."

"It's because I feel bad, Momma."

"About what?"

"Because of how they all act. It seems like they all have problems. They can't talk right. Their arms and hands don't work right."

Momma just laughed and laughed. She shooed me away with her hand and said, "I ain't gonna worry 'bout you."

Another day, I remember learning to play Dodgeball at recess. That's where you stand in the middle of a circle of kids and they throw a ball and you try to not let it hit you. But you have to understand, the way we played back then was with only one person in the middle at a time. When that person got hit, they got to pick the next person to go in the middle.

Being the one in the middle was the most fun part. Lots of kids wanted to get picked. When someone would get hit, they would all raise their hands and yell, "Pick me! Pick me!"

Well, after a few rounds I was getting picked a lot, so I felt pretty special. And the longer we played the more popular I was getting. But the more I was getting hit, the harder it seemed they were throwing the ball, so I eventually started to wish some other kids would get picked more. But they kept picking me.

After it started to hurt more, the next time I got picked, I just decided to not go in the middle. But they pushed me in anyway. And when I got hit and came out, they'd push me in again. That's when I realized when they pushed me in they were yelling the word, "Retard!"

I stopped feeling popular.

Eventually, the teacher eventually came out clapping her hands, yelling, "Class time. Class time." But she never said anything about how we were playing Dodgeball.

From that time on, none of the other kids wanted to walk home with me. My older sister, Sandy, had to walk me home. That was the rule of the family. She had to make sure I got home, even though we only lived two blocks away.

I tried baseball, too. But, I kept getting hit with the ball or the bat because I couldn't hear the coaches or the other kids yelling at me that they were throwing the ball to me.

Eventually, I noticed that when it came to games at school or parties, I was always picked last. I remember when they introduced us to whiffle ball. It was like baseball, but you didn't get hurt because the ball and bat were just made of plastic. Well, the teacher would pick the team captains, and they would get to pick the rest of the team. When they got to the last person, it was always me. But then those two would get in a fight over who had to take me.

That's when I would raise my hand and just ask to go do what I usually did at home, leave the family and go out in the yard and be alone. (I would play with the dog, Susie, and watch them have fun.)

So at whiffle ball, I just said, "I'll go over there and sit by the tree and watch."

And they would act all happy and say, "Oh yeah, you'll be our cheerleader!"

"Okay, I guess."

And that's the way it went for a few years.

But being retarded wasn't always bad. I got to the point in school I kind of liked it.

One day I got moved to a new class, and the teacher put me in the back of the room. All the other kids who were normal sat in the front. While they had to learn their ABCs and do math, I got a coloring book and some crayons and I got to draw pictures. That seemed like a lot more fun to me.

Apparently, it did to some other kids, too. One day a little boy raised his hand and said, "I want to sit in the back with Kenneth," and he pointed to me.

The teacher told him, "You can't sit there."

"Why not?" the little boy asked.

She said, "Because he's retarded."

At first the little boy looked disappointed, and kind of said, "Awww."

And then all the other boys and girls turned around in their chairs to look at me. I wasn't used to getting so much attention, and it was kind of nice.

Kenny turned slightly in his chair as he moved into character. He looked off into the imaginary faces of his classmates. His eyes took on an impish look of excitement. He sat up straight and waved excitedly to the crowd with both hands.

Some of them even waved back at me, but I could tell they were thinking about something.

Then they all started raising their hands at the same time, and the teacher said, "what, what?"

They said, "We want to be retarded too, like Kenneth!"

Kenny sat up tall and proud in his seat. He licked his lips and brushed out the make-believe wrinkles in his shirt as his eyes darted around the room at an audience of six-year-old admirers who weren't really there.

I knew then that I would be okay.

I must have been smiling all the way home that day, because when I got there, my momma was on the front porch and she said, "Well what are you so happy about?"

I clapped my hands and said, "I learned something new today."

She smiled back at me and said, "What did you learn?"

Then as loud and proud as I could, I said, "I'm retarded!"

"What?" Momma yelled out. "Who told you you were retarded?"

"The teacher, and the other kids," I told her. "And I like it!" I was still pretty proud of myself.

"Well, why do you like it?"

"Because all the other kids want to be like me!"

"No, no, no, no, no. Listen," she said. "we're gonna play a game."

"What kind of game?"

"You are to tell nobody you're retarded outside this house. You can say it here if you want, but not too often. Because you're not. Do you understand?"

"Okay, I guess."

That didn't last long.

A few days later, my daddy took me to 7-Eleven. That was a convenience store close to our house.

We walked in and Daddy asked the lady behind the counter, "Can you watch my boy here while I shop?"

"Sure, no problem," she said.

When Daddy walked off, the clerk looked at me and said, "What are we today?"

I thought that was a silly question. She's a grown woman and she doesn't know what she is? I thought about it for a minute. Then I looked around to see if Daddy was watching me. When I saw that he wasn't, I turned back to her and I told her in my big happy voice, "I'm retarded!"

But before I could smile too much about it, this big bear hand grabbed onto my shoulder and scared me.

"Oh, hi, Daddy," I said. Then I was embarrassed because I wasn't supposed to tell people I was retarded.

But I was still proud of it. And that wasn't gonna be the last time I told people I was retarded either.

Being different didn't have to be a bad thing. It just meant you were special. I needed to learn to make the best of it. And so that's what I've always tried to do.

Precocious isn't a word I would have used up to now to describe Kenny Tedford. But what just happened in that story struck me as nothing short. Both of his parents had told him to never use the word "retarded" and chastised him when he did. Of course, it was out of a genuine love and caring for him that they did. They obviously wanted to protect his self-esteem, and perhaps make sure that label didn't limit him from setting high goals for himself.

But there's an unintended consequence that comes with making some words taboo, especially as they relate to yourself. And that is that it gives those words power over you. You learn to fear those words. Those words hurt you because you've been told they're hurtful. So hurtful, in fact, that you're forbidden to use them yourself.

But what if you just embraced words that accurately described you and took them at face value? What if you didn't imbue them with so much power by avoiding or denying them?

Now, I'll admit the word "retarded" is so stigmatized today that's it's perhaps hard to see how it might be wise to simply embrace about oneself. But it wasn't that way in the 1950s. It would be like saying "cognitively impaired" or "differently-abled" today.

Instead of denying what was biologically true about himself, Kenny chose to embrace it, and, as he said, "make the best of it."

That struck me as a profound insight. And one I think we can all use in some aspect of our personal and professional lives.

Imagine your 7th grade child being teased as "stupid in math," because every year he makes Cs in the most basic math classes. He could respond by crying about it or starting a fight. Or, he can say, "Yeah, math's not my thing. But let me tell you about the poetry I'm writing!" The teasing immediately stops when your tormentors realize their criticisms don't hurt you.

And that concept could even be extended to embracing our failures at work instead of running from them. Like that project that you never could deliver. When it comes up in performance reviews or casual conversations with your peers (or your nemesis), you've got a couple of ways you could respond. You could deny it was your fault, blame it on other people, and generally downplay the impact of the failure.

Imagine how disarming it would be instead to say, "Yeah, I really screwed that one up, didn't I? Let me tell you what I learned from it..."

I started to like my new role as Kenny's student instead of his investigator. It was clear I was going to learn a lot more about life that way. And, as I think I had just discovered, a lot more I could apply to my professional life as well.

~ ~

The first story I ever remember being told in school was the story of Cinderella. One of the teachers came to get us and took us down the hall to the library.

Kenny turned to the side as he briefly became the teacher . . .

"Okay, everybody sit down and be quiet. Sit, sit, sit. . . Janet, pull your dress down! Bobbie, stop pickin' your boogers!"

And I was sitting there thinking, "Are we ever gonna get to the story?"

Well, eventually she got to reading the book to us. But when you can't hear very well, like me, it's hard to understand what's happening in the story. The teacher's the only one who can see the words and pictures in the book. Except, every time she got close to finishing a page, she turned the book around for us to see the picture. But I couldn't see the pictures and watch her mouth at the same time. And the way I'd learned to understand people was to read their lips, so I usually missed out on some of both.

I ended up going to the library later, and reading that book all by myself. The pictures and the colors looked so beautiful. I wanted it to all come to life. But I couldn't hear the joy of sound the way other kids did from the teacher's voice, so I found a table in the back, in a corner, so I could be all alone. And as I read the book, I would pretend. I would pretend and I *became* the characters. I became Cinderella!

I got out of the chair and down on my knees to scrub the floor. And then I acted like I was sweeping out the fireplace with an old dirty broom. And the soot and coal from the fire made me cough, so I coughed out loud a little. And I could hear the stairs start to creak as the stepmother started to come downstairs. And she yelled out, "Kenneth! Look at you! You're just a mess!"

Later in the story I became the fairy Godmother, and the little birds, and the mice, and the handsome prince, and all the other characters, one at a time. And that's how I got the stories to come alive for me.

Reflecting on that scene on the library floor later, it occurred to me that it probably looked a lot like the interviews I was having with Kenny. He doesn't tell stories like most people tell stories, verbally describing what happened. He performs them, stepping in and out of characters as quickly and easily as a Broadway actor in a one-man play.

As I thought about why that was, it occurred to me that it's at least partly due to his deafness. Dialog drives most narratives. So if you don't have access to all of the dialog, the way you interpret what's going on, and, therefore, what you remember about the story, are the non-verbal components: the look in people's eyes, the expression on their faces, their body language.

Kenny acts out the stories he tells because that's largely how he experienced them, as a physical production instead of a verbal narrative.

I made a mental note about my own work as a leader, a speaker, and storyteller. How much of the power of storytelling was I missing because I focus so much on the words that are coming out of my mouth? What else am I missing? And how can I stop missing it?

A few weeks later, one of the teachers read us the story of Snow White. There was a handsome prince in that book, too. That seemed to happen a lot with the stories they read to us, there was always a handsome prince around. And then we heard about the Old Lady Who Lived in a Shoe, and she had so many kids that she didn't know what to do. I don't think there was a handsome prince in that one. But all the kids were beautiful, and handsome, and perfect. Everyone in these stories all kind of looked the same and was shaped the same and had the same abilities.

So one day, while the teacher was reading us another story, I raised my hand and said, "Why is there nobody with a handicap in these stories?" That's what we used to say back when I was little, a handicap. Now we say someone has a disability. "And, I don't see any black people in these stories. And how come there aren't any Hispanic people, either?"

Then the other kids started yelling, "Yeah, that's right! How come? How come?" Then the teacher had to shush everyone again and get us to settle down. And I guess she didn't have time to explain it to me, because she told everyone to be quiet and told me to stop being a trouble-maker. But I wasn't trying to make trouble. I was just trying to understand. Why are all the people in the stories cute and perfect and all look the same? Why wasn't there anyone different? Why wasn't there anyone like me? Where did I fit in?

I ran home that day and asked my momma. "Momma! Momma! We read about the Old Lady Who Lived in a Shoe today. How come all the boys are always handsome and the girls are always cute? Can I be in fairy tales, too? Can there be someone like me in the stories?" But Momma was busy cooking dinner, so she told me to go talk to my daddy. I went out into the back yard to talk to my daddy. And I asked him the same question. "Why isn't there anyone like me in the stories?"

And Daddy goes, "Have you asked your mother?"

"Yeah, she told me to go ask you."

He said, "I tell you what, son. You know Mrs. So-and-so, your favorite teacher?"

"Yeah."

"Why don't you go find her at school tomorrow and ask her. She seems to do a good job explaining things to you."

"Okay, Daddy."

So the next day I went and found my favorite teacher and I asked her all those same questions. She pulled up a chair for me and asked me to sit down. She looked me right in the eyes, pointed to my heart, and she said, "Kenneth, you're a good storyteller. When you grow up, I think you should write your own fairy tales. Then you can put anyone in them that you want. There can be a deaf person, or a blind person, or someone in a wheelchair. There can be black boys and Hispanic girls. There can even be someone who's mentally retarded." That's what we called people with brain damage when I was little. Mentally retarded. Today we say they're "mentally challenged."

"I can?" I thought that was a great idea, and I wondered if I would ever do that someday when I grew up.

She said, "Yes, you can, Kenneth." And she smiled at me, and I smiled at her.

I thought about how much progress society has made in this regard in the last few decades. It's a rare movie or television show today that doesn't have a visibly diverse cast. I found that encouraging.

But I also thought about the less obvious examples, the background noise of experience that we barely notice, but that surely affects us, nonetheless.

I remember the first time it occurred to me something like that existed. I was working on a brand of disposable diapers and we were discussing the packaging. Someone in the room suggested we needed to change it and she was quite adamant about it. A host of voices chimed in to remind her that we'd changed the package a half a dozen times in as many years. "It looks just fine, thank you."

Her response was something like, "I'm not talking about the colors, Bob! Or, the words. Or even the bloody fonts! I'm talking about the picture of the blond-haired, blued-eyed, thumb-sucking baby boy on the front! Jesus, can we get a picture of a kid who doesn't look like you on the damn thing?"

It just hadn't occurred to anyone. Or, at least not anyone in a position to do anything about it. But, she was the new president of the business unit, so the problem got fixed pretty quickly.

More importantly, a roomful of people, including me, got a quick lesson on the background noise of privilege we wouldn't have noticed otherwise.

But I was even more happy that she liked the way I told stories. My mom and dad would tell me the same thing. They'd say I was funny and I told good stories. If we were at a family reunion or a party, they would always ask me a question in front of everybody because they knew I'd tell a story.

Like one time my momma just said, "Tell everybody what we had for supper last night."

And I'd go, "Why? Who cares?"

Then I'd hear, "Come on. Come on, Kenneth. We want to hear what you had for supper." I thought they were just doing it to make fun of me, because I was labeled 'retarded.' Like I was some kind of jester or a clown. I didn't learn 'til years later what it meant to be laughing *with* you, instead of laughing *at* you. Sometimes back then, I thought they were laughing at me. But now that I'm older, I know my parents loved me and they were laughing with me.

So I told everyone about the supper we had. I told them about the 'paghetti (because I couldn't say the letter 's' very well yet). And I talked about the meatballs, and how juicy they were, and what we talked about at dinner. I'd just make a whole story out of it. And the strangest thing was, while I was talking, nobody dropped a pin or anything. Everybody would just stand there and listen. And when I got done, everybody would start clapping.

I just thought, "Man, you people need to get a life."

When I was eight years old, I remember my daddy taking me back to that 7-Eleven to get some eggs and other things for my mom. We got out of the car and my father took my hand, and we walked up to the door. And right in front of us, as we were walking in, was this woman who was fat, I mean super big. And to an eight-year-old boy, she was huge! And she had a bright colored dress on. And I started laughing.

Then my father said, "What are you giggling about?"

And so I told him. I said, "That's a *fat* woman! That's a *fat* woman!"

Well my daddy got down on his knees and put both hands on my shoulders. He turned me around and made sure I was looking at him. It kind of scared me, because I could tell he was upset. Then he said to me, "Don't you ever, ever make fun of other people like that! How are you gonna like it when other people make fun of you?"

"What do you mean?" I asked.

"What are you gonna do when people start calling you 'retarded, deafy, stupid, slow'? What'll you do then?"

"Why would they do that? I'm not stupid."

He said, "I didn't say you were. But I'm gonna tell you right now, when you get older, people are gonna make fun of you.

You're different, Kenneth. You're different. I'm gonna do my best as your father to teach you to love yourself. And you're doing fine. But you should never, ever judge someone else like that. Treat them the way you want people to treat you."

I just said, "Okay, Daddy, I won't do it no more."

And he said, "Oh, I'm not finished with you yet, boy. We're gonna go inside and you're gonna go directly to that woman and tell her you're sorry."

"What!? I ain't doin' nuthin' like that!"

And my father said, "Excuse me? Do you know who you're talkin' to?"

So I said, "Yes, Daddy."

"Okay, then. Come on inside and you're gonna apologize."

"But, Daddy, I'll be embarrassed to talk to her now."

He said, "Good! You should be." And then he took my hand, and we went inside.

Oh, I do like this man! As a parent, I found an enormous amount of wisdom in that last comment from Kenny's father. When we do things shameful or embarrassing, we should feel shame *and* embarrassment. *That's what gives us the motivation to not do those things in the future.*

The fact that apologizing to the woman would be embarrassing wasn't just not *a reason to let Kenny avoid it. It was actually part of the reason he needed to do it. He needed to feel the shame and embarrassment that came with it in order to learn.*

Within a few days of this interview, I found myself using that line with one of my own kids. I was explaining how something he'd done was unfair to someone. After listening, he complained, "Awww. But now I feel bad."

I responded, "Good! You should. Now, just sit with that feeling for a few minutes. It'll help you not do that again."

I never got the opportunity to meet Kenny's dad. But he'd already made me a better father twice, and we were only a few hours into the interviews. I wondered what else I might learn from him before we were done.

We walked up to the woman, and he got her attention, "Ma'am, ma'am."

She turned around and said, "Oh, what a cute little boy. How are you?"

And I started feeling really bad. Here she was saying something nice to me and I'd just called her a fat woman. My daddy just smiled and he looked at me and said, "Do you have something to tell the lady?" I looked up at her and I almost started crying. I got behind my daddy's legs but he pushed me back around front. He said, "Look up. Look at her." Then he said to her, "My son can't hear very well, so he has to read your lips. But he has something to tell you."

The lady looked at my father, and then she looked at me. Then she handed him her shopping basket. She reached down and put both her hands on my shoulders. And she had the most beautiful smile, and sparkly eyes. And she goes, "I know what you wanna to tell me."

I said, "Oh no you don't, I haven't told you, yet."

Then she started tapping my nose with her fingers, like she was gonna do a magic trick. Then she said, "I sho' do know what you goin' tell me."

"What am I gonna tell you?" I asked.

"You goin' tell me I'm a very fat woman."

Kenny's mouth dropped in a look of shock and humiliation as he recreated the scene for me.

And then I said, "No! What did my daddy tell you?"

She said, "I don't know yo' daddy. But I been called a fat lady befo'. I been called a pig, and a whale, and I even been called a whopper."

Well, that made me even more sad, and I told her, "That's not nice." And that's when I could tell I was crying, because I felt a tear come down my right cheek. And I told her, "I'm sorry. I didn't mean it." And she smiled at me again with her big beautiful smile. And then she bent down and gave me a big hug. She squeezed me so tight I couldn't breathe! "Ugh. . . okay, okay." Then when she pulled back, she said, "You the sweetest thing. I'm glad you learned your lesson. God bless you."

Then she turned around and got her basket back from my father. And she said, "Thank you, sir. That made my day." And she went on to finish her shopping.

That lady always stays with me. She keeps me in place. Ever since then, I try not to judge other people, how they look, what they do, how they talk, how they live. She's a part of me now. And it's a good thing, because it turned out my daddy was right.

"Right about what?"

About getting picked on and bullied. Seems like everybody gets bullied at some point in their life. Little kids and grown-ups. And not just someone like me. Normal kids, too. But I've probably got more experience at it than most people.

"Tell me about that. What was it like getting bullied? And how did you handle it?"

Well, the first bullying I remember was in the first grade in Dallas. We went on the bus to see the symphony orchestra. Sometimes when they would have a big performance that people would pay a lot of money to go see, they would let school kids like us come in early and listen to them do a rehearsal for free. That way, if they messed up it didn't matter as much.

That's the day I fell in love with music! I can hear musical instruments a little. And I like hearing people sing, even though

I don't understand what they're saying. But I read lips, I'm an oralist. That's how I understand people. And it was beautiful!

I've heard the human voice referred to as the most finely tuned musical instrument. But I'd never considered that analogy very thoughtfully. Listening to Kenny now, it suddenly became obvious how you might appreciate a beautiful singing voice even better if you weren't distracted by being able to understand the lyrics. It would be like me listening to an Italian opera and being able to focus solely on the amazing range and control of a master performer precisely because I don't speak Italian.

I had to laugh at myself. This deaf man was a more astute aficionado of the human singing voice than I was.

If that wouldn't humble me, not much would.

Well that day we went to the orchestra, it just happened to be raining. When we got back, all the kids got off the bus and were waiting for their parents to come pick them up.

I was standing there, and all of a sudden, this kid in my class named Jimmy came up to me and started making fun of me.

Just as he had before, as Kenny told the story, he mumbled, bent his right hand awkwardly at the wrist, and started slapping it against his chest, parroting the mockery of his bully.

Back then I didn't talk so good like I do now. But he made it sound even worse than it really was.

And he kept walking closer, so I started to back up. Then I noticed behind me was another kid down on his hands and knees. I guess Jimmy was gonna push me over the second kid, because that's what bullies did back then.

And still do, I thought to myself. Apparently some forms of torment never go out of style. I remember being on the receiving end of that exact maneuver myself in grade school. And my son Ben assures me that it's alive and well today. In fact, he said they even have a name for it now: "Table topping."

When I saw the second kid, I turned around to try to get out of the way, and I tripped over my own foot. I landed in a puddle of mud, because it had been raining. I had mud all over me and my clothes.

So I got up and was cleaning the mud off, and I heard some kids screaming, "Hit him! Hit him!" I looked up and they were holding Jimmy by the arms. (The other boy had already run off.) But they held Jimmy up and kept telling me to hit him.

I could have used a few friends like that when I was getting table-topped.

I looked at all of them and asked, "Why?"

"Because he pushed you in the mud!" they said.

I said, "No he didn't. I tripped over my own feet."

One of them yelled, "Hit him anyway! He's a bully! Hit him!"

So I told them, "He didn't do anything to you. He was doing it to me. And he didn't push me over anyway."

About that time, the teacher came over and told everyone to break it up. She asked me, "What happened to you?"

"I slipped and fell in the mud," I said.

The kids started yelling, "No, it was Jimmy! Jimmy pushed him!" Jimmy just stood there, really embarrassed.

I told the teacher it was okay. "I just live two blocks from here, and it's stopped raining. I can walk home and change clothes." By that time, I had a friend who walked home with me every day instead of my older sister. So we walked home and I changed clothes.

And then I told him I wanted to go to the TG&Y store. That's what we called a "five and dime" store back then. They sold a little bit of everything, but I mostly got candy there. You could fill up a nickel bag full of whatever candy you wanted. It only cost five cents, that's why they called it a nickel bag. These days, when I tell people about the nickel bag, they think I'm talking about drugs. But that's not what it meant back then.

Anyway, when we got there I went in and bought two nickel bags of candy.

When we left the store, my friend put his hand out and he smiled real big. "What are you smiling for?" I asked him.

He said, "Candy, of course. You're not gonna eat both those bags all by yourself, are you?"

"No," I told him. "But it's not for you."

"Well who's it for, then?"

I told him, "It's for Jimmy."

"Jimmy!? The one who pushed you in the mud?"

I said, "He didn't push me in the mud. I fell in the mud myself. How many times do I have to say that?"

"Well, he was gonna push you anyway."

"But he didn't," I told him.

"But he's a bully!"

So I looked at him and I said, "You know what? You're right. He is a bully."

"And you're still gonna give him a bag of candy?"

"Yeah, I am."

Then nobody said anything for a little bit. And I could tell he was sad that he wasn't gonna get any candy. So I gave him the other bag, *my* bag of candy.

He took it. But he looked sad and said, "Well, now I feel bad."

And I said, "Good! You should."

Kenny's father would have been proud to hear that.

Then he reached in the bag and pulled out a sucker. "You want a sucker, Kenneth?"

"No, thanks."

Then he said, "Well, I'm going home now."

He left, and I walked back to the playground at the school. When I got there, there was Jimmy, going around the merry-go-round, all by himself. And he looked really sad. So I walked up to him. He saw me coming, and jumped off the merry-go-round and said, "I don't want to fight. I don't want to fight."

I said, "I don't either, Jimmy."

"They pushed me into that," he said. "I didn't want to bully you. Except, well, you do talk funny, Kenneth."

I said, "I'm just different, I guess."

Then he asked, "Well, why do you talk that way? You don't seem to be retarded."

I told him, "I'm not. At least I don't think so." (Remember, I wasn't supposed to tell people I was retarded outside my house.) Then I said, "But even if I was retarded, it's cool. Because I don't have to study so hard like you. I get to color with crayons all day."

"Oh yeah . . . well, they were pushing me to bully you."

"I know, Jimmy." And then I handed him the nickel bag of candy.

He said, "What's that for?"

"For you."

"Me? Why me? I was mean to you."

"Not really. You just said it. You were pushed into doing that."

"Well, why are you giving me candy?"

So I told him, "Because you need a friend, somebody that likes you. I can tell you're not happy. But I'll be your friend."

So he took the candy and he asked me to sit down by him on the merry-go-round. Then he opened the bag and held it out to me, and he said, "Pick whatever you want. We'll share." So I reached in and got what I wanted and we started eating candy together. And we talked. He told me about his life. He had it pretty rough at home. He didn't have two nice parents like most of the kids had. And sometimes they pushed him around. So it seemed like he learned to act like a bully because that's how he got treated at home.

And that's the day that my bully became my best friend.

Apparently it wasn't a more protective set of friends that I needed when I was getting table-topped at school. It was a nickel bag of candy. Or, more rightly put, the wisdom to show a little kindness to someone who probably needed it more than I did. But that wasn't wisdom I had, until now.

Conventional wisdom in my generation was that if you stood up to a bully, they'd always back down. In fact, my most vivid memory of a successful encounter with a bully involved exactly that sort of testosterone-filled response strategy.

I'd been on the receiving end of an endless stream of taunts from a kid we'll call "John" when I was in the fourth grade. Day after day. The guy was relentless. I complained about it to my father one night when his drinking buddies were over. The boldest (and perhaps drunkest) of the bunch was a guy named Jerry.

Jerry put his arm around me and said, "Look kid, here's what you gotta do. You get to school early tomorrow and wait for this John character to get dropped off. Then you walk up to him, you get in his face, and you say, 'John, you and I are either gonna be friends, or we're gonna be enemies. And you need to decide which it's gonna be, right now!"

The assumption was that that kind of bluster and bravado would scare the crap out of the little shit and he'd be my best friend for the rest of the year. Well, I must have delivered my lines just right, or maybe gotten lucky, because it pretty much worked out exactly that way.

Worst case scenario, I figure it could have resulted in me getting punched in the face. After all, those were the days before school shootings were a real concern.

Either way, in giving advice to my own boys about how to deal with bullies, I decided I liked Kenny's solution better. At least for plan A. If that didn't work, I suppose they could always switch over to drunk Jerry's bluster plan.

Chapter 3: The Magic Crayon

When I was in the second grade I started what they called art therapy. Back then, a psychiatrist came to school once a week to visit some of the kids and look at our drawings. He was supposed to figure out if we were crazy or were gonna stab somebody or something. And that's how he determined how bad they were with brain damage. I don't know how you can figure that out from looking at drawings, but that's what they did anyway.

Well the day I met him, he came in and said, "I'm your psychiatrist."

I didn't know what that was, so I said, "What's a psychiatrist?"

And he said, "We're gonna see if you're smart or not."

"Okay."

So then he asked me for one of my pictures. Most days my teacher would tell me to draw a picture of what I did the day before. So I showed him a picture I'd drawn of me on a seesaw. He looked at it and asked, "What did you draw?"

I said, "a seesaw."

"And who's on the other end?"

"My Mama," I told him.

"Hmm. Creative. Creative . . . B+."

And I'm sitting there thinking, "Where did this man get his degree? I mean, he's gonna tell me I'm smart because I can draw a seesaw?"

Well, anyway, it went on like that for a few days. Then one day he came in, and I drew another picture. This time it was a butterfly. He looked at it and asked me, "What's that?"

I wondered if he was gonna ask me that every time. I thought psychiatrists were supposed to be smart. So I thought that was a funny question. I asked him, "You don't know what a butterfly is, and you call yourself a psychiatrist?" I didn't know how much longer he was gonna be able to keep his job if he didn't even know what a butterfly was.

Well, I guess he didn't like that question because he shushed me. Then he said, "Hmmm, not very colorful, or creative." And he wrote a big 'D-' right on my drawing. I thought maybe he was just mad because I was being a smart aleck. That wouldn't bother me as much as getting a D- because I couldn't draw. Anyway, I rolled up my paper and put it in my backpack.

I kept thinking about that the rest of the day. I wondered if they were right about me. Maybe I'll never be anything but a retarded boy. I didn't think so. But those doctors were smart people.

After school was over, I left class and started walking down the hall. One of the other teachers stopped me in the hallway. She got down on her knees to talk to me and said, "What's wrong, Kenneth? You look so sad."

I told her, "I can't even draw! I got a 'D-' on my drawing, and that's the thing I'm best at."

She asked if she could see it. So I took out my drawing and showed it to her.

She said, "He's very pretty. But he looks a little sad. Can I see your box of crayons?"

So I pulled out the box and showed her. It was a tiny little box of four crayons.

"You mean like the kind you get at a restaurant for kids to play with before dinner?"

Yeah. Like that. Only one of mine was missing. So it was really a box of three crayons that leaned over a little. She opened it up and looked inside. The three colors I had were black, white, and gray.

She said, "Are these the only colors you have, Kenneth?"

"Yes, ma'am." I was a little embarrassed because I knew the other kids had bigger boxes with more colors. But I'm just the retarded boy in back, so I figured that's all I deserved.

That really pissed me off.

Having opened up countless boxes of those restaurant crayons for my own kids, I knew those weren't the original colors in the box.

It was a strange feeling. I was sitting in front of a man fourteen years my senior. Yet, I was feeling aggressively protective of him like I would one of my own children. And not just the mature, rational, humane sort of protective. But an instinctual, Papa Bear, rip-someone's-head-off kind of protective.

I wanted to punch someone in the face!

And I wasn't even sure which I found more objectionable. The fact that he only had a four-pack of crayons to begin with, when everyone else had larger boxes. (How the hell does that happen?) Or the fact that somehow only the most colorless of colors had migrated their way into Kenny's box. Were the other kids stealing his crayons when he wasn't looking? Were they trading him for their boring colors when their pretty ones got too short and dull? Or was he giving them away willingly to win friends who probably wouldn't return the gesture?

I didn't know, and I wasn't clear-headed enough to ask. Not that it mattered. None of those reasons would have made me feel any less angry.

Then she told me to follow her into her room, and she sat down at her desk. She reached into a drawer and pulled out a huge box of crayons with every color you can imagine, and she gave it to me! Then she found some extra sheets of paper and rolled them up and put them in my backpack.

She got back down on her knees again like she did in the hallway and said things to me that I'll never forget. She said, "Kenneth, I want to tell you something. You are very creative. When you talk, even at your age, you tell the most amazing stories. You seem to love all the kids, even the ones that make fun of you."

She even said she thought I was funny. I thought she was making fun of the way I talk, so I got kind of sad. But she said she didn't mean it that way, and that I would understand it when I was older. So then I felt better.

Then she said, "I want you to go home and think about this, that you are important, and you have a gift. And then I want you to draw your butterfly again. Use any colors you want this time. And when you're done, you think of a story to make your butterfly come to life." Then she hugged me, and sent me on my way.

I wasn't sure what she meant about the story and making the butterfly come to life. But I did what she said and thought about it. A few days later, I was at the park playing. All of a sudden, I was surrounded by butterflies. Dozens and dozens of butterflies. All over the place. And one of them landed on my hand. And they were beautiful. The one on my hand was bright yellow. It was almost like he was saying to me, "Look, dummy. I'm yellow, not black and white."

Then a blue one landed on my shirt. And then a red one. And I started thinking about other times I've seen butterflies land on people like that. One time was my Uncle Larry. He never seemed to smile. I thought he was always grumpy. But one day when we were visiting him and on a family picnic, a butterfly landed on his shoulder. And he got the biggest smile you ever saw! All it took was a beautiful butterfly to make him happy instead of grumpy.

So the next time that psychiatrist came to see me at school I was ready for him! He asked if I had any new drawings to show him. This time I gave him a brand new picture of a butterfly that I made with all my new crayons. It had red and yellow and blue, like the ones I'd seen in the park.

He looked at it and said, "Wow! That's wonderful, Kenneth. It's beautiful, it really is." Then he got a funny look on his face. He said, "And is that a woman on the back of the butterfly?"

"Yep," I told him. And I had a big smile on my face because I knew what I was about to say next.

"Well, who is she?"

I told him, "That's my momma." And now I was about to bust because now I was telling my story and the best part is about to happen.

"What's she doing there?"

And that's when I said, "She's there so she can fly around the room here and make sure you give me an A+ this time."

The teacher's tenderness had been soothing my anger for the last few minutes, so by the time Kenny got to the part where his mom was flying around the room on a butterfly, I was able to let out an audible laugh. Not a hearty laugh, mind you. But the kind that was muffled by the lump in my throat and sent a conflicting message with the tears in my eyes.

Yes, part of me was still angry about the crayons. And part of me hated the psychiatrist. But the bigger part of me was cheering for the little boy inside the man across from me. And what a sweet victory it was.

Well played, Kenny Tedford. Well played.

That was the first time I ever saw that psychiatrist smile. And then he got that look in his eyes like he was maybe gonna cry, but he didn't. He just said, "What a beautiful story." I guess a story doesn't have to be long to be a good story.

Then he took out his red marker and cupped his hand around it so I couldn't see what he was writing. He scribbled something at the top of my picture. Then he rolled it up gave it back to me. He told me, "Put this in your backpack and don't look at it till you get home."

Well, let me tell you, it wasn't easy to walk all the way home without taking a peek in my backpack. When I got there I ran straight back to my room, pulled out the paper and unrolled it. And there at the top of the page was a giant red A+! I was so happy!

That's when I learned one of the most important lessons I've ever learned in my life. That I could do things just as good as other kids as long as I had the same opportunities. Give me the same crayons, and I can be a great artist. Give me the same education, and I won't have to sweep floors my whole life. I can do anything I want.

And with those words, Kenny brought my emotional roller coaster ride to a sobering and fitting conclusion. I'd laughed. I'd cried. I'd seethed in anger. And I'd cheered for joy. All in the course of a few minutes time.

But what I was left with was a sense of comprehending something I'd been struggling to understand about Kenny Tedford since the day I met him. In fact, it was one of the main reasons I embarked on this journey to begin with: How on Earth could someone like Kenny Tedford have such a positive outlook on life? And I think I'd just found one of those reasons in a dour psychiatrist, a merciful teacher, a beautiful butterfly, and a box of crayons.

Not surprisingly, this seemingly small victory turned out to be one the turning points in Kenny's life that made him uniquely who he is today.

I suspected I'd find more as our interviews continued. (And I did.) But this was one of my first moments of satisfaction that I think I'd found one of the secrets to his success. One of the buried treasures in his life that makes him so rich in spirit.

I couldn't wait to see what jewel got unearthed next.

~ ~~

I guess a lot of interesting things happened at 7-Eleven. There was another day I was in the car with mom and dad and we went there to go shopping. When we got there, a man was walking out the front door with a bright yellow coat on. Daddy said something about his coat that, to me, made it sound like it was magic. So I jumped out of the car and ran up to the man. I grabbed his coat and pulled it up to my head and pressed my best ear into it.

The man reached down and pulled his coat away. I grabbed it again and leaned my head into it again. It wasn't working, so I started shaking it a little to see if I could get it to work. The man reached down and slapped my hand away. And about that time, I saw my daddy jump out of the car and start marching over to me the way he did when I was in trouble.

Daddy walked up to the man and said, "I'm so sorry, sir. Very sorry." But I was still trying to get it to work, so I was still shaking his coat, and trying to put my other ear up to it. Eventually, Daddy pulled me away and said, "Let go of the man's coat, Kenneth!"

I let go and the man kind of straightened his coat up and looked all bothered with me. Then he said, "What's going on here?!"

My father started to explain, "I'm sorry. See, my son . . . well, see, he doesn't understand expressions like that . . ."

And he wasn't making any sense, so I just said, "Daddy, it's not loud at all. I don't hear anything!"

Well, the man looked down at me, and then up at my daddy. Then he said, "So . . . you're teaching your kids to make fun of other people, are you?"

"No, of course not, sir. I'm very sorry. I . . ."

But the man interrupted Daddy and said, "Well, you think my coat is loud, do you?"

My dad said, "I'm sorry, let me explain. My son takes everything we say literally. I didn't mean to insult you."

Well, the man put his arm on my shoulder and said, "Son, you're a good boy. I'm sorry I got upset with you." And then he walked away.

It's the kind of thing I never could understand. "That shirt is loud. That coat is loud." Why can't ya'll just say "bright?"

In addition to writing, this was obviously one of Kenny's other cognitive idiosyncrasies: difficulty understanding metaphors and analogies. It made me realize how meaningless it is to say that someone has a "mental disability." What disability, exactly? An inability to learn math? Diminished facility with abstract concepts? Verbal challenges? Everyone's disabilities are unique, just like everyone's abilities are unique.

And, once again, I liked the way Kenny's father dealt with this situation, accepting, nonjudgmental, and straightforward: "Kenny doesn't understand expressions like that. . ."

And once again, my own parenting suffered by comparison. I couldn't help but remember one of my most shameful parenting moments involved a similar challenge with metaphors.

I was at a restaurant having lunch with my family. During the conversation, I used what I thought was a simple metaphor to explain something. I can't even remember what it was now. But one of my boys didn't understand, so I repeated myself, thinking that surely he just hadn't heard me properly the first time. When that and two other attempts to explain didn't work, I got frustrated and blurted out something like, "Seriously!? Are you that stupid?"

The regret set in before the words were even done coming out of my mouth. My wife stopped me immediately and shot me a look that told me I'd crossed the line. An understatement if ever there was one.

I looked over at my sweet boy just in time to watch him literally hang his head in shame as he began to cry.

It was one of those moments that I could never undo, but that I'd have traded almost anything I owned if I could.

How could I have been so callous?

I beat myself up for years over that misstep. But today, as I considered Kenny's story of the loud yellow coat, for the first time I understood perhaps why I'd made such a grave error. Both of my boys score well above average on academic and mental acuity tests. But I'd made the assumption that meant they were basically like everyone else, that they weren't unique in any of their mental abilities, or disabilities. And that wasn't true.

And why should it be? My wife and I both made straight A's in college. But I get lost in my own neighborhood, and my wife struggles with junior high math. Those are our disabilities. The whole family accepts them for what they are and acts accordingly. We even laugh about it every time it comes up ("Don't ask Dad for directions, and don't ask Mom for help with your math homework.")

And for one of our children, at that one point in his life, he struggled with metaphors. I'd seen it before. I just didn't accept it like I did my own struggles. A mistake I hadn't seen clearly until just now.

I wondered how Kenny's father would have handled that situation at lunch with my son. And I wondered if he'd ever flown off the handle or done or said anything he'd live to regret. He was human, after all, so I'm sure he had.

But these were all just things that raced through my head as Kenny told his story. The only thing I ended up saying out loud was, "I like your dad a lot. Tell me more about him."

I remember Daddy always had grease all over him when he came home from working at the railroad, so he was probably some kind of mechanic or engineer. But that's not what I remember thinking when I was a kid. Words like 'mechanic' and 'engineer' didn't mean anything to me back then. What I remember him telling me was much more exciting.

Back in those days we had hobos. They might live out in the woods or on the streets. But they would ride from town to town on the cargo trains looking for work or a place to stay. Once the cows got taken off the cattle cars, the hobos would jump in and get a free ride. There was always a lot of hay they could use for their bunk bed.

Daddy's job, the way I remember it, was to go from car to car checking for hobos. He had a lantern he carried with him at night so he could see in the empty cattle cars. And he'd write down the train car numbers after he checked them. That way, if they found hobos at the next stop, he'd know they got on after the train stopped in Dallas.

The cool part was, when he'd checked the last car, he'd stand on the side of the caboose. They don't have those anymore. But that was the last car on the train. And it was really small and was always painted bright red. Then he'd take his lantern and swing it out to the side so the engineer knew they were cleared to go. I thought he had the coolest job in the world.

He worked the evening shift from three to eleven. But bedtime was nine o'clock on school nights, so we usually didn't get to see him until the next morning before school.

But one night in December, my momma said, "Kids, do you want to stay up and wait for Daddy to come home?"

"But we have school tomorrow, Momma."

"I know," she said. "But I think you should get to stay up and see Daddy."

We were all ready for bed and in our pajamas with the little footies connected to the bottom. I hated them, really. Pajamas suck. But getting to stay up for Daddy was exciting. And it was a week before Christmas, so we were all happy and in a good mood. We stayed up and played games and watched a movie. It was like a special treat.

When Daddy got home he came into the kitchen. He had grease all over him from working on the trains. He unzipped his jumpsuit and took it off. Put his lunch pail on the counter. It was one of those old-fashioned ones that was like a rectangle on the bottom but rounded on the top to fit a Thermos bottle. Momma took it and pulled out the rest of the coffee and leftovers and cleaned it up. Daddy smelled like grease.

He put his hands on his hips and looked down at us. He looked like a giant. But he was our hero. Then he said, "Come here!" And we all ran over and jumped up in his arms and hugged him.

Then I grabbed him around the neck. Even then I loved to wrestle with my daddy. So I got him in a headlock, and he said, "You think you can hold me?"

"Yeah, Daddy!"

So he got on his knees and said, "Try again." And I don't know if you've heard of them, but we called them a knuckle sandwich. That's when he'd make a fist and rub his knuckles on my head. I'd say, "Okay, Daddy, I give up." And he'd smile and call me a "cry baby," and we'd laugh and hug.

So we did all that and then he stopped and said, "What are y'all doing up at this hour?" I thought it was kind of funny that it took him that long to ask.

Momma said, "I just think they needed to see you, honey."

"Well, thank you, honey," he said. "So what's been going on with everyone?" So everybody told him what we did that day; Momma; my older sisters, Sandy and Dora; my baby sister, Mary; and my baby brother, Robert. My other brothers and sisters had grown up and moved away by then.

We all had a good talk. Then everyone gave him a hug. I was last, and he popped me on the butt and said, "Now get to bed, boy." I gave him a big hug around his neck, and then started to walk off to my room. I turned around before I got there and he was still on his knees, leaning back on his heels, looking at me. He said, "I love you."

I said, "I love you, too, Daddy," and I went off to bed.

When I woke up the next morning, I was alone. That was strange because all of us kids slept in the same room. Then I realized it was already 8:30. And I thought, "My goodness, we're supposed to get up at seven to get ready for school!" So I jumped up, still in my pajamas with the little footies. I opened the door and walked down the hall, and there was a room full of people. There were some older men there smoking. Some of my dad's best friends from the train station. Back then, people smoked in the house. Seemed to me like everyone smoked in those days. And everyone was talking.

I started walking through the room, between people's legs, to look for my momma. I didn't know what was going on, because some of the people were laughing, but some of them were crying and others were hugging. As I got near the kitchen, I could see my mom on the phone. Then all of a sudden, she let out a wail of a cry and started to faint. One of her friends grabbed her and set her in a chair. She dropped the phone as she was sitting down, and somebody picked it up and finished the conversation.

I tried to run to her, but somebody grabbed me and swooshed me up, and took me out to the front porch. It was my sister, Sandy. I asked her what was going on. And she said, "Daddy passed away."

"What do you mean, 'passed away'?" I hadn't experienced death before, at least not with a person.

She tried to explain it to me in a nice way that a child who was labeled 'retarded' and 'slow' and didn't understand words very well could understand. But she was only two years older than me. So she said, "Daddy bought the farm."

Well I jumped up and started clapping and laughing all excited. My sister grabbed me and pulled me forward with an angry look. She said, "What's wrong with you? What's wrong with you?"

I said, "Daddy bought the farm! Daddy bought the farm! Now we can move from here and live on a farm!" I loved animals, especially farm animals. I was crazy about horses.

Then my sister said, "You're crazy! He didn't buy a farm. Daddy died!"

I said, "I know. You said that. But I don't know what you mean." I was still excited because Daddy bought a farm.

She was just so mad at me. She yelled, "He kicked the bucket, Kenneth! He kicked the bucket!"

And I got quiet and looked up at her.

She said, "Now do you understand?"

I said, "No. I mean, if Daddy kicked the bucket . . . I hope he didn't hurt his foot."

Sandy said, "You're impossible! Just impossible!" Then she said, "Come here. . . Do you remember your turtle?"

I said, "Albert?"

"Yes, Albert. You know, the one that died just last week. What did Daddy tell you happened to him?"

"He said he went to turtle heaven."

"Right," she said. "That's what death is. Remember? We had to bury him."

"I remember," I said.

Then she said, "You remember the goldfish?"

"Oh yeah."

"What did we do with them?"

"Well, when they died, we flushed them down the toilet."

"And Daddy told you what?"

"That they went to fish heaven."

"Right. And they're happy . . . Well, that's where Daddy is. He's in people heaven."

"Ohhh," I said. "Okay."

Then she told me to go inside and put on my clothes. So I did.

The day went by pretty fast. But some parts of it seemed like it was in slow motion. I walked around the living room, the dining room, and around the house. It was full of people. Friends of my father. Relatives and family. It was awesome. In a sense it was like a big party.

That afternoon, we all had to dress up in our best Sunday shoes and socks. My white shirt. Bowtie. Vest. My little hat. And shorts. You could wear shorts in Dallas in December because it was pretty warm there. Plus, I never liked wearing pants.

We were about to set off to see my daddy in the funeral home. The real funeral was a couple of days later. But they let some family and friends come in early to see Daddy, so we loaded the car and headed out.

When we got there, I asked a lot of questions. I guess I always talked a lot and had a lot of questions. "Why is Daddy layin' there in a box? Why is he in his Sunday suit? What's the box for? What're they gonna do with the box when we leave?"

I even remember when it was time to leave, I ran back in to get the casket. Everybody said, "Kenneth, what are you doin'?"

I said, "Well, we can't leave Daddy here all night. It's cold! He's gotta come home." They got angry with me. But I was just trying to understand.

Mostly, I just watched all the people talking. I remember it was the same thing that was happening at our house. People gathered around crying and hugging and telling stories about my dad. Of course, a lot of it I never understood. But the plain and simple things that I know, that I could read from people's lips, I remember. Things like, "I love you." But I remember a lot of "I wish . . . I wish . . . I wish . . ." And "If only I had told him . . . If I had only given him a hug . . . If I'd only told Mr. Tedford what a wonderful job he did at the train station . . . If only . . . If only . . . If only."

And I realized then how sad it must be for people who never share how much they love someone. It's just a simple three words: I. Love. You. And you never know when someone will be gone forever. Then I thought about how lucky I was the night before. Because those were the last words I ever spoke to my father, and the last words he ever spoke to me. That became one of the most memorable evenings I spent with my father. Because in a way I got to say goodbye.

The doctors said he had a massive heart attack. It was one week before Christmas, December 17, 1961. He was 37 years old.

I was a blubbering mess and so was Kenny. We both needed a mental and emotional palette cleanser. And a cup of coffee wouldn't do it. I needed a full reset. So we took an early dinner and promised each other not to talk about anything too serious for the rest of the evening, which we somehow managed to do.

When we resumed our interviews the next day, the story continued. . .

The next day I woke up early in the morning. The sun was just coming up. I looked around the house, and there was nobody there. I heard Susie barking really loud outside. And then I heard a door slam. I walked into the kitchen and there was a note. It said, "Kenneth, I've gone to get some food. I took your brother and sisters with me. We'll be back soon. Please keep the doors and windows locked."

So I made sure the door was locked. Then I went in my parent's bedroom and saw that the window was open, and the curtains were blowing in the wind. I walked over and closed it and locked it. And about then I got this strange sense that someone was in the room with me. And there was this strange odor, a smell. And I've smelled that smell before, but I didn't know where.

When I turned around, I saw him hiding behind the tall dresser. It was a man with a hat pulled down over most of his face. He was wearing an old, dirty overcoat. And he pulled a knife out of his pocket, like from the kitchen. I tried to scream, but nothing came out. So I just started running around the bed and headed for the door. And just as I got to the door, he reached up and grabbed me by the hair on my head. He pulled my head back and the knife came up in the air . . .

And that's when I woke up. Soaking wet with sweat. And crying. I didn't understand at first that it was just a dream, because the smell was still on me. That odor. So I went to take a shower to get the smell off of me. I didn't understand it. But at least the smell washed off. What I couldn't get rid of was a strange feeling that it was somehow my fault that my daddy died. I didn't know why that would be. But it just seemed that it was.

That wouldn't be the last time Kenny had that dream. And it would take him another twenty-three years to figure out what it meant. But that reason turned out to explain a lot of what happened to him in the intervening years. It even explains much of who he is and what his life is like to this day.

~ ~

At some point in my journey to understand Kenny Tedford, it occurred to me that I might get some ideas from other people with disabilities. So I started reading some well-known authors with disabilities, and used those insights to ask better questions of Kenny. One of those questions turned out to be one of the most important to ask because, to Kenny, it was one of the most important to answer.

"Kenny, I've been reading Helen Keller's autobiography. She said that the most important day of her life was the day she met her teacher, Anne Sullivan."

"Yes," he said, very matter-of-factly. He was obviously familiar with the story.

"How about you? Do you have a most important day of your life?"

Unlike most of my questions, this one gave Kenny some pause. At first, that pause was to consider the question and think through the many options for what the best answer might be. But I could tell the moment he settled on the answer in his head. The expression on his face turned from contemplative to melancholy. And that's when I knew I'd asked a good question.

They say my momma was an abusive alcoholic. But I don't remember much of it that way. It just seemed to me she was quiet a lot. And she always had a headache. Which really meant she was hung-over from the night before.

But I do remember the time she threw an iron at my brother, and it went right past my head. And then there was the time she went out on the front porch and fired a shotgun to scare off one of the neighbors she was having an argument with.

I guess things like that did happen from time to time. When they did, Sandy would send us all out into the front yard, and she would stay behind and call our older brother, Terry. Then she would come out last. And then, Terry would come and save us in his red Volkswagen Super Beetle. We'd see his headlights coming and knew we'd be okay.

But the day I remember the most was very different than those days. And I guess you could say it was the most important day of my life. But first, you have to understand that every Saturday morning at 10 o'clock, Mighty Mouse came on TV. Mighty Mouse is who I wanted to be. If you've ever seen Mighty Mouse, or heard about him and know what his purpose is, you know his theme song was, "Here I am to save the day!" That's what I wanted to do. Even when I was a kid. I wanted to save everybody's day.

I remember Momma asked me one Saturday, "Why do you like Mighty Mouse so much, and not Mickey Mouse, or Donald Duck, or any of those other characters?"

I told her, "'Cuz, Momma, I'm gonna be Mighty Mouse."

"Why's that, Kenneth?"

I said, "'Cuz I want to save everyone's day. I'm gonna make everyone happy."

She must have liked that answer, because she said, "Where on earth did I get you? She liked to say that a lot when I said something smart.

"I told you, from the front porch, Momma!"

She laughed and laughed. "Stop saying that. You're my son, you silly boy."

Well, a few days later I noticed Momma didn't feel very well. She'd been having headaches. But these were different from her normal headaches. She was laying on the couch with a wet rag on her head. Everyone was begging her to go to the doctor. On Thursday she finally went to the hospital to see a doctor.

And then on Friday, it was odd. Momma was just as sweet as can be. She even made our favorite food. And then on Saturday morning, of course, I was watching Mighty Mouse. And before the show was even over, she came in and said, "Come here, Kenneth."

"But Momma, Might Mouse isn't over."

"I know. But I need to talk to you."

We went out on the back porch. Momma sat in her chair, and had her coffee. She said, "Come here," and patted her lap.

I protested, "Momma, Mighty Mouse is still on."

She just patted her lap again.

I climbed up and sat on her lap sideways like I normally did. But she didn't want me that way. She picked me up and put one of my legs on each side of her so I was facing her. She smelled like peppermint, which was different, but nice.

I complained again, "Momma."

But she just shushed me.

I looked at her, and she looked at me. And she said, "I want you to know I'm sober."

"Huh?"

"I'm not drunk, Kenneth. And what I have to tell you is important."

"What's wrong, Momma?"

She said, "Nothing's wrong." But she had tears in her eyes while she was talking. One fell onto her cheek and I reached up and wiped it away.

"But you're crying, Momma."

"Shhhhh. Listen to me," she said.

"Yes, ma'am."

"I just wanted to tell you how much I love you."

"Sure. I know that, Momma. Why are you telling me this?"

"You're the man of the house now. Daddy's been gone for a while. And someday when I die, I want you to look after your baby brother and baby sister."

"Are you gonna die, Momma?"

She said, "Oh no, no. I'm gonna live to see you have grandkids! I'll be a great-grandma!"

"Oh. . . well, what's wrong?"

"Nothing. I just wanted to see your beautiful face. And tell you how much I love you."

"Oh. . . I love you, too, Momma."

Then she leaned over and kissed me on the forehead. That made bright red lipstick marks on my face.

I said, "Ma-muuh!" You know, the same way you probably did when you wanted your momma to stop kissing you.

"Shhhhh."

Then she said, "Whatever you do, just remember that your heart," and she poked me in the chest, "is bigger than your head."

I just said, "Awwww."

She goes, "What's wrong?"

"I said, "I don't want my heart to be *that* big!"

She just laughed and hugged me. "My boy, my boy," she said. "I'm not gonna worry about you. You're gonna be fine. You're gonna do great things when you grow up."

I asked her, "How do you know?"

She just shushed me again. I guess she wanted to do all the talking in this conversation. "Trust me," she said. "But I want you to forget me. I haven't been a very good mom to you."

I tried to interrupt, "Momma . . ." but she just shushed me again.

"Just hear me out . . . I wish I'd been a better mom. But there is one thing I'm gonna tell you. You're the most precious thing in my life . . . and I'm proud that you're my son. No matter what anyone else tells you. You don't believe them."

"Yes ma'am."

Then I saw that she was crying again, so I reached up and wiped another one of her tears away. Then she said, "Okay, now go play."

Kenny's voice started to break as his own eyes welled up with tears. He turned his head slightly and stared off into the distance. But unlike his other stories, this wasn't a performance.

"But, Momma . . ." Now I was the one trying to stay.

Then she started to kiss me again all over my face, so I guess I changed my mind and tried to squirm away saying, "Momma!" Well that got her to laugh, so I grabbed her by the neck and hugged her, and said, "I love you, Mom."

She said, "I love you, too." And she let me go.

His voice cracked, and he paused for a moment to compose himself.

Two days later, it was Monday. When I came home for lunch, she was lying on the couch with a bad headache again.

She was groaning in pain. But she made me my favorite meal anyway, homemade chili and a grilled cheese sandwich with onions and tomatoes. Not everyone else in the house liked it that way. But I did, so she made it for me.

I could hardly eat it because I was worried about her. But she kept saying, "Eat. Eat. You have to go back to school."

I said, "No! No! I want to stay with you."

"No, you're going back to school. You need to be educated."

"I'll be fine, Momma."

About that time, my older sister, Sandy, came home. As she was walking by the couch, Momma reached up and grabbed her hand, and said, "Sweetheart." My sister looked down at her. And Momma said, "Make sure Kenneth goes back to school." And she looked at me, because she knew I would be reading her lips. "Make sure he goes to school. He needs his education. . . but I want you to stay." And then she told me, "You listen to your big sister, Kenneth."

Sandy put my stuff in my backpack. And I finished eating. I kissed Mom, and told her I loved her. And I went back to school.

When I got home from school, they told me she was in the hospital. An ambulance had come and taken her.

Four days later she died.

Some people told me she had a brain tumor. Years later, they told me it was an aneurism that killed her. Either way, my momma died on Friday, May 18, 1962. She was forty-three years old.

Sometime that week I woke up in the middle of the night. I smelled that same smell I smelled the night my Daddy died. It scared me, so I got up and ran into my parent's room. But nobody was there. Then I noticed that the bedroom window was open and the curtains were blowing in the wind, so I went over and shut the window and locked it.

When I turned around, the man was there. The same man as before. He was wearing that same old, dirty overcoat. And he pulled a knife out of his pocket, just like before. I tried to scream but nothing came out. I just started running around the bed and headed for the door. And just as I got to the door, he reached up and grabbed me by the hair on my head. He pulled my head back and the knife came up in the air.

And that's when I woke up again. Soaking wet with sweat, and crying, just like before. Only this time, I didn't go take a shower. The smell was gone. But I remember thinking that it was my fault my momma had died. I know it doesn't make sense. It didn't to me either. But I just had that feeling.

When we went to the funeral, I remember hearing a lot of the same words I did when Daddy died. "I wish I'd said this . . ." or "I wish I'd done that." Even one of my sisters had gotten in an argument with her right before my mother died. And she wished she'd ended it by telling her, "I love you."

But I treasure those last moments with my mom, and they changed my life. She'd never sat down to talk to me like she did in those last days, really talked to me, eyeball to eyeball. Sincere. With compassion. She never did that with me. She was always drinking, or sad, or depressed, or complaining. She slept a lot. It took me years to forgive my mother for that.

We did a lot when Daddy was alive. We'd go on picnics and things. But I think his death was the last straw for her. She loved him dearly.

I always assumed she was ashamed of me. Kids would say, "Your parents don't love you, they don't want you." I've even been told, "You're the reason your mom is an alcoholic."

But that moment was beautiful. She made that moment to make me feel important and loved . . . and that I had the biggest heart of anyone in the family.

Kenny's voice had started breaking again in these last few sentences as the emotions overcame him. I felt incredibly humbled to have him share such a personal moment with me. But also, a little guilty. When I asked him about an important day in his life, I was assuming he'd tell me about his favorite teacher, or an award he earned. But this? Who was I to force him to relive such a painful experience? And how long did I think I had the right to let it continue?

Hearing his voice crack even more, I decided it was time to take a break and move on to the next topic. I was infinitely grateful that this kind, gentle man had shared such a deep and painful memory, and I didn't want to intrude any further. I thanked him and pushed the keyboard away.

But he wasn't done.

Sometimes when I want to quit . . .

He was sobbing at this point.

Sometimes when I want to quit life, I think of that moment. When I'm feeling unworthy. When I think "I can't do this," I think of that moment. And I know that I was loved. That I am loved. That I am worthy. And that I can do this. That one moment of honesty and love gets me through a lot.

Chapter 4: Back of the Bus

Well, I guess you can't have five kids living in a house without a grownup. After Momma died, somebody had to figure out what to do with all of us. And that was a problem, because nobody in the family had much money or room to take us.

My half-sister, Betty, was the oldest of all of Momma's children from her first marriage. She was all grown up and had six kids of her own, so she couldn't take us all.

Aunt Jessie and Uncle Larry had a two-bedroom house in Memphis. But they had a daughter plus Aunt Jessie's mother living with them, so Larry told her we couldn't stay there.

When they all came to Dallas for momma's funeral, Betty packed up all our things to move. Dora was going to live with Betty since they were full sisters from Momma's first marriage. Sandy (11), Mary Bess (7), and Robert (5) were all scheduled to go off to orphanages. And I was gonna be sent to an institution, because orphanages didn't take kids with disabilities. So that was basically going to be the end of my family, with all of us either dead or shipped off to different places.

But I guess when Jessie got to see all four of us little kids together, she couldn't bear the thought of us being split up. Over the next week, Jessie and grandma convinced Larry to let us all come to Memphis and live with them. They completed all the background checks, got approval from the neighbors, and filed for status as foster parents.

The day we arrived in Memphis, everybody came out to the driveway to greet us. We were just getting out of the car. Everybody had big smiles. And they said, "Welcome to your new home!" Aunt Jessie and grandma were giving us all hugs and kisses.

Uncle Larry started hugging everyone, too. Except, when he got to me he just patted me on the head and walked past me. I thought, "What am I, a dog?" Then, I saw Aunt Jessie say something to him, and he came back and kind of hugged me a little. So I was glad I wasn't in an institution. But I could tell something wasn't right between me and Uncle Larry.

Eight people was a lot to live in a two-bedroom house. But the state provides money to foster parents, so Larry was able to have a third bedroom and second bathroom added to the house eventually. I spent the next eleven years of my life in that home, on Tatum Road in Memphis.

I was pretty excited to move to Tennessee. I heard they were nice friendly people with all that Southern charm. Turns out they were mostly like everyone else.

There was a park just down the street from our house where I met some kids. They came up to me like . . .

At that point, Kenny executed what had now become a staple of our conversations, the mumbling and slapping an awkwardly bent hand against his chest.

And I was thinking, "Oh my God! These poor kids. They got the same problems here they did in Dallas! It must be in the water."

I went home feeling kind of bad for them. And my foster mother said, "What's wrong? Who's pickin' — I'm calling the school — who's pickin' on you?"

I told her, "Nobody's pickin' on me."

And she asked me, "Then why are you upset?"

"Because everybody I talk to keeps walkin' up to me mumbling," and I showed her how they were acting. "Their arms don't work right. They can't even talk."

She just laughed. She goes, "I ain't gonna worry about you."

Well, I thought that was strange because that's the same thing my mother said back in Dallas. And I said, "I hope somebody worries about me." You know? But I knew then that Aunt Jessie was gonna be good to me.

Uncle Larry was a different story. I could tell right away he didn't want to have anything to do with me. And he would yell at Aunt Jessie, and call her names. Plus, if she didn't cook his bacon the way he wanted it, he'd throw it at her.

One day, I was trying to work on my reading. I love to read. But I couldn't understand all the words, so I went to Uncle Larry to ask for help. He was in his recliner, reading the paper. I asked him to help me. And he just said, "Why? You're retarded. You're just gonna get a government check. You don't need to learn any of this stuff." Then he went back to reading the paper.

But later on, when Robert wanted to go outside and play catch, he said "Sure," and jumped right up.

About three weeks after we moved in, I had my first argument with Uncle Larry. I was on the floor, laying on my tummy, reading the comics in the Sunday paper. He came in and stood over me. All I saw was his legs in front of me. I looked up. He looked down. And he yelled, "I told you to mow the yard! Now, get out there and mow it!"

I just said, "Later," and put my head back down to read the comics.

He yelled out, "What!? I'm gonna. . ." and I looked up. And when I looked up, his hand was raised. So then I kind of stood up real quick. I was only eight years old. But I thought I had to protect myself.

And I don't know what made me say this. But I just said, "If you hit me, I promise you, you'll be sittin' on your big, fat butt!"

Well, he couldn't believe I said that. He started huffing and puffing. Then he yelled out, "Jessie! Jessie! Get in here!"

And she came running into the room and said, "What? What?"

He said, "Deal with him!" And then he stomped out of the room.

She came over to me and said, "What are you doin'?"

"Nothing!"

"Well, something just happened."

"Uncle Larry asked me to mow the yard. And I told him I'd do it later. And then, he started to slap me."

"He actually hit you?"

"No, but he had his hand raised like he was goin' to."

"All right then. I'll talk to him about that. But, Kenneth, he won't get mad at you if you'll just do what he says. Now, please, go mow the yard."

So I went out to mow the yard. I guess I learned a lesson that I should obey my aunt and uncle better. But it made me think Uncle Larry wasn't gonna be a very good foster father.

~ ~

I don't remember ever going to church until after my parents died. But Aunt Jessie told me a story about the first time I was ever in a church. And it was the day I got off the incubator. Probably the greatest thing my momma ever did.

Aunt Jessie said that when my momma and daddy were driving me home from the hospital, they passed a little white chapel with a pointed roof and a cross on top. Presbyterian. She saw it and said to my daddy, "I want to go into that church." Daddy thought that was strange since they never went to church. They took me in and Daddy was like, "Okay, what do you want to do now?"

They walked up to the altar. Momma picked me up and held me up high, and gave me to God.

Aunt Jessie said I was the only one of Momma's nine children that she dedicated to God. But Momma knew she would have issues with her drinking. And she probably thought all my problems would make life hard for us both. I guess she wanted all the help she could get.

I found out Aunt Jessie was a very religious woman who loved to go to church. I thought she was a religious nut-and-a-half. Every time they even vacuumed the church for a wedding, we would go help.

The thing is, about going to church, you have to understand what it's like from an eight-year-old boy's perspective, a little deaf boy with brain damage who doesn't understand a lot of language. It was strange.

I remember the first time I went to church with them. I was sitting there on the pew, but I couldn't understand much of what anyone was saying. I liked the singing, though. But back then, they didn't have a lot of instruments. It was just an organ. To me, it just sounded like a low humming. It was like a funeral every time I went to Sunday service.

And they would sing. And pray. Then sing. And pray. And then the preacher would get up and preach. And then pray. Sing and pray. Sing and pray. And at the end of everything that they would say or sing, they said something that surprised me. I thought, 'Oh . . . this is weird."

And then they passed around the offering plate. And my foster mother told me, "Put your nickel in. Put your nickel in."

So I put my nickel in. And then I started moving all the coins and fishing around to the bottom of the plate. When she saw me, she smacked my hand. And then she said, "What are you doing?"

Kenny delivered Aunt Jessie's line in a way that looks like screaming but only sounds like a whisper.

So I started to tell her, "I'm looking for —"
But she shushed me.
Then she asked me again, "What are you doing?"
So I said, "I'm trying to tell you, I'm looking for —"
But she shushed me again. I guess it was supposed to be a quiet time, and deaf people can talk too loud sometimes.

Kenny, playing Aunt Jessie, waved his hand dismissively in a way that meant, "Never mind," but that young Kenneth knew also meant, "We're gonna talk about this later, young man."

Well, at the end of the service, you know what they did? They passed the offering plate around again! I couldn't believe it. But I didn't dig around in it this time, since I got in so much trouble last time. But I saw what they did with all those plates. After everyone filled them up, some people took them all and stacked them up in the back of the church.

As soon as church was over, I asked Aunt Jessie if I could go outside. She said, "Sure, go!" but not in the happy way. It was more in the way you'd say it if you just wanted to get rid of someone.

I ran down the aisle, all the way down to where all the plates were stacked up. I ran up to them to look inside and . . . they were empty! I thought, "Oh, man! They're gone!" So I started picking up the plates on top and moving them so I could see the ones underneath.

Aunt Jessie saw me and ran over and smacked my hands again. "What are you doing? That's embarrassing! Are you looking for money?"

"Noooaah!" I said. "Who cares about money?"

"Then what are you looking for?"

"Al-monds."

"Al-monds?"

I nodded and said, "Mm-hmm."

"You mean almonds? Why are you looking for almonds?"

"Because ya'll do all during church service."

"What are you talkin' about?"

"Well, at the end of every song, every prayer, and the sermon, everyone keeps sayin', 'aaaaaal-monnnds.'"

"Ugh. Kenneth, we're sayin' 'A-men.'"

"No, you're not. You're sayin' 'aaaaal-monnnds' real long and slow. I'm watchin' your lips! Anyway, I figured when they passed the plate, when you put money in you'd get almonds. Only I didn't get any almonds. So I thought I'd come back here and look for 'em."

So then she wasn't mad at me anymore. In fact, when she got back from the grocery store that afternoon, she gave me my own little bag of almonds. Then she smiled at me and pretended to scold me. She wagged her finger at me and said, "Don't you ever do this again. You stay out of those offering plates."

I smiled back and said, "Yes, ma'am." I decided I really liked Aunt Jessie.

One Sunday, the sermon was about "Love your neighbors." I couldn't really understand the preacher that well. But I could read the bulletin. It always had a little paragraph of what the preacher said, so I could understand a little of it.

Well, we came home after church that day, and everyone was eating. And the TV was on. It was showing some people protesting something. It looked like a bunch of white men, all wearing a white shirt and tie, like they'd been at work. Apparently, they were protesting that a black family was moving into their neighborhood.

Uncle Larry looked over at us all and said, "Bunch a' n-words."

Only he didn't just say 'n-word'. He said the whole word. And you know what word I mean, right?

I nodded.

I'd never heard that word before, so I said, "What?"

So he said louder, "N*****s! N*****s!"

I could tell already I didn't like that word. I didn't know what it meant. But, just the way he said it. So mean and angry. I could tell it was an ugly word.

Aunt Jessie whispered, "Larry, stop it."

But he just said, "Well, they need to know. Theeeey need to know," pointin' at us.

So I asked, "Know what?"

"About n*****s!"

"What's a n****r?"

"Them! Black people! You're gonna call them n*****s, like everybody else."

I thought that didn't sound much like the sermon we just heard about "Love your neighbors." But Uncle Larry never did go to church with us on Sundays, so I guess that's why he didn't know about that.

But it still didn't make sense to me. We knew lots of black people in Dallas. We had neighbors who were black. Some of the men my daddy worked with and drank beer with and played cards with were black. They were friends. They would all hug us when they left.

And then there was Martha. Martha was our housekeeper. She was a big, heavyset black woman. She was a better cook than my mom. And she had the most beautiful, angelic voice. When she was making breakfast, she would sing these beautiful songs. Momma couldn't make breakfast on account of her headaches. Martha was a wonderful woman.

Then, one day, Momma tried to get me to do something, and I said, "I'm not doin' that. Momma said I don't have to!"

She said, "Momma told you that? I'm your Momma!"

"I know that. But Momma. You know. . . Momma."

"Who are you talking about?"

"Martha!"

Momma's eyes got big and she took a big breath and looked really mad. She said, "Did she tell you to call her 'Momma'?"

"No. But she's like a momma. She's a great cook. She sings like an angel. And she gets me ready for school in the morning."

The next morning, Momma was cooking breakfast in the kitchen.

We never saw Martha again.

That got a loud laugh out of me, and for a moment, I enjoyed the humorously transparent nature of Martha's dismissal.

But then I thought about her more deeply. What a wonderful thing that she was able to be part of the mother to Kenny that his real mother wasn't able to be. And I wondered what her best dish would taste like. I wondered what it would be like to hear her sing Kenny's favorite song. I liked this Martha, even though I'd just met her sixty seconds ago.

And, so far, I liked Aunt Jessie, too. I hoped that she would love him like Bessie Faye, sing for him like Martha, and raise him to be the strong, independent man like Kenny's father had.

But she'd have to do it on her own. Lord knows Uncle Larry wasn't going to be much help.

But Aunt Jessie knew how hard it was on me at school, being the deaf and "retarded" kid. She knew I would sometimes cry because the other kids didn't want to play with me, or because I couldn't understand what people were saying around me. Or because Uncle Larry didn't want me.

She told me one day, "You're gonna come to know Jesus."

I said, "Okay." But I didn't really know what that meant.

The church we went to was a Methodist Church, and we had a new pastor there. He was from Germany and he was a really big man. And to a little nine-year-old boy like me, he seemed ten feet tall! Plus, he was a military man. He scared the you-know-what out of me.

And he kept talking about Jesus. "Get saved! . . . He's watchin' you . . . Every move you make." And it seemed like he was always pointing at me when he said those things. Like he was saying, "You're a bad boy, Kenneth! You need to come up here and get saved."

I actually got saved three times in my life. The third one was a charm. But that wasn't until I was 17.

The first time was when I was nine, at that Methodist Church. I noticed that near the end of church they would ask people to come up to the front to get saved. And a lot of us kids would sit together, so I'd see them go down the pew to go up to the front to get saved. I wasn't really sure what that was all about. But when they came back they always had a brand-new little red Bible. And I would see Aunt Jessie with her hands together like she was praying, but she was looking at me. I knew she wanted me to go with them. And I did want one of those little red Bibles.

So one day, I said, "Okay" and I followed the rest of them down to the front. They sprinkled our heads with water. And they did give me a little red Bible. But I told the pastor that I didn't really want to get saved, because it just didn't make sense to me. I mean, think about it. Here I was born deaf. Can't see right. Brain damage. Both my parents died when I was eight. And my new foster father says he doesn't want me. But there's this Jesus guy in charge of everything, who's supposed to love me. Right.

~ ~

One day, not long after we moved to Memphis, Aunt Jessie wanted to go shopping, and I got to go with her. I guess we didn't really have malls and shopping centers in the part of town where we lived. We had to go all the way downtown. They had famous stores there like JC Penney's and Macy's and Sears & Roebuck. They were huge! Like a block long. And they were spotless.

But my grandma and Aunt Jessie never drove the car. And I guess Uncle Larry didn't want to have to drive us downtown and wait for us to go shopping. So we had to take the bus.

Now, I'd never been on a bus before. Actually, I'm not even sure I'd ever seen a bus in person when we lived in Dallas. Aunt Jessie got me dressed, and she got all prettied up. It was so much fun back then. We went outside and she held my hand as we walked down to the bus stop. I was so excited to ride on a bus.

It was in the summer, so it was really hot outside. But the bus came pretty soon and we got on. We sat right up front near the bus driver. There was a little plastic wall between him and us. And Aunt Jessie told me to behave because we were in public. So I sat there quiet like, just looking around. And then after a while, I tapped Aunt Jessie on the arm. She looked at me, and I said, "Aunt Jessie, why are all those black people back there?"

Now, when you're deaf or you can't hear well, you tend to talk really loud. So it probably sounded like I had just yelled that across the bus. There was a man and woman sitting across from us. The man put his paper down and looked at me like I had just done something really bad. I looked around and all the people in the front of the bus near us were white people. And most of them were looking at me funny, too, just like that man.

Then the bus driver turned around and told Aunt Jessie, "You hush that boy up. Hush him up!" Then Aunt Jessie shushed me.

A little bit later, the bus stopped and an old black lady got on. She had a cane, and could barely get up the stairs on the bus. So I got up to go help her, because that's what I thought you were supposed to do with old people who can't walk very well. But that man put his paper down again and looked at me the same way again. And the bus driver yelled at Aunt Jessie again and said, "Get that boy down!" She grabbed my pants and pulled me back.

I said, "But we need to help her." But Aunt Jessie just shushed me again.

The old lady put her money in the bucket and started to walk passed us. And when she did, she looked at me real nice and smiled and said, "It's okay, baby. It's okay." Then she kept walking. But the bus driver took off, and she almost fell down right in front of us. I reached out to grab her arm to help her from falling down. It probably didn't help much because I was just a little kid. But she reached up with her other hand and put it on top of my hand and held it for a while.

And, for some reason, that made the man with the newspaper and some of the other people get all mad again. The bus driver yelled out, "You better get that boy in control!" Aunt Jessie told me to sit down. And the old lady told me "It's okay, it's okay" in a sweet, quiet voice.

Then two black men stood up in the back of the bus and came to the front to help the lady. And the bus driver told them they better sit down and get in control, too, like he did me. I was getting upset, because my daddy always taught me to help people. And you remember how he told me not to make fun of people when I told that lady she was fat? Plus, we had friends in our neighborhood in Dallas who were black, and I don't remember people treating them like this.

Then things kind of settled down a little. I could feel a cool breeze coming from the back of the bus. It was a hot summer day, and every time someone got on the bus, all the hot air came in the front door and made it hot where we were sitting. And I was getting all sweaty, so I got up and told Aunt Jessie I was gonna sit in the back, and I started walking down the aisle. She reached out and grabbed my pants again and pulled me back and sat me down. Now she was actually mad at me. She said, "What are you doing?"

"I'm going to the back."

"You can't."

"Why not?"

"That's for the blacks only."

I said, "Boy, are they lucky." At that point, I don't think anyone was talking on the bus except me and Aunt Jessie because they were all looking at me.

"What did you say?"

So I said even louder, "I said, 'Boy, are they lucky.'" And by then I was kind of mad. I looked around the bus and then at the man with the paper across from me and I said, "Y'all are a bunch of idiots."

Kenny's mouth dropped wide open and his eyes got big as he stepped briefly into Aunt Jessie's character. Or the man across the aisle. Actually, I suppose it could have been just about anyone on the bus at that point.

I said, "It makes no sense. All the air-conditioning is back there. They're a lot smarter than all of you people are. I wanna sit back there with them."

About that time the bus stopped and the doors opened. Aunt Jessie jumped up and grabbed me by the arm and pulling me to the front. I said, "Is this our stop?"

Aunt Jessie said, "Nope. But we're getting off right now." And she pulled me off the bus. We got outside and she said, "You're gonna get us killed, Kenneth." As the bus was pulling away, I looked up through the windows at the back of the bus, and there were all these black people looking at me clapping and cheering.

We had to walk three or four more blocks to get to JC Penney's.

When we got home, she sat me down in the kitchen and gave me a glass of milk. She said, "We can't ride the bus if you behave like that, Kenneth."

I still didn't understand why the black people got to sit in the back with the air conditioning, so I asked her.

"Because they do, Kenneth. That's all." I told her I would be better. But it still didn't make sense.

I realized later that Aunt Jessie was just trying to protect me. My mother was the same way. They loved me dearly and wanted to protect me from things they thought would hurt me. My father loved me, too. But he never tried to protect me. He wanted me to skin my knees, so I'd learn to put on a Band-Aid.

And when bullies would pick on me at school, he'd say, "Well, what are you gonna do about it?" And, if I did something wrong that he warned me not to do, he'd say, "I told you there'd be consequences. You made your bed. Now you have to sleep in it."

I never understood that, him telling me I had to sleep in the bed. So I'd tell him that wouldn't fix anything because the problem was still going on. Then he'd ask me, "What do you need to do?"

"I don't know."

Then he'd say, "Change the sheets, Kenneth."

Well, I still wasn't done figuring out how to sleep in the bed, and now he's telling me to change the sheets. But I finally understood it when I got older. I needed to make the changes myself, not point fingers at everyone else.

At the time, I just thought he was mean. But now I know that was his way of making sure I grew up to be able to take care of myself.

I guess parents can have different ways of taking care of their children.

Well, the next day at school, I guess it was still bothering me that I didn't understand about the black people on the bus. When we were at lunch, I was sitting at a table with a bunch of other kids, eating a bologna sandwich with milk. I loved bologna sandwiches. And I just asked them, "Did ya'll know that black people sit on the back of the bus?"

And they all looked at me funny and said, "Of course."

"But, whyyyy?"

One of them looked at me and said, "Because they're n*****s."

I must have looked confused, because they said, "Don't you know what n****r means?"

I said, "Yeah, my Uncle said it means black people. But why do they have to sit on the back of the bus?"

And eight-year-old kids will tell you the straight truth , exactly what they think. They told me what their parents had been saying at home. They said "Because n*****s are lazy, worthless, they want to be given everything for free, free jobs, free education. Free everything!"

Then some of them asked me if I was a "n****r-lover."

I asked, "Why don't you like them . . . what did they do to you?" But I never could get a real answer. One girl told me they were smelly, so I asked her if she'd ever been around a black person, and she said no. So I asked, "Well, then how do you know they're smelly?"

She got all mad and stood up and said, "I don't like you. I'm gonna eat somewhere else," and she stomped off. Some other kids did the same thing. But that was okay, because there were other kids who heard what we were talking about. They came over and sat with me and said, "Good for you."

So I got to make some new friends with people who thought more like me. They were trying to get answers, too.

One of them said, "My daddy doesn't like black people. But I've never met one, so I don't know what I'm supposed to think." I told them that when my foster father found out I was playing with black kids at school, he threatened to send me to the orphanage. And I told him, "That's fine. I'd rather be in the orphanage with people who love me than with someone who doesn't."

They thought that was funny, but I'm not sure why. I didn't think it was funny, and neither did Uncle Larry. He just yelled at Aunt Jessie, "Jessie, the boy's talkin' back to me again!" And she came running in to take me off to the kitchen. That's how she'd protect me, from my own mouth, I guess. She said, "Kenneth, you be nice to Uncle Larry. He's tryin'."

"Tthhhppt! Doesn't look like he's tryin' to me."

I still couldn't figure out what was so different about black people. Another day I was at the park with Aunt Jessie. I went up to the water fountain and they had two of them. One of them said, "Whites Only" and one said, "Colored." I went to the colored fountain and took a drink. Then I stepped over to the white fountain and took another drink. Aunt Jessie looked at me and said,

"What are you doing!?"

I just said, "They both taste like water. It tastes the same."
Then I looked behind the fountains and there was just one little
pipe that went to both of them, so I said, "It's all coming from
the same place, Aunt Jessie."

Then she shushed me and we had to leave.

I never did get a good answer to my question about why
people didn't like black people. I'm sixty-five years old now, and
I still haven't gotten a good answer.

FOUR DAYS WITH KENNY TEDFORD

*Less than a month after we got married, my wife and I had our first big
fight. My college roommate's brother was coming to town and needed a place
to stay. Plus, we were friends and I wanted to visit with him. Naturally, I
assumed he'd stay with us in the second bedroom in our apartment.*

Wrong.

*My wife was an only child, and an introvert. Sharing space with me as
her newest family member was unfamiliar enough. But sharing our tiny
apartment with a complete stranger, even for only a few days, was simply
out of the question.*

Our argument was short and decisive. I lost.

*That was twenty-four years ago. And like most healthy couples, we
make each other stronger. I've adopted some of her more appealing qualities,
either through determined effort or sheer osmosis. And I'd like to think she's
adopted some of mine, one of those being comfort with strangers. But it takes
work, and it doesn't come naturally for her.*

*So I know how difficult it must have been for her to be told that I
wanted this old, deaf, partially blind, partially paralyzed, cognitively
impaired man she'd never met to come spend four days in our home so I*

could interview him. We didn't fight about it. She agreed immediately. But I knew I was asking a lot.

More important to her now than her own insecurities with strangers was her desire to make Kenny feel comfortable in our home, and not knowing exactly how to do that. Would it be awkward and uncomfortable for him here? While she definitely wanted him to feel welcome during his visit, she wasn't excited at the prospect of feeling responsible for making sure he did.

My fourteen-year-old son, Matthew, an introvert like his mother, was similarly apprehensive, but for his own unique and imaginative fourteen-year-old reasons. Apparently, my description of Kenny came across to Matthew as something like, "Hey, there's this crazy old deaf guy who was just released from a mental hospital who's gonna come stay with us for a while. Isn't that great?"

In truth, Matthew wasn't afraid of Kenny. He just didn't know what to expect. And, like a lot of introverts thrust into unfamiliar social settings, he doesn't like not knowing what to expect.

Then there was my nine-year-old, Ben, my patently extroverted, hyperactive, nonstop talker. When I asked Ben what he thought about Kenny coming to visit, his response belied the fact that he was not only indifferent, but found the question so oddly obvious that it bordered on boring. He said something like, "That's fine. When's dinner?"

So there we were. The anticipation in my house for Kenny's visit ranged from apprehensive to indifferent. Not exactly the most enthusiastic audience. My only solace was that Kenny had no idea what he was about to face.

Meanwhile, Kenny was experiencing his own fears in anticipation of the trip. Some were professional, like: will he have enough stories to fill the time, and would I find them interesting. But most of his fears were personal. They ranged from petty, ("Will my slippers squeak on the floor?" and "Will they hear me snore?"), to more consequential ("Are they going to be comfortable around me, and will they accept me for who I am?").

I guess we'd all find out soon enough.

Chapter 5: Learning to Talk

I found out in Memphis they have 7-Eleven stores, just like we did in Dallas. Well, one day Aunt Jessie took me there with her to shop.

When I went in, the woman that worked there looked at me and she goes, "Who's that cute little fella?"

Before Aunt Jessie could say anything, I looked up and I said, "I'm retarded."

The woman kind of looked me up and down. Then she looked at Aunt Jessie. And Aunt Jessie said, "He ain't mine. I found him on the road." Then they both laughed about that for a bit.

Well, we got home and Aunt Jessie said, "Why are you tellin' people you're retarded?"

I said, "Because that's what they call me at school. That's what they call me in the playground. And as a matter of fact, that's what my brothers and sisters call me."

"Well, don't you listen to any of them!" she said. "You're not retarded. But you are gonna have to learn to speak better and understand what people are saying to you."

I said, "Is that why you're always grabbin' my chin and shakin' my head back and forth?"

"Yes. Because every time I say something, you need to turn and look at me. You have to read lips better."

I go, "But why?"

"Because that's the only way you're gonna be able to communicate with other people."

"But a lot of times you got bad breath," I said.

Well I guess that wasn't nice. She pointed her finger in my face and goes, "Bad or not, you're gonna learn!"

And so after that, everyone in the family would grab my chin when they talked to me and made me look at them. My older sister Sandy would say, "Look at me, Kenneth, when I'm talkin'."

I'd say, "You're ugly," and that usually made her let me go.

But Aunt Jessie was right. I did need to learn. And the schools I was in weren't always very good at helping, even though they tried.

Like up until I was eight, I was always in Special Ed classes. Some of the reason why was because of the brain damage I had. But mostly it was because I was deaf. It's hard to learn when you can't hear or speak well.

I was what people in the deaf community called an "oralist." That meant that I read people's lips and tried my best to talk to them instead of using sign language. And without any training, you just learn to improvise. Just like if I was born with one leg, I'd learn how to get by with one leg.

One way I did that was by watching TV. When nobody else was in the room, I'd turn the TV up really loud and put my ear up on the speaker and try to make the same sounds.

Or, I could read the lyrics to a song and memorize them, like "Jesus loves me this I know / for the Bible tells me so . . ." And then I could watch when other people sang, and I could see how they did it.

A great way deaf kids can learn today is from closed captioning on TV shows. You read the words and then watch how they move their mouths. But we didn't have that back when I was a kid.

But it's better if you get special training where they know how to teach deaf people to talk. I'd just never had anything like that when I lived in Dallas.

Well, when we moved to Memphis, I went to the same school as my brothers and sisters. But Aunt Jessie started to notice that I didn't have homework like the others. Everyone else came home with math homework or reading or they were learning the alphabet. I just came home with pictures. That's how she figured out they'd placed me in Special Ed classes again. Well, that made Aunt Jessie mad and she started raising Cain with them.

She wanted me to be in regular classes so I would learn more and be like the other kids. But they said I couldn't go to what they called a "mainstream" class unless I learned to talk better. So Aunt Jessie put me in a special speech class for deaf people.

When I started speech lessons, the first thing I had to learn how to do was make the sound, "pah, pah, pah, pah, pah," in front of a candle. I don't know if you've ever done it, but they put a candle in front your mouth to make sure you're doing it right. When you do it right, the candle flickers a little. But they didn't explain that very well. So when they got the candle in front of me, I just looked at it and blew it out.

My teacher goes, "Blow that thing out again, I'm gonna light your nose."

Well she lit the candle again. I looked at her, and I like my nose so I didn't do that again. Eventually, I learned how to pah, pah, pah, and I realized it was the beginning of learning to talk.

I went to that class on Monday, Wednesday, and Friday after school for an hour. We did the candle thing. And sometimes she would put my hand on her throat so I could feel what the vibrations should feel like.

But I was the only deaf person in the class. All the others had some other kind of disability. Some of them had a hair lip. Some had Downs Syndrome. Some were mentally challenged. But we all had to learn to speak right. So we'd sit around in a circle and all say the letter sounds together. Sometimes it would sound like some of the kids were moaning or groaning. And the teacher would stop us and say, "John, you're not doin' it right. You sound like you're suffering. Relax, and say it right." Then when he said it right we could keep going.

I was learning a lot. But I didn't like being in the class. All the other kids would walk by the room when they were leaving school. And they could see us through the little window in the door and see what we were doing. Some of them would make funny faces in the window, or ask me the next day, "Why are you in that retarded class?"

But I kept taking the speech classes anyway.

As I listened, an uncomfortable thought occurred to me. I thought about all the schools I'd attended, and the fact that everyone always knew where the Special Ed class was, even if you never went there yourself. It was the one with construction paper taped over the little window in the door. I always assumed it was to keep whatever they were doing in there a big secret. But now I realized the secret they were keeping wasn't what they were doing. It was who was doing it. And the reason was to avoid exactly the kind of teasing and tormenting Kenny was talking about.

Then, an even more uncomfortable thought occurred to me. I wondered if I was ever the kid who asked the question, "Why are you in that retarded class?" Was I one of the reasons why that paper was taped over the window? Or, are my kids part of the reason those windows are probably still papered over today?

I wasn't certain I really wanted to know the answers. But I knew they were important questions to ask.

I made a mental note to have a conversation with my kids about it.

~ ~

One day Aunt Jessie and Uncle Larry came in the bedroom and shook me awake like they were very excited.

"Kenneth! Kenneth! Wake up!"

"What? What?"

"Today, we're gonna go get you a hearing aid!"

"A what?"

"A hearing aid."

I said, "A what?" again. Then Aunt Jessie pointed at me and smiled. She knew that I understood what she was saying. Sometimes if I pretended I didn't know long enough, people would leave me alone. And I was still sleepy so I thought she'd just let me go back to sleep.

It didn't work.

So she said, "Get dressed. We've gotta get on the bus. . . It's your birthday!" It was September 17th, 1962. I was nine years old.

I said, "O-kay."

"And, we got a surprise tonight."

"I know, a birthday party."

"Well, if you don't behave, we may not have a party. Now let's go and get your hearing aid."

We got on the bus, and of course I kept asking her, "What's a hearing aid? How does it look? What does it do?"

"Just wait 'til we get to the speech center."

"Okay."

Well, we got there. And it was kind of scary. When we got off the bus, she took my arm. We walked toward this really old building. I stopped.

Aunt Jessie said, "What? What is it?"

I pointed at the building and said, "I don't want a hearing aid."

"You need one to hear."

"Can I just be deaf and not hear nobody?"

"No."

So she pulled me. We walked in, and it smelled like a hospital. And all these people were wearing white smocks, with a name tag, everybody. I was like, "This is scary. I wonder if she's gonna have me admitted." You know, like for crazy people? Then all of a sudden they took me into this room, and then a nurse came over. "Kenneth, come with me. We're gonna take you to a small room. We're gonna test your hearing."

Kenny got a bashful, childish look on his face, and looked up as if the nurse was standing right there in the room with us. Obviously, he'd been afraid to go in.

They said the room used to be a bank vault, and it looked like it! It had a big, heavy round door, and a window cut in the wall. When she opened the door . . .

With that, Kenny scrunched up his face, grabbed a fistful of air, and appeared to pull mightily on the imaginary vault door. Then he made the sounds of creaking iron and the whoosh of the airtight room taking in a welcomed breath.

. . . it looked really cramped inside. She looked at me and she said, "You, in."

I said, "Me? No, thank you." And I just squeezed onto Aunt Jessie's arm.

She goes, "You, in!"

And Aunt Jessie pulled her arm out and pushed me away a little.

"Me? No."

Aunt Jessie gave me another push. And the nurse got down on her knees and said, "It's okay. I'll go in with you."

So I went in. There were some toys on the ledge. I thought that was pretty cool. But there was padding on the wall, I guess to make it soundproof. And it was really small, like being on a submarine. So it was still kind of scary.

The nurse walked out and shut the big, heavy door behind her. I walked over and pushed on the door. But I was locked in. Then the nurse knocked on the window. I looked over and I could see her and two other people through the window. And Aunt Jessie was there, too.

Kenny stepped into character and flashed an exaggerated, toothy grin my way and waved excitedly.

But she looked at me like she did when I was being silly.

Then the nurse sat down on the other side of the glass. She turned out to be my speech pathologist.

She waved at me and goes, "My name's Janice." She was talking into a microphone and there were speakers in my room for me to hear her.

"Okay."

"Can you hear me well?"

"Barely."

She turned it up. "HOW ABOUT THIS? HOW DOES THIS SOUND?

"A little too high," I told her. And she brought it back down.

She said, "How about this? Does this sound okay?"

"Yeah."

"Great. Do you like the toys?"

"Yeah."

"Pick one and wind it up."

I picked up the monkey with the drums. That was my favorite. I wound it up and he started playing the drums. Then she asked me if I could hear the drums. And, of course, I couldn't. Then she told me to listen close. I held it up to my good ear. That was my right one. And I could hear a little tiny "boom, chunk, boom, chunk." I told her that.

Then she had me do the same thing with a wind-up alligator and tell her what I could hear. I think she was impressed that I could make some of the same noises with my mouth that the toys made. Aunt Jessie told her that I learned to do that from watching the Milton Berle Show on TV.

Then the lady said she was gonna say some words. But she was gonna cover her mouth up with a little board so that I couldn't read her lips. I was supposed to tell her what she said. She said, "banana. . . orange. . . baseball . . .mittens." Things like that.

I tried my best to understand. But I had to really focus. I could catch some of the words, like banana. I hear that word a lot, and I'm not totally deaf. But I couldn't get enough of them that I could actually carry on a conversation without watching someone's lips.

It's funny. I had a hearing evaluation just five years ago and they did the same test with the same list of words. It started with 'banana.' I couldn't believe it. I got to the point that I started telling them the words before they said them to me. They thought I was a mind-reader or something.

Anyway, back in the bank vault, the lady played sounds from different instruments and asked me what they were. The first one was violin music. Only I didn't know the word for violin. So I just moved my hands like I was playing the violin, and she said I got it right. Then she played piano music. Then she wanted to know if I could tell the difference between an electric piano and that other kind. . . What's the one with the stick that holds up the top?

"A grand piano?"

That's it. A grand piano. The electric piano is what they called a synthesizer back then. And the grand piano is the kind with the stick that holds the top open. Back then electric pianos didn't sound the same as a piano at all, so I could almost tell the difference.

That's why I love music. And I especially love listening to the orchestra. The 'symphony,' they called that in Dallas. Because there aren't any words, I can just enjoy the music.

Then the lady said, "Now, we're gonna see if you can read my lips."

I said, "Okay. I been doin' it ever since I was born." Then I saw Aunt Jessie through the glass, so I waved real big again.

The lady looks at me and she said, "I'm gonna say something to you that almost everybody can understand. Even you should be able to understand this, I hope." She goes, "I'm gonna turn off the sound, and you do exactly what I'm gonna do. Are you ready?"

She turned off the sound. She looks at me, and she mouthed the words "I love you" three times.

And I knew she didn't really love me, because I had just met the woman. So I looked at her with the kind of smile you do when you really don't mean it. Then she turned up the mic volume and said, "Did you see what I did?"

"Yes."

"Now you repeat back to me what I just said."

So I did the same thing she did. I mouthed "I love you" except I only did it two times.

She looked confused and started slapping the microphone. "Is your mic on over there? I can't hear nothin'. My speaker's not workin'."

"I think it's workin' fine," I said.

"Oh, I can hear you now. Now, do it again. Somehow I think there's a wire loose or something. Do what I just did."

I saw my foster mother again.

Kenny shot me another toothy grin and exaggerated wave.

I gave Janice a thumbs up and then mouthed "I love you" two more times.

She's going, "Something's wrong with the mic. Is anything wrong over there?"

"I don't think so."

"Oh! What is going on?"

"I don't think nothin's goin' on. I'm doin' what you told me to do."

"Let me see if I can get my director. I need to get my boss."

Kenny laughed, and kept a mischievous smile on his face as he continued. I found myself enjoying the story all the more because I could tell how much he was enjoying telling it.

So a minute later, he comes in. They brought a technician, the electrician, and there they all were on the other side, pulling wires and playing with it. I'm just looking through the window at them with big eyes, but I'm still in that little vault. And I thought, "Does it take this many people to help to get me to talk?"

Now, all of a sudden, she looks up, "Well everything's workin' on our side. Let's do this again because I want my boss to see what you're doin', how well you progress. Do what I just did."

Another embellished smile and wave from Kenny.

Then I mouthed "I love you" three whole times this time. And this time the director and everybody else started smacking the mic. And he said, "Now, there it is, it must be your mic."

And I go, "I don't think anything's wrong with my mic."

"What are you doin' over there?" they asked.

"I am doin' exactly what you told me to do."

Aunt Jessie was over there looking at me with kind of a mean look on her face. So I thought I'd better tell the truth. I said, "I did exactly what you told me to do."

She said, "Well, what did I do?"

You said, "I love you."

"Well, that's it! That's what I said. Why didn't you say that?"

"I did, but you told me to say it the way you said it. When you said it, there was no sound."

You won't believe it, but I went through four counselors just to get that hearing aid! I had so much fun.

Kenny and I both had a good laugh. "So what'd you find out from all those tests?"

The tests all determined that back then I was what you'd call "hard of hearing." That means that I could hear a little bit. And with hearing aids, I could hear a lot better. But things still didn't sound the same as what you hear. The hearing aid makes things louder. But to me, you'd still sound like Donald Duck talking with a mouth full of marbles.

Today, I'm what they call "profound deaf," because my hearing has gotten worse.

That confused me a little. I remembered earlier Kenny saying that he had "severe deafness." So I did some research. Most sources I found use that description for hearing loss in the 71 to 90 decibel range, which is Kenny's range, and reserve the descriptor "profound deaf" for people with hearing loss above 90 decibels. But not all audiologists use the same descriptors, and sometimes the words are interchanged. What's important is that his hearing loss is significant enough that he can't follow conversations, even with hearing aids. He has to read lips or use sign language. And his hearing has continued to get worse over the course of his lifetime.

I'd be sitting in church and people would say, "Do you hear something buzzing? What's that noise?" It was my hearing aid. As my hearing got worse, I kept turning the volume up and up. When you get it all the way to 10, it's so loud, other people can hear your hearing aid and it sounds like a whistle or a buzzer. That's how you know you need a better hearing aid. Or better ears.

They make better hearing aids today than they did when I was a kid. But they're really expensive. You can spend $5,000 to get a good pair. Only some of the insurance companies won't pay for them. It's strange, because they'll pay $100,000 for you to get cochlear implants, but they won't pay $5,000 for hearing aids. I never understood that.

Anyway, I finally got fitted for my hearing aid. They make a mold of your ear so it fits real comfortable and fits just your ear. They even finished it and gave me one to test that afternoon. It was amazing! Here I was, nine years old. I put that hearing aid on. You know, you stick it in your ear and it had a long wire, and you put the big part of it in your pocket. That's where the microphone is. I didn't really like it because that tells people when they see it, he's deaf, because the wire's there, right? So I thought, "How can I hide it?" And I figured out a way to do that.

Then I started to test it out. But I realized when I was going down the hall that I could hear a funny noise. And I said, "I'm hearin' noise, it sounds like scraping."

She's goin', "Oh, it's your shirt. It's rubbin' against the hearing aid."

"Ohhh." So I took it out of my pocket. Then I went over and I wanted to get some water, and for the first time as I leaned over to get a drink, I could hear it. "What's that?" I said.

She goes, "That's you drinkin' water."

Then, somebody opened the window, and I heard whistling. You know, different kinds of whistles. "What's that?" I asked.

"That's a bird, whistling." And then I saw Aunt Jessie and I can hear that she's crying. She said, "He can hear!"

And I was happy for her being happy. But I was thinking, "I don't like it." Because I'd already learned what all those words and sounds sounded like to me, through my ears. And now I was gonna have to learn them all over again. But it turned out to not be that bad. In fact, I think it was fun.

I guess it all went pretty well with the hearing aid and the speech classes. In January, they put me in one mainstream classroom with "normal" kids for the rest of the school year. The next year, they let me go to all mainstream classes. But they made me do the second grade again so I could catch up to the other kids. And I kept taking the special speech class, even though I still didn't like the other kids seeing me through the window and making fun of me.

At first, being in mainstream classes turned out to be frustrating. I was the only deaf kid in the school. And it was frustrating because I had to deal with more people coming up to me and mumbling and slapping their hand up to their chest like they were disabled.

But then I found out that the best thing to do is to teach them what my problem actually was. And then when they finally find out what my hearing aid does they understand better.

The first time I tried that it didn't go very well. As I was taking the hearing aid out, I was saying "And this is . . ."

And this kid interrupted. He said, "Hey, that's a radio! Man, let me see it!" And the kid jerked it out of my ear and put it in his ear and started dancing around. And then he's like, "I don't hear nothin'. What channel you got this on?"

"Zero."

"Is there a zero channel?"

"For me, it is."

"What kind of music did you hear?"

"Loud mouth like you," I said. "Maybe you should let me explain what it is. It's a hearing aid!"

You know back then, they had — even today I think they still have — transistor radios. You know, you hold it in your hand. Now, they're called iPods or Smartphones. Now I see everybody wearing them, and they look like everybody's got hearing aids. At least that's what they look like to me. It's just a little Pod with a wire that goes in your ear. I wish everyone had all those back then, because I would wear my hearing aid and I wouldn't look so different.

Another time a boy took it out of my pocket and put it in his ear to listen. He was one of the boys teasing me. Once he had it in his ear, I grabbed the microphone and yelled in it. Oh, he jerked it out of his ear so fast! I thought that was funny. My teacher did not. She said I could damage his ears. I got in a few fights that way. So I had to stop doing that.

I didn't wear it all the time, though. When I was on the wrestling team, I couldn't wear it because you had to wear the helmet and there was no place to put it on the uniform. Plus, it would probably get broken. Same thing in football. But sometimes I didn't wear it because I was just embarrassed. And I liked it when my hair was long because it kind of hid the earpiece. By the time I was about to graduate from high school, the technology got better. I got the kind that went behind your ear, so it wasn't as easy to see it. But back then, it was still kind of embarrassing.

Imagining Kenny on the wrestling team reminded me of going to my son Matthew's wrestling matches just a year earlier. And one meet in particular jumped straight to mind.

Those mats have a 28-foot diameter circle that defines the wrestling area. The coaches sit in chairs just outside the circle. But they're not allowed to get out of their chairs or come in the circle. Well, at one point in this match, his opponent had Matthew on his back and close to being pinned. Our coach slid out of his chair and got on his hands and knees to shout some instructions to Matt. The referee immediately waved him back, even though he was still outside the circle and only a few inches from his chair. A little picky, I thought. But those were the rules.

After the match, there was about an hour until Matt wrestled again, so I watched some of the other matches. At one point I noticed one of the coaches running all the way around the circle to coach one of her wrestlers, waving her arms around like mad. It was the same referee, so I knew he was about to send her back. But he didn't. I thought, "What an idiot! How could he miss that? She was all the way on the other side of the circle?"

A minute later, she ran back to the other side to get closer to her wrestler. But this time she even stepped inside the circle waving more signals! I thought, "What the hell? When it's my kid getting pinned, that ref plays by the book. But this kid's coach gets to run all over the mat!"

There was no way the ref hadn't seen this. She was right in front of him. I started to think, "Why is this happening? What could be a legitimate reason why this coach is allowed to skirt the rules, but Matt's coach wasn't?"

And that turned out to be the right question to ask.

I started looking, and honestly hoping to find, a good reason. Not an excuse, or someone to blame for the oversight. But a reason that

*would make me slap my forehead and think, "Duh! That makes sense."
And that's when I saw it, like a blinding flash of the obvious. The
reason the woman was allowed to be in places coaches were forbidden,
was because she wasn't a coach. She was a sign language interpreter.*

*The boy was deaf. His coach was across the circle in his chair
where he was supposed to be all along, shouting instructions to the
interpreter, who signed them to the boy.*

*Suddenly my son and his coach didn't seem unfairly treated at all.
Duh!*

*It was a pivotal life lesson for me: It's amazing what good sense
we can find in other people's behavior when we don't start with the
assumption that they're an idiot.*

~ ~

A few months later, I started looking forward to Halloween.
The week before, we were all excited, trying to decide how we
were gonna dress up. I wanted to be the meanest and scariest
monster you could think of. But back then, we didn't have all the
fancy costumes like they have today. We didn't have two-headed
monsters, with eyeballs popping out, and blood and guts
everywhere. We only had five monsters then: Frankenstein, The
Werewolf, Dracula, The Mummy, and The Invisible Man. And
that's all I can remember from those days.

*Kenny rattled off that list of costumes like a sportscaster going
through the starting lineup. I wondered how on Earth a man in his 60s
could recall the full suite of ghoulish Halloween options so readily. I can't
remember what I had for breakfast this morning. But then I remembered
how he experienced life — quietly. Even though his eyesight was definitely
compromised, his hearing was worse. Maybe he remembers what he sees
better than other people because that's mostly what he has access to?*

*Or, maybe it was because he just stayed interested in childhood
longer than the rest of us.*

Either way, I knew my mother had dressed me up as at least three of those characters in Halloweens past. So I was excited to see where this story would take us.

Well, Halloween night came. It was a crispy night. The moon was out and it rained a little. Not a lot. Just sprinkles. And we were supposed to go trick-or-treating and then get to go to a party. We were gonna get to bob for apples, and play games, and win prizes. And there was gonna be a bonfire. What more could a kid ask for? I was just bubbling with excitement.

I couldn't wait to put on my monster costume. I didn't know what Aunt Jessie had created for me. But she told me she had made the best one for me.

Then after dinner, around 6 o'clock, my sister came running in to get me. She put her hands on her hips and said, "Come on! Aunt Jessie's got your costume ready!" I hadn't heard Aunt Jessie yelling for us all.

So I came running into the living room and saw all my brothers and sisters putting on their costumes. Sandy was a witch. Mary was Cinderella. Robert was dressed up like a vampire. And I thought those were all cool. And I said to Aunt Jessie, "What's my costume?"

And she pulled out a white bed sheet and said, "Here it is!"

I didn't know what kind of costume that was, so I said, "What else?"

And she said, "This is it."

"That's it? A white sheet? But I want to be a monster."

"Oh," she said, "but you're gonna be scary. You're gonna be a ghost!"

"A what?"

"A ghost." And she threw it over my head and my brother and sisters started laughing and giggling.

I pulled it off and said, "But I can't see where I'm going."

"Patience, Kenneth. Patience," she said. "Now, put it back on and I'm gonna poke for your eyes."

I said, "I don't want you to poke for my eyes!" But she put it back over my head anyway. Then she started feeling around for my eyes, and she poked one of them! I screamed, "Owww!"

She said, "I'm sorry. I'm sorry." Then she took out a marker and make an 'X' mark over both eyes. She pulled the sheet off, and everyone was laughing.

I said, "That's not funny."

She said, "You're gonna be fine."

Then she cut out two big holes where my eyes were and put it back on me. I looked at myself in the mirror and I did look like a ghost. But I looked like Caspar. He's a nice ghost. I still wanted to be scary.

So Aunt Jessie said, "Wave your arms, and run around, and make scary noises like a ghost. Say things like, "I'm gonna get you! I'm the scary ghost of Halloween Night!"

Well, I decided that sounded pretty good. Maybe even scarier than being a monster! So I said okay. She made my sisters promise to walk with me. I couldn't see very well with the sheet over me, and I couldn't hear traffic noise. So they said they would make sure I didn't walk out into the street and get run over.

So about 6:45 it was time to go trick-or-treating. My sister grabbed my hand to hold it. I pulled it away and told her, "I'm a big boy. I'm nine years old. You don't have to hold my hand." So she let go. We walked out into the neighborhood and it seemed like there were hundreds of kids in the streets, and walking up the drives, and knocking on doors. It was awesome! It was already a great night, and we hadn't even gone to the party yet.

About an hour later, my bag was starting to fill up pretty fast. We had all kinds of really cool candy. It was so neat. And about that time it started to rain again. So my sheet was sticking to my body. And my glasses were even getting a little wet under the sheet. Since I couldn't see through them, I just took my glasses off and stuck them in my back pocket.

We all started to walk toward home when a friend of ours walked up and said, "Hey, who's going to the party at Sharon's house?"

"We are! We are!" everybody started yelling.

So somebody yelled out, "Last one there is a rotten egg!" And everyone took off running. So I started running behind them, too. But I couldn't keep up. Well, I didn't want to be a rotten egg. So I decided to take a shortcut to Sharon's, because I knew the neighborhood pretty well. But I still had to run.

So here I was, this little boy with a sheet over his head. Can't see very well. Glasses in his back pocket. Running through backyards in the dark, and in the rain. And I can't hear. Now this was an adventure!

Then I saw it, the shortcut. It was through Mrs. Andrews' backyard. So I started running even faster. Well the next thing I know, there was an even darker shadow-like thing in front of me. But I kept running anyway, right into . . . Mrs. Andrews' rose bushes!

I had to fight my way through, and ended up cutting myself from the top to the bottom. But I got through it. I did it! And when I got to the other side, it seemed like I was even more wet than before. Those rose bushes must have been really wet.

Well, anyway, I started running again. I didn't want to be the last one to Sharon's house and be a rotten egg. When I got to Sharon's house, I saw most of the other kids already there in the yard. And I was so excited to start bobbing for apples and having candy and hot dogs and popcorn. As I walked up the driveway, all the other kids started turning around and looking at me and gasping. "Oh my goodness, Kenneth! What happened to you? . . . Kenneth, what happened?" And I was thinking, "What is wrong with everybody?"

I didn't know how to answer, so I just kept walking. But they started following me and asking me what happened. Then my friend's mother came out and she started screaming for her husband. "Mercy, mercy, oh my God!"

Well, that got my attention. I said, "What is it?" And about that time, my sister ran up to me and said, "Kenneth, what happened? Who did this to you?"

"Did what to me? What is everyone talking about?"

Then my sister reached up and grabbed the sheet and ripped it off my head. She looked at my face and said, "Put your glasses on! Put your glasses on!" So I reached into my pocket and pulled out my glasses and put them on. And the first thing I noticed when I put them on was that my hand was all red. Actually, it was bloody!

Then I looked at my arm and I saw thorns from the rose bush sticking out of my skin. And the same thing on my legs. Crazy me, I was wearing shorts. And then they showed me the sheet with the eyes cut out. And it was bloody red all over it. And I looked at the faces of all the kids and grown-ups staring at me, and they all looked scared to death.

And at that moment, a big smile came on my face. And someone asked me, "Why are you smiling, Kenneth?"

So I told them, "Two things! One, I wasn't the rotten egg. See! Here comes Jimmy now. He's last, so I'm not the rotten egg!"

"Really," someone said. "What's the second thing?"

"Look at me! And look at my sheet! I got to be the scary monster after all!"

~ ~

Christmas Eve came that year. It was our first Christmas in Memphis, after Mom and Dad died. And we always had a tradition that we got to open one present on Christmas Eve. We could pick any present we wanted. But it had to be from a relative. It couldn't be from an immediate family member. We could only open those the next morning. And, of course, we didn't get presents from Santa Claus until the next morning, either.

Well, that Christmas Eve, I chose the present from my grandma to open. It was a blue Tonka truck. It was made of metal, and I loved it. I still have it to this day, and the box it came in.

When it was Mary's turn to open her present, she tore off the wrapping paper and looked inside. But, instead of being happy, she started to cry. And then she started complaining. Uncle Larry just looked at her and said, "What's wrong with you, girl?"

Mary pulled the present out of the box, and it was a nightgown. But I guess it was a color she didn't want, and it made her cry. And Uncle Larry said, "You ungrateful little . . ." and he raised his hand.

That's when Grandma jumped up in between Larry and Mary. She said, "Don't you dare slap that girl!" And Uncle Larry looked so mad, like he was gonna fight someone. Then he pushed Grandma over, and she fell right into the Christmas tree!

I knew a lot of men who'd like to push their mother-in-law into a Christmas tree. But I didn't know any who'd actually done it.

"What did you do when that happened?"

We did what we always did when there was trouble. We all jumped up and ran out the front door. Sandy gathered our coats and brought them outside, because we were still in our pajamas with the little footies. We just stood there in the middle of the yard, hugging each other, freezing, and waiting for Terry to come get us.

But then Sandy told us, "We're not in Dallas, anymore. Terry's not here to save us."

Chapter 6: "When I grow up..."

A couple of years later, I decided to get saved again. Only, this time it was my idea. I'd started to learn a little more about what salvation was all about. I still didn't really understand it all. But they gave out an even bigger Bible, so that was nice. And the second time turned out to be the fun time, so I'm glad I did it.

By then we were going to a Baptist Church. There they didn't just sprinkle you with water. They had a huge bathtub called a baptistry that you got dunked in. It was way up high behind the stage and above where the choir sings. And the preacher there was ten feet tall, just like at our last church. And he was kind of big and scary, too. And he shook his finger at me just the same.

Well the day I was going to get saved, he called all of us together and said, "If you're gonna get baptized tonight, make sure to bring your underclothes. Boys, bring your white underwear."

And I said, "I'm not going up there just in my underwear!"

He laughed and said, "It's okay. You'll have a robe on."

"Oh. . . okay."

So that night we all went in the back and lined up at the baptistry. The pastor stood there and explained how it was all supposed to work. But since I couldn't hear, I didn't understand it all.

At this point, Kenny stepped into character as the pastor. He looked down, as if to a crowd of children, and pointed off to his right to an imaginary baptistry. And then he started mumbling in an effort to mimic what it sounded like to him. It was a mish-mash of letters, sounds, and half-words, delivered in quiet, muted, and garbled tones. I was witnessing Pastor Duck with a bill full of marbles!

He went through a full fifteen seconds of instructions in this way, first pointing to the right, then the left, then using his fingers to indicate the walk down into the baptistry. I could almost make out what the instructions must have been. Yet, certain that I wasn't completely sure what they were supposed to do.

It was a brilliant fifteen-second performance that left me understanding exactly what Kenny had witnessed, and the impossible situation he was in.

I thought about what an incredibly useful skill that was, to be able to create such a deep, visceral level of understanding in another person. To be able to put them so squarely in your shoes and experience the world as you experienced it. Even as a professional storytelling coach and author, I knew my stories fell short of his performances in that regard. There are some things words will never be able to communicate as well.

So while part of me was still marveling at his performance, another part of me was envious. And I wasn't sure what to do with that, but I knew I'd spend some time figuring that out.

All the kids nodded their heads, except for me.

Well, eventually it was my turn. I walked over and looked up at him.

Pastor Duck looked down and mumbled while pointing to the baptistry.

I didn't understand, so I just said, "Huh?"

More mumbling and pointing from Pastor Duck.

So I looked out into the audience and I could see Aunt Jessie. She was just shaking her head.

Here's a little piece of advice: Never point when you're trying to tell a deaf person what to do. They'll just go exactly where your finger goes.

Well, the pastor pointed to the water again and kind of grunted. So I walked up to the edge, and I thought, "Why not?" And I dived in just like at the swimming pool.

I looked up from my keyboard, looking for some indication of whether or not that was intended as a joke.

Much to my satisfaction, it was not.

When I came up for air, I swam to the other side and pulled my head up and looked out. Well, apparently the tub was too full, because the water had gone flying over the wall and splashed all over the choir.

I laughed and shook my head in what must have looked like disbelief. If it had been almost anyone else telling me this story, I wouldn't have believed it. Only it was Kenny Tedford telling me. So I did.

They didn't look too happy about it. But for me, I was excited because I got baptized!

I looked for Aunt Jessie, but I couldn't see her. I thought maybe she was hiding to pretend she didn't know me. Then I turned and looked up at the pastor. He looked like he wanted to choke me. Then he walked down the steps into the baptistry with me. He had a mean look on his face and he held his finger up and motioned for me to come over to him. Then I got kind of scared, but I walked over.

He tried to explain to me again what was supposed to happen, but I didn't understand any better this time. Then he grabbed my hand and covered my mouth with it. And I thought he was trying to drown me!

Despite my previous laughter, this is part of this story I found the most comical. Imagine trying to explain to a nine-year-old child,

without using words, what full-immersion baptism is, and to prepare
them to undergo that ritual themselves. Only two scenarios seem
plausible to me: A) they'll understand it only a little, and will be
frightened to death when you explain it because it'll look like you're
trying to prepare them for a drowning. Or, B) they won't understand
at all, and they'll be frightened to death when they're in the baptistry
and find themselves the victim of an attempted drowning.

No other options seem remotely plausible to me.

Kenny was experiencing option B.

Well, eventually I figured out that he wasn't a murderer, and I let him cover my mouth. Then he bent me backwards into the water. And apparently, what I didn't understand was that there was a piece of metal at the bottom of the baptistry. You're supposed to hook your feet under it so they stay down while he's dunking you. But I didn't know, so I didn't do that. So, when he bent me backwards, my feet came flying up and out of the water and wiggled around. That splashed water over the walls again. And the people in the choir were getting wet all over again.

I came up and looked for Aunt Jessie and couldn't see her. I thought maybe she'd left the church. But it turns out she was there the whole time, hiding behind the pew.

And that was the second time I got saved.

~ ~

When I got to the fifth grade, they had this big sign on the wall that said, "What do you want to be when you grow up?" And they gave all of us a big yellow piece of paper and told everyone to draw a picture to put up on the wall under the sign. Well, of course, the first ones that got hung up looked like a fireman, policeman, a teacher. One of them looked like a murderer but I don't think that was right.

Then when it was my turn, the teacher looked at my picture and she made a funny face. She held it up in front of the class. One student came to hold one side of it and another one came to hold the other side. And the teacher said, "Kenneth, explain to the class. What is this? What is it you want to be?"

I'd drawn a picture of a podium with the American flag and the Tennessee flag behind it. And there was a little stick figure of a person behind the podium, and that was me. I said, "Someday, I'm gonna be a speaker to change people's lives, so we can learn to love one another and quit labeling people."

My teacher looked at me and she started laughing. But not laughing really hard like someone had just told a funny joke. More like a fake laugh people do when they think you said something that wasn't very smart.

So I said, "What's so funny?"

Then she got on her knees, and she patted me on the head. People pat me all the time. I think that's one reason why I'm bald today. So she was patting me and patting me, and I tried to shoo her hands away like there were flies buzzing around my head. "What are you doing?" I asked her.

She goes, "Class, this is a typical thing that's never gonna happen. Kenneth will never be able to be a motivational speaker or speak to a crowd because he can't talk well and he's retarded." And she said, "The most that you will ever do, Kenneth, the most you will ever do, is that you will be able to sweep a broom at McDonald's."

That comment triggered my mental brakes and brought my train of thought to a full stop. I had a hard time imagining a teacher speaking to a special needs student that way, or any student for that matter. Thankfully, today, it might be next to impossible to find a teacher who would say such a thing.

But in 1965 in Memphis, Tennessee, it wasn't that hard. She probably thought she was being honest with him and saving him the pain and frustration of unrealistic expectations. Whatever the reason, it was a common one, because those kind of low expectations were set for Kenny by many adults in his day, not just his teacher.

I wasn't sure what was so wrong with working at a place called McDonald's. It sounded like a nice place. But I didn't think it was nice what she said about the broom. And I was kind of a smart-aleck kid by the time I got to the fifth grade. So I looked at her, and I said, "Well, you can ride it."

Oh my God! She grabbed my ear. She pulled me up. "You are going to the principal's office right now!"

So we got to the principal's office and she asked, "What's going on? Why are you pulling that boy's ear?"

"He just told me I was a witch."

I looked up and I said, "I didn't say you was a witch. I just said 'ride it.'" I really never thought *a witch* because I wasn't smart enough.

She went on to tell the principal about my drawing and what I said, and then goes, "I want him punished."

The principal said, "I'll handle him. You go back to class." So the teacher went back to class. And the principal got on her knees and looked at me. I just covered my head, because I knew what she was gonna do.

"What's wrong?" she said.

"You ain't pattin' me on my head."

She said, "I'm not gonna pat you. I'm gonna give you a hug." And then she hugged me.

"What's that for?"

"'Cause I hate that woman."

I grinned from ear to ear. That principal simultaneously gave voice to what I was thinking at the moment, and saved my faith in the teaching profession of the 1960s as well.

Well, I didn't think adults were supposed to hate each other, especially a principal. So I go, "Why?"

"Well, she's always puttin' kids down. But I been watchin' you since you been in this school. You have a gift. You're very creative, and I saw some of your drawings. I can't even draw that good. But if that's what you want to be, a motivational speaker, and change people's lives, we're gonna have to do one more thing."

"What's that?" I asked.

"You need to take your speech lessons more seriously. So you can learn to talk better."

I smiled and told her, "Yes, ma'am. I will" cause I knew she was right.

And I did. I tried hard and kept taking those classes until I was in the seventh grade, until I could talk pretty good like just about everyone else.

~ ~

One of the great things about moving in with Aunt Jessie was that my grandmother lived with us, Grandma Tedford. Some days, she would take us out to her brother's house on the farm and tell us stories.

But we had to earn the stories. She'd say, "Don't just sit there. Grab a bag of corn and start shuckin'." And we'd have to pull the husks off the corn. I hated that part, because they were all stringy and the strings would get all over you. But sometimes it was peas, and we'd have to take them out of the hulls. And the peas were purple, so our fingers were all purple when we got done. But it was all worth it to spend time listening to Granny Tedford's stories.

When we worked, she'd let us ask questions about our mom and dad and she'd tell us stories about them. So one day I had a question for her. I could tell that Uncle Larry was ashamed of me. And I thought maybe I made my daddy ashamed, too. So I asked her if he was.

Grandma Tedford looked down at me and she said, "Young man, let me tell you about your daddy." Then she sat me down on the porch, and she sat down next to me real close. She looked at me right in the eyes and she said, "I'll never forget when I got the phone call. Your father called to tell me your mother had just fallen down a flight of stairs. I was in shock, because we didn't know if she was gonna lose the baby."

And, you have to understand, when you're deaf, you pay really close attention to facial expressions. Because you have to, to understand. You can't hear the tone of voice, and you miss some of the words.

That comment explained a lot about how Kenny told his stories. He frequently paused in between sentences, or sometimes mid-sentence, just to deliver the facial expression of one of the characters. In fact, he could carry on an entire conversation between two characters with nothing more than alternating looks and body language changes as he stepped in and out of each character.

And now it was clear to me why. I'd assumed it was something he learned in an acting class or that he picked up from watching the Milton Berle Show as a kid. But now it was clear that studying facial expressions and body language was a large part of how he understood conversation, because he didn't have access to all the words or inflections of voice. He used those visual cues when telling a story because that's the way he listened to stories.

So I was paying close attention, and I could see that Grandma Tedford was getting sad telling me the story. Her eyes were getting a little wetter and a little redder.

I didn't want her to be sad. But I was glad she was telling me anyway. People didn't usually talk about bad things in families back then. So it was hard for me to learn about my own family, and especially about me.

Then she goes, "And your father was upset, too. He was afraid he would lose you before you were ever born. And I was concerned about Bessie, too."

I didn't know who that was, so I said, "Who's Bessie?"

"Bessie, that's your mother."

"Oh yeah. I call her Momma."

"Right. Right. Well, we were all worried about your momma, and about the baby. That was you."

And that's when Grandma told me the story I told you in one of our other conversations. The one about how the doctors told daddy that I had brain damage and that he should probably just send me away to a home. And that he got up in the doctor's face and said, "What'd you say about my boy?" Do you remember that one?

"I remember," I said, smiling.

Then Grandma told me that when she got to the hospital, daddy was handing out cigars to everyone. That's what men did back then when they had a baby and they were proud.

And not only that, but she told me, "Your father was so proud of you, that he named you after himself. That's why you're Kenneth Lee Tedford, Junior. So you carry that name with pride, okay?"

I smiled and said, "Yes, ma'am, I will." And I have ever since.

~ ~

I think my little brother Robert could tell that Uncle Larry didn't like me. And even though he was only a little boy, sometimes he would get Uncle Larry to be nice to me. Like one time, Uncle Larry asked Robert if he wanted to go fishing. And Robert told him, "Only if Kenneth comes with us." That was pretty cool. My little brother looking out for me.

Uncle Larry looked at me and said, "You don't want to go fishing, do you?"

I love nature, so I said, "Yeah! I want to go!"

He said, "Fine." And we all got in the car and went to the lake.

He had lots of fishing poles in the trunk. When we got there, I reached for one of them. He pulled it out of my hand and said, "No. You use this one." And he handed me a cane pole. That's just a long pole with a string tied on the end of it with a hook. He gave me a few worms in a can, and said if I ran out I could look for more in the ground.

Now, you have to understand that Uncle Larry was a famous fisherman. He'd even been on the cover of a fishing magazine, so lots of men wanted to go fishing with him all the time. And he had a reputation to uphold.

So he told me, "You go to the other side of the lake to fish. I've got some other men coming to fish with me and Robert on this side." So I went over to the other side. I put a worm on my hook and started fishing. I could see him and Robert across the lake having a good time. When the other men showed up, they pulled out an ice chest and were laughing and talking. I just sat there on my side, crying. I didn't understand what was wrong with me. Why he didn't want me to be with him.

But, I had fun fishing anyway. And, as it turns out, God helped me get my little revenge. When it was time to leave, Uncle Larry and Robert started waving at me from across the lake. I had all the fish I'd caught on a string, so I picked up my cane pole and the string of fish and started dragging them behind me around the lake.

When I got there, one of the men looked at me and his eyes got really big. He turned to Larry and said, "Hey Larry, come look at this!" I probably had twenty or so fish on my string. Just little bitty fish. But it was so many that I couldn't pick them up. That's why I had to drag them. Then the man said, "Show him what *you* caught, Larry."

Uncle Larry just said, "Shut up."

"Come on, show him!"

"Shut up! Get in the car, Robert."

Then, one of the men just opened the ice chest and reached in and pulled out one little fish. That's all Uncle Larry had caught. I thought that was pretty cool.

On the way home, he yelled at me. He said that I was an embarrassment, and made him look bad in front of the other fishermen. I could tell he wasn't happy with me. But I didn't know what the word "embarrassment" meant. If he'd told me "you stink," I'd know what to do about it. I'd go take a shower. But I didn't know how to fix being an embarrassment.

And if it wasn't clear already that Uncle Larry didn't want me around, it got pretty clear soon enough. When I was thirteen, I got the mail one day and saw a letter addressed to "The Parents of Kenneth Tedford." It was from the Mentally Retarded Reformed School in Kentucky. I opened it because I saw my name and thought it was my right to read it. The letter was to tell my parents that there was a spot open for me in the fall. As soon as I read that, the meaning of that word "retarded" became crystal clear. That word was something shameful. It was not a good word at all, but a word that brought shame to my family, so much so that they wanted to get rid of me. Someone had contacted this school and asked if they had room for me.

I went to Aunt Jessie, handed her the letter and told her I hated her. She looked really confused. She took the letter, read it, and said, "What in the world is this?" Then she thought for a minute, and said, "Damn that man. Damn him!"

She went to find Uncle Larry and threw the letter at him and started yelling. All I remember him saying was, "I think it's best that we put Kenneth away. He'll be with his own kind." Then Aunt Jessie came back to me and got down on her knees. She took her hand, grabbed my chin, turned it to her. She said, "Kenneth, you are going nowhere. You are staying right here. You are my pride and joy." With tears running down her cheek, she said, "You will do great things. You are very creative, and you tell great stories." She tore the letter up, gave me a hug, and whispered into my good ear, "I love you."

She got up crying, walked to her room, and closed the door.

I knew then that I would do great things. But at the same time, the damage had been done, I understood what it really meant to be labeled "retarded."

FOUR DAYS WItH KENNY TEDFORD

It's about a five-hour drive from Kenny's house in Jonesborough, Tennessee to mine in Mason, Ohio. So he arrived in the early afternoon, an hour or two before our boys got home from school. He took a few minutes to unpack and Lisa made us both a snack and some tea before we started the interview. But when the boys got home, I told him I had to spend some time with Ben, and invited him to make himself comfortable. He chose to follow us out to the patio and plant himself in a chair to watch whatever was about to happen next.

We have a trampoline in our backyard with a seven-foot-tall safety net around the perimeter. When I was Ben's age, trampolines didn't have safety nets. And if they did, it would have seemed like overkill, and way too unmanly for a young boy to consider using. As a parent today, I wouldn't consider anything else. More to the point, Ben and I found a way to turn the otherwise uninteresting safety net into a critical part of our play.

We called our game "squishy ball." It resembled one-on-one volleyball, with Ben on the trampoline and me outside on the ground as we took turns hitting a ball over the safety net. The height of the trampoline plus a good bounce gave Ben a five- to six-foot height advantage over me. Even for a nine-year-old, that was more than adequate to give him a competitive advantage. That pleased Ben to no end, which made my inevitable defeat worth every minute.

Kenny sat patiently and watched with an unusual focus.

I couldn't imagine what would be so interesting about a man playing a silly, made-up game with his son. Especially if it was standing in the way of Kenny getting to do what he'd just driven five hours to do. But he was enthralled, nonetheless. Every time I glanced over my shoulder, there he was, sitting with a huge grin on his face, intently watching every bounce and spike, cheering and applauding each point, regardless of who earned it.

Having such an enthusiastic audience made our play even more enjoyable than usual. Like it was the first televised squishy-ball tournament! I wondered what made it so captivating for Kenny.

I didn't know it at the time, but that's something I'd find out over the next four days.

Chapter 7: First Love

School had just started in September of 1971. My sophomore year.

I was in art class next to my best friend, Tommy. Tommy was like a dear friend, a brother, a boosome buddy. We did everything together.

Kenny's pronunciation of 'bosom' was too precious. I fought back a smile.

So there we were in art class. And all of a sudden, everyone turned and looked at the door. Of course, I didn't hear anything, but I turned to look and see what it was. And there was the teacher standing in the door.

She said, "Quiet, class, quiet. We have a new student starting today. I want you all to make her feel welcome. Her name is Brenda."

She had long blonde hair and blue eyes. A nice figure. And she had the most beautiful smile. And skin like alabaster stone. She looked like a princess. Of course, all the guys had their mouths hanging open, thinking, "Wow!" Some of those boys had their girlfriends in the same class. And they were hitting the boys on the shoulder, saying, "What are you lookin' at?"

And a lot of that was going on, so the teacher shushed everyone. And then she told Brenda to go over and sit in the empty seat right next to me and Tommy! Well, Tommy and I watched her walk all the way over and sit down. Then we looked at each other and we both had a big smile on our faces.

And just as I was about to lean over and tell Tommy that I wanted her to be my new girlfriend, Tommy leaned over to me and said, "Kenneth! Kenneth! Guess what?"

"What?"

And Tommy said, "She's gonna be my girlfriend! I'm gonna ask her out!" And right then my whole bubble just busted. My dream girlfriend, or at least my dream date, just disappeared. I didn't want to hurt Tommy's feelings and keep him from being happy. So I just said, "Good for you, Tommy!"

But then after class, I asked, "How do you know Brenda's gonna be your girlfriend?"

"Oh, I know she is. We're gonna be perfect together! But I'm gonna need your help."

I said, "For what?"

"For getting Brenda to like me!"

"What? Tommy, I can't get nobody to like you. You gotta do that yourself."

"Aw, come on, Kenneth, you know I'm shy."

"I know, Tommy. But that's not how you get a girl. You're gonna have to speak up."

"But she's so pretty. I'll mess it up. I need your help. Please!! You're my best friend."

So I told him, "Well, okay, Tommy. I'll do what I can."

And he said, "Thanks. You'll do great. Everyone likes you 'cause you're funny."

A few days later, Tommy came over. It was on a Saturday, and Saturday is when Tommy and I would work out and wrestle. So we had just finished wrestling in the front yard, and we were just lying there on the ground enjoying a cool September breeze. And Tommy said, "Kenneth, I need you to do something for me."

"What is it?"

"I just bought a big teddy bear for Brenda."

I said, "Good for you! When you gonna take it to her?"

"Take it to her? No, no, no, no. *I'm* not gonna take it to her. *You're* gonna take it to her."

"What? Tommy, I can't take the teddy bear to Brenda. She'll think it's from me."

"No, no, no. You don't have to say anything. You don't even have to see her. Just leave it on the front porch."

"But are you gonna have a note or a letter on it? How's she gonna know it's from you?"

Tommy said, "I'm gonna wait till Monday in class to see if she likes it. And if she does, then I'll let her know it's from me."

"Tommy, that's just crazy," I told him.

"Aw, come on, Kenneth. You promised you'd help me . . . Please!"

Well, he was right about that. I did promise I'd help. So I told him I'd do it. So he ran into the house and got the teddy bear and brought it outside. And it was big! Almost as big as me! So I put it in my car and drove it home. I took a nice hot shower, all the while wondering how I was gonna get the teddy bear on the porch without getting caught by Brenda.

Around 5:30pm, I drove over to Brenda's house with the teddy bear. It was cool that night, and the sun was just starting to go down. I took it out of the car and walked up to the front porch as quietly as I could. I wasn't sure if I made any noise or not, being deaf and all. I laid the teddy bear in the corner by the front door. Then I turned around and started to walk off. But then I heard the sound of someone yelling something. I looked around, but I didn't see anybody. So I started to walk off to my car again. But then I heard the yelling again, except this time louder. I could tell it was someone's voice, but I couldn't tell what they were saying.

I turned around and there standing on the porch was a man with his hands on his hips, looking at me. I just smiled, and swallowed real hard, wondering who this man was standing on

Brenda's front porch. And about that time, he started walking towards me, and he said what turned out to be, "Hi, I'm Brenda's father."

"Excuse me?"

"I'm Brenda's father. Who are you?"

"I'm Kenneth."

"Kenneth, do you have a last name?"

I tried to answer, but not much came out. "Uh...Ted-, um, yeah, Ted-, Ted-. . ."

"Don't be nervous. What's your last name?"

I tried again. "It's Ted-, um, it's Ted...ford. Tedford."

"Ted Ford?"

"Well, it's actually Ted-ford. T-e-d-f-o-r-d. Junior. Tedford, Jr."

"Oh, okay. Well, what are you doing here? And what is that on the porch?"

Well I must have looked at him funny, because I thought that was the silliest question I'd ever heard. Then I asked, "You've never seen a teddy bear before?"

I suppose maybe he didn't like that. He said, "Wow...a smart aleck, huh? I know what a teddy bear is. But why is it on my front porch and not in your arms? Is it for me?"

"No! It's for Brenda."

"Really? Well go get your teddy bear and I'll get Brenda and you can hand it to her yourself."

I tried to explain, "Oh, no, no, no. I'm not givin' it to her —" but he interrupted me.

"No excuses. No young man is gonna give my daughter a gift without presenting it in person. It's just not proper. If you want to date my daughter, you'll have to give her the teddy bear yourself."

I tried to explain again. "But sir, it's not...I'm not really giving...I mean I am, but it's not. . ." But he'd already stopped listening and walked back to the porch and opened the door for me. So I picked up the teddy bear and went inside with him.

I followed him through the foyer and down a hallway to the living room. He yelled up the stairway, "Brenda! Breeeeeenda!" Then I heard her say something back. And he said, "There's a young man down here. He wants to see you." Then she said something back. And he looked at me and said, "She's on her way down."

Then he asked me if I wanted some water or tea. And I figured that was my chance to explain again. So I said, "Look, I didn't mean to give her . . . I mean, I want her to have it, but . . ."

And he just interrupted me again and said, "You need to stop being so nervous, young man. It's all fine. She'll be down in just a minute." And then he walked off to the kitchen. And about the time he left, Brenda was coming down the stairs. When she got the bottom and came around the corner, I felt like my heart just stopped beating. There I was, staring at Brenda. Me! I'm the first guy in our whole school to be standing in Brenda's living room. Oh, my goodness!

I was just standing there with that big teddy bear. And Brenda says, "Ohhhh, is that for me?"

"Um...ah, yeah," was about all I could manage. I was so nervous. I handed her the teddy bear, and she squeezed it and kissed it.

And then she said, "Oh, it's so precious! Thank you."

"Oh, no, no, no. See, it's not that I'm giving it to you...except, well, of course I'm giving it to *you*. It's just — "

Then Brenda interrupted me, just like her daddy, and said, "Oh, you're so sweet" And right then, she leaned over and gave me a kiss. A beautiful wet kiss on my cheek. I couldn't believe it! I just got kissed by Brenda. This brand new princess at our school kissed me!

And then it hit me. I've got to explain where the teddy bear came from, from Tommy, not me. Oh, I'm gonna kill him for getting me in this mess! I told him this wouldn't work!

So I said, "Brenda, I've got to tell you about the teddy bear—"

"Oh, you don't have to explain anything. I love it, I love it!"

"But it's not—" And at that very moment, Brenda's father came back into the room.

"Well, Brenda, how do you like it? That sure is a big teddy bear, isn't it?"

"It sure is, Daddy. Kenneth is so sweet."

I tried to explain again. But I guess I was just so nervous in front of Brenda I couldn't make any sense at all. Then her daddy said, "Does this boy talk like this all the time?"

And Brenda said, "Well, he doesn't in class. He talks pretty good at school. He's the boy I told you about, Daddy, who's deaf."

"Oh yes, I remember you telling me about him. Well, you speak pretty good, Kenneth."

"Thank you, sir. I had some training. Six years of training. . ."

"Oh, okay. Well do you work?"

"Yes, sir," I said. And I took another swallow in my throat. "Yes, I work at Big Star grocery. I'm a bagger."

"Well good for you. And that is really sweet of you to give my daughter a teddy bear. But it's starting to get a little late. And she has some homework to do. You probably have some to do, too."

I told him, "Ah, yeah. Yes, sir. I do. But I really need to tell ya'll about the teddy bear."

But then he gave me one of those answers like people give when they didn't really understand everything I said. It would be better if they just asked me to repeat myself. But I think sometimes people don't want to embarrass me. So he just said, "Yes, it is a beautiful teddy bear, Kenneth. And I can tell she appreciates it. I hope that I see you more often."

"But—"

"Run along now, young man."

So that was that. I walked to the front door. Brenda hugged me. Her daddy shook my hand. And I went out the door. I walked to my car, and I was so confused. I only knew three things for sure: I was in love. I got kissed by Brenda. And Tommy is gonna kill me Monday! What did I get myself into?

But then I realized. Why should Tommy be the only one good enough to date Brenda? Maybe she could like someone like me. After all, I'm the one she kissed.

Well, I drove straight to Tommy's house. He asked me how it went and if she liked the teddy bear. I told him what happened, and he got really angry. I can't say that I blame him. We got in a fight right there in the front yard. He told me he hated me, and I got in my car and drove home.

It was one of those situations where I just didn't know what to do. Tommy was my best friend. We had class together. We ran track together. Wrestled together. We were like brothers. I just hated what I'd done.

But I was absolutely in love with Brenda. And that overcame my friendship pretty quick. I'm not sure if that's the way it's supposed to be, or if that's the right thing to do. But that's what happened on that day.

I was sad all weekend. But when I saw Brenda on Monday, Lordy, Lordy. I was so happy. So we started going out. Going to drive-in movies. Things like that. I think she respected the fact that I wasn't just trying to have sex with her, like the other boys. She would tell me how all the other boys always tried to have their hands all over her, even if they'd just met. And her mother raised her to be a lady, so she wasn't like that.

And we would read the Bible together. I liked that.

We dated for about a year and a half. We even talked about getting married, and looked at wedding rings. Nobody told us we couldn't. But her family wanted her to be able to go off to college. And my friends told me I should date other people before getting married. So, like a lot of teenage relationships, we eventually split up.

But I'll always remember my good friend Tommy, and my first love: Brenda.

~ ~

Early in the process of our interviews, we created a list of interesting events and stories throughout his life. Then at each meeting, we'd pick up where we left of on the list and continue to work our way through them, sometimes in nothing more than random order. But there was one story Kenny avoided telling me every time it came up on the list.

When I finally cornered him on it, he explained his hesitancy this way. . .

People are always trying to get me to do an adult show. You know, like those midnight camerays?

I drew a complete blank on what he meant by "camerays," and it must have showed in my face, so he continued . . .

You now, that's when you do adult stories. At many festivals they have a cameray. It's like a play or a movie where a woman is dressed all up and dancing around like her clothes are gonna fall off . . .

"Oh, a cabaret?"

That's the word. Well, this is a story like that. It's probably just for grownups. I call it the pussycat story.

My mind went all kinds of places trying to figure out how on Earth Kenny Tedford would have a story about a burlesque show. Was he in the show himself somehow? And if so, how did that happen? Or perhaps he just met someone who was in the show? Either way, it was sure to be interesting.

While I was in high school I played on the football team. Kingsbury High School in Memphis. I was seventeen years old, and in really good shape. And if you know anything about sports in high school, you know that whenever practice is over, all the boys take a shower together in a big room. Usually somebody would take a wet towel and wind it up and snap it at you like a whip. We had fun.

Well, one day, we finished practice and were all taking a shower. And I couldn't see very well in the shower without my glasses on. But I could see well enough to tell what one of the other boys was saying. He said, "I got some pussy last night."

A familiar twinge of uncertainty and disappointment hit me after those last words. Could it be this simple? Was all that talk of a "cameray" just Kenny's inimitable way of saying this story had some foul language in it, and was therefore for adults only? Or was I actually going to get to hear a racy tale of a midnight cabaret, an illicit meeting, and a proper coming of age story? I'd have to be patient to find out. But I was prepared for anything. He went on. . .

And I thought that was a pretty odd thing to say. But then some of the other boys started talking about "getting pussy," too, and seemed like they were bragging. So I just watched and listened. Well that went on for a few more days after practice. And then on the fourth day, one of them looked at me and asked, "Hey, Kenneth, you gettin' any pussy?"

And I still thought that was an odd question to ask, but I said "Yeah, sure."

Then all the guys started looking at each other and looking at me. "You did? When?"

"I don't know. Maybe just the other night."

"What! Who with? Come on, tell us!"

Well, I could tell they were talking about girls, and I didn't know anything about that, so I just said, "I ain't tellin'." And then they started giving me high fives. And that didn't make any sense to me, but I felt pretty cool so I didn't complain.

Now, as Kenny's biographer, I was certain he hadn't done anything like that at this point in his life. But my mind was racing to where this story might go, and why he felt the need to pretend he was having sex.

A few days later, after school, I met my cousin Jeff at the Minute Man to play pool. I don't know if they have those anymore. But it was awesome! Best hamburger joint in the world. And we could play pool at this one. Anyway, my cousin's my age, and he can read me like a book. We're playing pool and then sat down to eat. And he says, "Hey, somethin' botherin' you?"

I wasn't sure I wanted to talk about it. But I said, "Well. . . yeah, sure."

"What is it?"

"Well, the guys in the shower this week, they keep talking about their cats."

My cousin goes, "So. Why does that bother you?"

"Well, I don't know. They're makin' a big deal of it. They seem to be getting their cats at night. Mostly on the weekend. . . And all their cats seem to be girls."

And his mouth dropped open. And then he started to laugh.

"What's so funny? Do you know what they're talking about?"

"I think I do. I'm starting to connect the dots. Are they actually saying that they're getting 'cats'?"

"Um. No, not exactly."

"Well, what are they saying?"

So I told him, "They say they're gettin' 'pussy.'" And we had a black pussy cat at home and everyone knows what a pussy cat is.

He said, "Kenneth, you're hilarious! This is a great story."

"What are you talking about?"

"Kenneth, they're not talking about pussy cats."

"Well, sure they are. They keep saying, 'pussy.'"

Then he said, "Do you know about women's body parts?"

I said, "No." I guess maybe I should have. I was seventeen years old after all. But I didn't.

"Do you know the function of this part of a woman's body?" And he pointed to his chest.

And I said, "Oh, boobs? Yeah, I know about that."

He said, "Okay, do you know about the bottom part?" And he pointed to his pants.

"No."

"Okay. Well, you might get sick if you don't like talking about this stuff. But I'm gonna draw a picture on a napkin." And by this time, he wasn't laughing anymore. He was really trying to help me, because he really cared about me. And he drew a picture of a woman below the waist. And he told me what it was called, and how it worked.

I looked at it and said, "Oh, my God!"

"What's wrong? I didn't mean to make you feel bad."

"No, no, no. You're not making me feel bad. I told all the guys I've been getting' pussy every other day!"

I'd pay good money to see the look on Kenny Tedford's face when he realized his mistake.

I'd pay slightly less to see the napkin.

Jeff just freaked out laughing, more than I've ever seen before. Then he raised his hand up to give me a high five. And I said, "I'm not high-fiving you. I just humiliated myself in front of them!"

"Are you crazy? This is great! Most of those guys probably look down on you and just think you're retarded or slow. How have they been treating you since then? Are they being nicer to you in the last couple of days?"

"Well, as a matter of fact they have. One of them even wants me to double-date with him and his girlfriend."

He said, "You see what's happening. They're starting to see you as just a normal kid like them."

"Normal?"

He said, "Well, maybe not normal, but let me put it this way. It ain't a cat. You did great. Leave it alone. And don't tell them what we just talked about. And I'll tell you something else. Out of twelve of those boys all saying they got it, maybe only one actually did. The rest of them are just bragging. They haven't done anything you haven't done."

"Seriously? Why?"

"Oh, boy! Let's talk about that another time. Let's finish our game of pool."

And so we never talked about it again.

The guys eventually figured out that I hadn't really been having sex. But things like that happen to me a lot. Getting confused about words. Especially when they were about body parts and sex.

Like we used to go to McDonald's or Shoney's after all our football games and track meets. Hamburgers cost a quarter back then. The golden arches came all the way to the ground. Not just over the building like they do today. And back then, they had girls that would bring your meal to your car on a tray and they were wearing skates.

We'd always sit by the window and look out. We'd watch the cars pull in and the people walk by. And back then pickup trucks were cool. You were a man if you had a pickup truck. And the cars were beautiful! Not like they are today. They had big headlights, and some older ones had tail fins.

I remember eating my hamburger and watching a car or truck pull in and a couple get out and walk in. And the guys with me would say things like, "Whoa! I love those headlights." And I'd say, "Me, too! Awesome!" And then another car would pull in and people get out, and they'd say the same thing.

Well, then a truck pulled in. And the headlights were big and really bright, so I pointed to it and I said, "Those are awesome headlights!" All the guys just looked at me like I was crazy or something. Then they started looking around, and there was a waitress that had just walked by and they spotted her. Then they were like, "Ohhhhh, yeah! Nice headlights." But they were looking at her instead of the truck, and I just thought that was strange.

Then they started talking about watermelons and cantaloupes. And I knew McDonald's didn't sell watermelons or cantaloupes. So I was even more confused.

Fortunately, I saw Jeff that night. He can always tell when I'm confused, so he asked me what was wrong. I told him about the headlights and watermelons. He just shook his head and started laughing. "Okay, Kenneth. I got another story to tell you. They weren't talking about the cars and trucks."

"Yeah they were. They said it every time a car pulled up."

"No. Was there a girl in the car every time?"

"Well, come to think of it, yeah. Yeah, there was."

Then he held his hands up in front of his chest like he was a girl. And he said "head-lights" really slow. And then I got it.

I said, "Same thing with the watermelons and cantaloupes?"

"Yep. Same thing."

I was always afraid I'd say the wrong thing in front of people because I didn't understand these words. Thank God for Jeff.

~ ~

My eighteenth birthday was coming up. One day, four or five of the football players came up to me and said, "We got a surprise for you for your birthday."

"Oh yeah? What is it?"

"Well, it's not really a present. But your birthday's comin' up." Then one of them said, "My cousin Sarah's in town. She likes bein' around people with disabilities."

"Really? Does she have disabilities?"

"No, no, no, no. She just works with kids and likes people with disabilities. That's all. Anyway, she's in town, and I've got plans already, so I can't show her around. We thought you might want to take her to the drive-in. You can get your station wagon, right?"

"Well, that's the only car we have, sure."

"Cool. Here's the address where she's staying." And he handed me a piece of paper.

So the next night I showed up at that address to pick her up. I knocked on the door and she opened it. And she was a knockout! I'm not joking. She was just beautiful. And really built.

She looked at me and giggled and said, "Oh, you're cute!"

I said, "Well, thank you." Then she leaned over to hug me. I thought that was strange because we hadn't met before, so I just stuck out my hand to shake her hand instead.

Then we walked to my car and I opened the door for her. She said, "Oh, what a gentleman!" like nobody had ever opened her door before. I thought everybody did that. Anyway, we drove to the drive-in. There was a line to get in, so we had time to talk and get to know each other. "Where are you from?" That kind of thing.

But I noticed she kept looking at me funny, like she was thinking, "What's wrong with you?" But what she said was, "You're just so nice." Then a minute later she said, "Are you lookin' forward to later tonight?"

"Yes! I can't wait to see the movie. I haven't seen this one."

She said, "Oh, the movie. Yes, that'll be nice."

Anyway, we eventually got in and I parked the car. I asked her if she was hungry. Then I went to get us some hamburgers and French fries and came back to the car. It was getting dark now, and the movie was starting. But just the advertising, with the hot dog dancing across the screen. That kind of thing.

I was sitting there talking to her and drinking my soda.

Kenny made a long, slurping sound.

And I looked over at her, and she was unbuttoning her blouse! But she was still talking to me. And she went to the next button, and the next one!

I said, "What are you doing?"

She just smiled and said, "It's okay. You wanna get in the back seat?"

I thought that was even stranger than unbuttoning her blouse, so I said, "Why would I want to get in the back seat? You can't see the movie from back there."

She just started laughing, and said, "Oh, you're so funny! They told me you were a funny guy."

I still didn't understand, so I said, "Okay, I still don't know what you're doing. Why are you takin' off your blouse?"

"To get in the back, silly."

"But, why are we getting in the back? I paid a lot of money for these tickets."

And just then she looked at me like she'd seen a ghost. Her eyes got huge. Then her mouth opened up and she covered it with her hand. She looked like she might cry. Then she said, "Oh my God! You don't know."

"Don't know what?!"

"I'm gonna kill 'em! I'm absolutely gonna kill 'em!"

I didn't know what to say, so I just sat there and looked at her. Then she said, "I'm your birthday present."

That didn't make any more sense, so I asked, "Why are you my birthday present?"

She said, "You don't know what I am, do you?"

"Yeah, you're my friend's cousin."

"No, Kenneth, I'm not. I'm a hooker. I was paid to have sex with you."

For some reason, I tried not to laugh. I was unsuccessful.

I said, "I know what a hooker is. But, I don't understand what's going on."

So she told me, "Your friends wanted to get a surprise for you. They said you're so straight and narrow. And they just wanted you to have a good time. I can tell you're really a gentleman. But don't you think I'm pretty?"

"Oh my gosh, you're gorgeous!"

"Well, then do you want to. . ."

"No, no, no, no, no!"

"But . . . you're not gay, are you?"

"Noooah."

"Oh . . . Well, then . . . you're eighteen, right?"

"Yes."

She said, "I started having sex when I was fourteen."

And I thought that was too much detail. But she kept going. And she really wanted to know why I didn't want to have sex with her. She said, "All the other guys I meet just want get in my pants."

I thought that was kind of silly, so I said, "Well, both of us can't fit in your pants." That made her laugh again. Then she got serious and told me that I made her feel like a respectable woman. She didn't feel cheap around me. And then she started telling me even more things about her life that I probably shouldn't know. She told me she'd been raped as a child by her uncle and her brother. She'd been in and out of foster care, through several families. There always seemed to be someone who took advantage of her, so she always felt worthless.

I just listened mostly, while she talked and cried. Then, when she was done, I told her I didn't think she was worthless. And she cried some more, and I cried with her.

We ended up leaving the movie and driving back to her house and parking in the street. We kept talking for several more hours. When we finally got done, she told me I was a jewel and that any woman would be lucky to have me. I thanked her because that was really nice.

Then she asked me, "Are you sure you don't want to . . ."

"No, no, that's okay. Really." I guess she felt guilty because she'd already been paid.

Then I walked her to the door. When we got there, she said, "Can I kiss you?"

I said, "Oh yeah!" I mean, I'm not totally stupid. Then she gave me the nicest, longest kiss I'd ever had in my life up to that point.

When we finished kissing, she said, "I love you," and walked inside and closed the door. I turned around to leave, and started walking back to my car. Then I heard someone screaming, so I turned around. She was running back towards me, and said, "Kenneth, do me a favor. When you go to school Monday, just smile."

"What?"

"Smile! We're gonna get them back. They're gonna pay for what they did."

When I got to school the next morning, all the guys were waiting for me outside homeroom. And they never do that. Seemed like half the team was standing there. When I walked up they were already high-fiving me and slapping me on the butt. And that's how you know you're in with the guys, when they slap you on the butt. They were all congratulating me and telling me, "We didn't think you had it in you!"

Some of them came up and whispered, "Later today, you can tell me all the details." I thought that was really strange. Even if I did have sex, does everyone just talk about that stuff with everyone else? Seemed kind of personal to me.

The truth is, I still didn't really know what sex was or exactly how it worked. But the rest of that year, all the guys were extra nice to me and thought I was really cool. Even the girls wanted to see me and talk to me more often. It's sad really. Just because they all thought I had sex.

~ ~

Usually it was just embarrassing when I didn't understand something. But one time it actually got me beat up.

My brother Robert finally got a date with a cheerleader that he liked. He was only 14 or 15 at the time, so they couldn't drive. Her father was gonna bring her over to our house and take them both to a dance. So Robert told me I better behave around her and be nice to her. And I was the older brother, so I guess I was supposed to understand things like this.

Well, when she got there, she came in and said, "You must be Kenneth."

I said, "Yes," and she went and sat on the couch, holding her purse. And I was staring at her. Actually I was staring at her chest. I guess that made her uncomfortable, because she held her hands in front of her so I couldn't see and said, "What are you doing?"

I just said, "Oh, nothing, nothing." So she put her hands down. But I kept looking anyway.

I still couldn't see what I was looking for, so I got up and moved closer. I sat down right next to her actually. Finally, I just reached up and put my hand on her chest. Her eyes got really big and she slapped my hands away. She jumped up and yelled, "Pervert! What are you doing!?"

I said, "Nothin'. But . . . it's not cold."

"What's not cold!?"

I said, "Your heart."

"My heart? What are you talking about?"

"Robert said you had a cold heart. But it doesn't feel that way to me."

Well, her mouth just dropped open and she made some funny noises. Then she opened the door and ran out to the car.

Robert came running downstairs. "I heard the door slam. Where is she?" I just pointed to the driveway. He ran to the door and yelled for her, but they were already driving off. He turned around and stomped up to me. "What did you do!?"

"Nothin'."

"You did something! Tell me what you did, step by step!"

So I told him everything that happened, just like I told you. When I got to the part about the cold heart, he jumped on me and started hitting me. It seems funny now, but I guess it wasn't at the time. He was really mad at me and was really trying to beat me up. Aunt Jessie had to come in and pull us apart.

She said, "What are you two fighting about!?" I still didn't understand what I did wrong.

But Robert said, "It's Kenneth! He's stupid!"

She said, "What did you do?"

I said, "Nothing!" So I told her the story.

She just started laughing. She said to Robert, "It's not your brother's fault. He takes everything we say literally. He doesn't understand when you use metaphors like that."

"I don't care! He shouldn't be touchin' her!"

She said, "I know. I need to talk to him about that. Kenneth, come with me to the kitchen and have some coffee." We always sat in the kitchen for talks like that. There was a small table where we would be close. She always took time to talk to me. She said, "You didn't do anything wrong. But you did in one way."

And I thought, "You can't have it both ways. It's got to be one way or the other, doesn't it?" But I didn't say anything.

Then she said, "A man never touches a woman's chest like that unless they're married." And she explained that a little. Then she went on to explain that a 'cold heart' just meant she didn't have any feelings.

So I said, "Well, why can't ya'll talk like that? Why can't my brother just say 'She has no feelings' instead of saying 'cold heart,' or a 'hard heart,' or 'no heart at all,' when I can feel their pulse? Words like that I just never understood growing up."

Poor Robert. I guess I really messed things up that time. It sure would have helped if people would talk about sex and dating. But back in the 50s and 60s, parents didn't talk about stuff like that with their kids.

That last comment reminded me of Hans Christian Andersen's story of the child telling the Emperor that he had no clothes. I had to agree with Kenny. Wouldn't we all be better off if people could talk more openly about sex and dating? And not just sex. This cultural prohibition we have against talking about sex, religion, or politics has just made us ignorant about all three. And when we shroud what little discussion we do have with euphemisms or a wink-and-a-nod, the people who suffer the most are children and people like Kenny who struggle to connect those obscure dots.

I found myself enjoying Kenny's childlike brand of refreshingly straightforward thinking. Maybe it's not so surprising that it took a child in Andersen's fable to tell the emperor he was naked.

~ ~

About the time all this was happening, Kenny had a life-changing religious experience. I asked him to tell me about that.

From the time I was born until I was eighteen, I knew there was something missing. I just felt empty a lot. Growing up as the "deaf, retarded kid" didn't help. And it probably seemed a lot worse to me than it really was. Sometimes when people would tell me I was "funny," what they really meant was that I was deaf and retarded. Like "funny in the head." But a lot of times they really meant I was funny and I made them laugh. But I didn't know the difference, so I always assumed they were making fun of me.

And I saw a lot of ugliness in the world, with people calling other people all kinds of names. Bad names for black people, Native American people. And they have some kind of name like that for Asian people, too.

"Mm hmm," I agreed, rather presumptively.

And I even remember being called a "cracker" one time, and I didn't know what that meant. I thought as long as you put peanut butter and jelly on it, you can call me a cracker all you want. I didn't know it wasn't a nice thing to say.

But I also saw a lot of ugliness in the church. People standing around and all they talk about was what everyone was wearing and who was dating who. "Did you see what she had on? I heard she was dating him!" Or they're talking about how bad the other churches down the road are. And I always thought, "Is anyone listening to the preacher?" I was, and I didn't even understand him. I had to take the verses home and look them up in the Bible and talk to Aunt Jessie to figure out what they meant.

And there were all these rules. Just like at home at dinner. You couldn't leave the table until everyone was finished eating, and we had to leave one hand in our lap while we ate. And that's hard when you're eating cornbread. At church it was "Don't bring the deaf guy. . . don't bring any black people. . . no long hair. . . no earrings." Rules, rules, rules!

All I wanted to do was know the truth. How could I find peace and just be me? Just me. I didn't want to be told, "You can't succeed unless you wear your hearing aid." Or, "You won't succeed if you don't talk right." Things like that. Or worse, sometimes when religious people would find out I have disabilities, they'd ask, "Who sinned? Was it your parents, or was it you?" Seriously. They thought my deafness was God's way of punishing me.

I guess because of all that, I never really wanted to be a Christian. It didn't seem like that good of a thing to be. The truth is, the first time I got saved, I just did it for Aunt Jessie. Plus, I really wanted that little red Bible. And the second time, when I dove into the baptistry, I just thought it would be cool to get in the water.

Well, around that time, I was dating a girl named Pam. We went to the mall one night to hang out with the other kids. We did that a lot. Around 8:30 we decided to leave. But I thought it was too early to go home. And then we saw this long line of people in front of the movie theater in the mall. There was a big sign that said, "Billy Graham production. . . *Time to Run*," and it said the movie was free! I'd never heard of a movie that was free before. But I guess that's why there was such a long line. And I'd heard about Billy Graham before.

I said, "Let's go see that movie." And so we did.

It was a story about a young boy and girl in love. The boy's father was a big man in town and everyone knew him, and even feared him a little. Everywhere the boy went, people would know him because of his dad. And when he would get in trouble, people would say, "Don't you know who his father is?" And then he wouldn't get in trouble. The boy didn't like always being his daddy's son, so he kept saying, "I just want to be *me*!" And I knew what that was like. Just wanting to be me.

The boy's dad was also rich, so the boy had everything he wanted; a car, a big house, lots of clothes. But his daddy never had any time for him. When he asked his dad to go do something with him, his father would just give him money and tell him to go have a good time.

The boy started misbehaving, like putting soap suds in the fancy water fountain in front of his dad's office. He even tried to sabotage the power plant where his daddy worked. It turned out, what he really wanted from his father wasn't the stuff. He just wanted to be loved. I knew what that felt like, too. Not the part about having all the stuff; the part about not feeling the love of a father.

And the girlfriend, in the movie, she got saved and became a Christian. She stopped sneaking out at night with the boy, and wouldn't have sex with him. She told him it wasn't right and that she'd found peace.

And there was another place in the movie where the kids who were saved were talking to each other about the bad things that happened in their life. "I'm trying to get off drugs. . . I'm trying to live better out of prison. . . my brother just died in a car accident." That kind of thing. But they told each other that none of that was punishment. It wasn't their fault. And it wasn't because they'd sinned. That's just life.

And I wanted to know what that was like. To not be told it was my fault that I was the way I was.

And I wanted to find that kind of peace that the girl found.

And I wanted to know the love of a father that the boy was missing. To be the son of a father who loved his boy and would always be there for him.

By the time the movie ended, I was in tears. I knew then that I wanted to know more about Jesus and accept him in my life.

Pam looked at me and she could tell. She'd been elbowing me in the ribs all through the movie and telling me to stop crying like a girl. Then, she asked, "What, are you gonna be all 'holy' now?"

But it didn't matter. I felt like I was floating. I felt peace. When the boy accepted Christ in the movie, I saw how easy it was. It wasn't about all the rules and policy. It wasn't about what clothes you wear or who you date. I needed to see the story for it to make sense.

At the end of the movie, I got up and helped Pam with her coat. Then, all of a sudden, the lights came on. *All* the lights. I don't know if you've ever been in a theater when all the lights are on, but you can see *everything*! Usually when you come in and, even when you leave, it's still a little dark with just a few lights on. This was strange. And really bright.

And there were these people down on the front row, and this one man stood up. He had a microphone, so everyone could hear him, except for me, of course. But he held it down far enough that I could see his mouth and tell what he was saying. He said he was the choir director for Leawood Baptist Church. And the other people on the front row were also from the church. Some were adults and some were teenagers. Pam wanted to leave. She said, "Let's go. They're startin' to preach."

But I wanted to listen, so I said, "No, let's hear what he has to say." And we sat down, along with most everyone else. Except about three or four people who left anyway.

And that's when the man said, "Is there anyone here who's suffered loss? Who doesn't feel loved? Who feels like they want to know Jesus like the young man in the movie? If so, come forward. We're here to help you and pray with you. We're not here to ask you for anything, or try to make you come to our church. We're just here to love you."

He didn't wave a Bible around. He didn't say, "If you walk out that door you're going straight to hell." He didn't say his church was right and all the others were wrong. No fire and brimstone. Nothing like that. Just an invitation. I'd never seen anything like that.

I went down to the front and got a pamphlet. I found out that Leawood was just down the road from where I lived. The next Sunday I started going to Leawood Baptist Church.

That turned out to be the most important decision I ever made.

"What did your family think about that?"

When I told them that I'd been saved, Aunt Jessie was ecstatic! But the rest of them looked at me like I was crazy. Sandy said, "Seriously, Kenneth? You've been a Christian your whole life."

Then Mary turned to Sandy (because Sandy was the oldest sister), and she asked, "What's the difference between Kenneth now and the way he was? He never cusses or swears. He doesn't chase girls. He won't talk about sex. People bully him, and he's nice to them anyway. What's gonna change now?"

I guess those were good questions. I didn't know what was gonna change about me. But I knew something had. And I was looking forward to finding out.

The next Sunday, I went to Leawood Baptist Church, and was baptized. It was the third time in my life. But it was the last time. Because I was finally doing it for the right reasons. And I knew what I was doing.

"I recall the first time you got baptized, it was getting sprinkled. The next time was immersion, when you dove into the baptistry and got the red Bible. What was the third time like?"

Well, they let us pick if we wanted to be sprinkled or submerged. And I picked to be submerged.

"You picked immersion?"

Yeah, I wanted to be submerged.

I've heard of some people, when they really accept Christ, end up kind of wrestling around on the floor, speaking in tongues, having seizures. But that's not me. That's not who I am. But I was hoping that when I came up from being submerged in the baptistry that I'd see a dove flying by or something.

Of course, I didn't. But that was okay because all the people were clapping, and my Aunt Jessie was right there, crying. And that was very rewarding to me. I know that was the greatest gift I could have ever given to her. And for her to know that I finally understood what she was telling me about at that little round table in the kitchen all those years.

Two weeks later, Pam broke up with me because she didn't want to date somebody who was so "Christian." But that didn't bother me too much, because I had Jesus then.

~ ~ ~

The next summer, I was working a lot at the Big Star. My boss' name was Mr. Stephens. He was a great man. He was the first person to give me a job working with the public. Before that I was a newspaper delivery boy, and I didn't have to talk to anyone.

It was July 3, 1972. The day before Independence Day. Aunt Jessie woke me up and asked me to drive her to the store. She still never drove the car herself. I said, "But Aunt Jessie, we just went yesterday."

She said, "I know. But I forgot some things."

So I got up and got dressed and in the car. Then when we backed out of the driveway, I started to go the way we normally went. It was a shortcut. But Aunt Jessie said, "Don't go that way. Go the long way. I need to talk to you and I need more time."

I thought, "That's an odd, and rather unsafe, way to arrange a conversation with someone who needed to read lips – and who was driving the car." But I just listened patiently. Things like that tended to sort themselves out later in Kenny's stories if I was just patient.

And, you know, I was a teenager, so I was huffing and puffing and complaining, and thinking, "Oh, gosh, here we go." But I did what she asked. And as we were driving, she started talking to me.

At first, she told me that she loved me. And that if she'd ever had a son, she'd want him to be like me. She said I had one of the kindest hearts she'd seen in anyone. Or, at least that's what I think she said. It was hard to tell, since I was trying to drive at the same time. Then she started crying a little bit, so I asked her what was wrong with her.

She said, "Nothin'. I just wanted to ask your forgiveness for talkin' bad about your momma." At first, I didn't know what she was talking about. But then I remembered that when I first moved to Memphis, I think she was kind of jealous of my momma. Because any time a teacher would ask me how I learned something impressive, I'd always tell them that my momma taught me, instead of Aunt Jessie. Sometimes she'd get mad and tell me my momma wasn't that great of a mom, and that she was an alcoholic.

I guess I never gave Aunt Jessie the credit she deserved for raising me, or teaching me anything. And it probably hurt her feelings, which is why she said those things about my mom. So I think that's what she was talking about.

I accepted her apology. And I told her she didn't have anything to apologize for. She'd been a great foster mom for me. Then she kissed me on the cheek. I asked her what that was for, and she said, "Just because I love you."

We went to the grocery store and then back home. I went back to sleep because I was exhausted, and I had to go to work that afternoon. She woke me up for lunch, and I ate. When I was walking out to the driveway to leave, she looked at me through the kitchen window. She said, "Don't forget the watermelon, because tomorrow is the fourth." I said I wouldn't forget. Then she said, "I love you." I just waved and got in the car.

My shift was supposed to end at nine o'clock that night. Around seven thirty, my brother-in-law Billy came by the store and said, "We need to go home."

I said, "But I don't get off till nine."

He looked really upset. His eyes were bloodshot.

Then my boss, Mr. Stephens, walked up to me. He said, "Take off your apron, Kenneth. You need to go home." My mind started going crazy, wondering what was happening. Our grandmother lived with us, so I thought maybe something happened to her.

We got in Billy's car. And he was crying. But he still

wouldn't tell me what was going on, so I started yelling at him. He was just leaving me in suspense. Then he told me that Aunt Jessie just died.

I told him "That's crazy!" and told him he was mean, and he shouldn't say stuff like that. But when we got home, there were already a lot of cars parked in the street. We went into the house and I saw grandma sitting on the couch. And it was just like when my daddy died. There were people all around the house and in the kitchen. All comforting grandma and Uncle Larry.

And I saw Sandy and Mary were crying.

I went out to the backyard and started screaming, having my own little fit. I was so angry. She'd become one of my best friends in the last year. And I knew one of her biggest dreams was to see me graduate from high school, but I still had another year left.

Kenny paused, and wiped a tear off his cheek. His voice trembled a little.

Looking back now, I'm grateful that I got to spend time with her on that July third, never knowing that by that afternoon she would die of a heart attack, just like my father. Of course, I don't know how she would have known it either. But somehow, God gave us that extra time together on that long route to the grocery store.

It's a lesson I kept learning. Whenever you get the urge to tell someone that you love them, do it. Don't wait. Even if you have to write it on a piece of paper and fold it and put it under their pillow. Or stick it in a lunch pail or lunch sack. Tape it to the mirror in the bathroom. That way they have to see it when they shave or wash their face. Let them know that you do love them. You'll never know when their time will come.

That night, I had the dream about the old man again.

Chapter 8: The Red Cross

Not long after Aunt Jessie died, Sandy and Mary went to live with our oldest half-sister, Betty. Robert went to live with Dora, the youngest half-sister. She was already grown now and had a place of her own.

But I stayed with Uncle Larry. I had one more year of high school, and I knew I'd be more likely to graduate if I stayed home. And I really wanted to graduate, because I still wanted to be that little stick figure guy behind the podium like I dreamed of as a kid.

I was still working at the grocery store as a bagger. But about the middle of May, I started getting bored. I didn't have enough hours at work, especially on the weekend. That's when most people do their shopping, so you make better tips. So I asked Mr. Stephens for more hours.

He told me he was sorry, but he couldn't give me any more hours. But then a few days later, he came back to me and told me he had an idea. He said, "I think you'd be great working with kids with disabilities." I wasn't so sure about that. But he said, "You have a great heart, Kenneth. You'd be great at it." Then he handed me a piece of paper with a man's name and address on it. He told me the man was the director of the Disability Center in town. Then he said, "I want you to go there tomorrow. He wants to talk to you about volunteering with kids with disabilities."

I said, "Fine." It didn't sound very exciting. But I wanted something to do. The next day I went there. I remember it like it was yesterday. I walked in and there was a swimming pool.

It had glass walls all around it. It was nice. I went to the ballroom, and it had a kitchen. Then I walked into the office and there was this woman there, and she said, "Can I help you?"

I told her I was there to see the man on the piece of paper. She said, "Well, he's at lunch right now."

I said, "Okay." And right then the door to his office opens and a guy comes out with a half a tuna fish sandwich in his hand. He said, "Can I help you?"

Those last four words were delivered while Kenny pretended to have a mouthful of tuna sandwich.

I said, "I'm Kenneth."

He said, "Oh, you work with Mr. Stephens."

"Yes, that's right."

"Great! He said you would come by. Your swim trunks are in the locker room. They're red."

"Huh? What swim trunks?"

"Yeah, I can't talk right now. I'm on a long-distance phone call. Just go ahead and put them on. The bus will be here any minute." And then he went back into his office.

Kenny looked around the room with a confused look on his face, as if he was back in that place and time.

I looked at the woman and she said, "It's okay, go on. If they don't fit, we have another you can try."

So I said, "What are you two talking about? I don't want to go swimming."

"Of course you do," she said. "That's your job, isn't it?"

Kenny stepped out of office lady character and into young Kenny, stared at me with a dumbfounded look on his face, then jumped right back into office lady. . . .

"Now go on, the bus is pulling in right now." So I went into the locker room, and sure enough, there were some red swim trunks. I put them on, and they fit. I walked out to the pool, and there was another guy there laying out life jackets. His glasses were even thicker than mine.

When he saw me, he came up and said, "Are you Kenneth?"

"Yes," I said, and I walked up to him.

We shook hands, and he said, "Well, okay, are you ready? This is gonna be fun."

I told him, "Nobody's talkin' to me. I don't even know why I'm wearing these swimming trunks. And why am I in the pool area?"

"You know why you're here. We're both lifeguards."

"What?"

Then I looked up at the wall and there were all these kids with their mouths and noses all smushed up against the glass looking in. Kids with Down Syndrome. Kids with M.S. Kids with cerebral palsy. A kid in a wheelchair. And all the parents were with them. And the other life guard asked me, "Are they all here?" I guess he couldn't see them very well.

I said, "Yeah, they're all here."

"Okay. We're gonna have about thirty kids. Are you ready?"

"But. . . but. . .I can't be a lifeguard. I'm not trained for that." But they all started coming in, so it was too late. The other lifeguard got in the pool, and I went over to help the kids in. Some of them had trouble walking or getting out of their wheelchairs. And I helped some of the boys get out of their shirts. The good thing is, there were lots of mothers in there with us to help out.

Well, there was this one boy named Kyle. He was about fourteen years old. And when he pulled his blue jeans off, I could see that he had a fake leg. It looked like plastic, but in the shape of a leg. And then he unsnapped a couple of straps and took his leg off! Then he just put it in the locker along with his clothes. He didn't have any crutches, so he just started hopping over to the pool on one leg like it was no big deal!

About that time, some of the kids already had their lifejackets on and started jumping in the pool. This was all so new to me. I couldn't wait to see what the boy with one leg was gonna do in the pool, so I got into the water and introduced myself. I said, "Okay, my name is Kenneth, everybody. Just call me Kenneth, not 'Mister.' I'm not old." And they all started laughing.

"You are too, old!"

"No, I'm not."

"Yes, you are!"

I could tell already I was gonna like them.

Well, once we had all the kids into their life jackets, most of the parents left. But there were a few kids left who were too scared to get in the water, so I went over to the steps where they were all standing. One of them was even crying. I got some of them to try one step at a time, and then they'd jump back out. Then two steps, and back out. Then three steps. I had to hold some of their hands so they wouldn't be afraid.

One of them I had to pretend that he was getting into the ocean to make it exciting and take his mind off being afraid. "Is there a shark in there!?"

"No. No sharks. It's okay."

Two more steps and he was in the water, and shouted "I did it! I did it!" He was so proud.

Pretty soon, I had all of them in the water and having fun. They were climbing on my back and jumping off. And I decided they should all have a partner that they stayed near, to watch out for each other. Even though they had life jackets on, that seemed like a smart thing to do.

By the time their parents came back, none of them wanted to get out.

My first day as a lifeguard was a huge success! And I had a great time, too. Plus, I got to learn a little about all their disabilities. I got to be a lifeguard twice a week; and later, three times a week.

One of the things I liked to do the best was talking to kids who were feeling picked on or depressed because of their disability. I got to tell a lot of my own stories of when I was little and I got bullied. That always seemed to help them feel better about themselves.

Other times I just had to think of a way to get them to feel special. Like this one little boy who told me the other kids made fun of him because he had one arm shorter than the other. I said, "Well, that makes you pretty special, doesn't it?"

"Why's that?"

"Well, how many of them have a short arm?"

"Nobody."

"See there," I told him. "You're unique." And that got him to smile.

One of my favorite times at the Center was chaperoning at the dances. When I was in high school, I used to teach dancing and, I don't know how you say the word, colorography. Especially for the school plays. Anyway, I knew a little bit about how to get kids to dance who didn't want to or didn't know how.

This one little girl was at the dance in her wheelchair. None of the boys would dance with her. But her dad was there, so I went over and told him he should ask her to dance. He just said, "She's in a wheelchair. She can't dance." So I asked him if he minded if I asked her.

"Sure, go ahead."

I went up to her and said, "Hey, Betty. How are you?"

Kenny looked down, stuck out his bottom lip, and with as pouty a face as I'd seen in a while, said...

"Nobody wants to dance with me."

I bowed, and took her hand and said, "May I dance with you?"

She smiled really big and said, "Sure!"

She unlocked all the wheels, and I pulled her wheelchair out to the dance floor. The music was already playing. And I held one of her arms up in the air and held her hand still. And with my other hand I grabbed the arm of her chair and I swung it around in a circle. She was twirling! And she loved it, so I did it again and again. Finally, one of the guys with Down Syndrome came over, and said, "I want to dance with her! I want to dance with her!"

I politely bowed out and went over to stand next to her father. He said, "That was pretty good." So I guess I'd done okay.

But the time I remember the most was with Kyle. It was close to the end of the summer. I came in and found several of the boys over on the bench near the pool. Most of them were laughing. But Kyle was sitting down at the other end all by himself crying. I went over and sat down by him and asked him what was wrong. He said, "The other boys are making fun of me because of my leg."

"What do you mean," I said. "What are they saying?"

"They're saying I'm not a real person. I'm not a whole person because I have a fake leg."

I leaned over and said quietly, "You want me to tell you a secret?"

His eyes got really big and he said, "Yeah, what?"

"Well," I said, "we can't tell the others," even though I knew they could hear me. "You have the best thing that they don't have."

"What do I have?"

I said, "You have a personal baseball bat."

"A baseball bat?"

"Sure. You have a personal baseball bat. You take it wherever you go. None of them have one." And by then, all the other kids were looking and listening, so I said, "You want to play some baseball?"

He said, "With my leg?"

"Yeah."

I went over to the office and grabbed a piece of paper and started wadding it up. I came back and said, "You know how you usually take your leg off and stick it in the locker? Well, this time, let's play a little baseball with it."

Hey said, "Okay," and took his leg off. But I could tell he was confused, so I walked away from him a few feet, and I held up the wad of paper like I was a pitcher on the mound. He stood there for a few seconds, and then his whole face lit up. He picked up his leg and held it like a baseball bat. I threw the wad of paper, and he took a big swing — Boom! He sent it flying across the room.

As soon as that paper hit the ground, every other boy in the room was jumping up and yelling, "I want to do it! I want to do it!" I just moved away. The next thing I know, Kyle was hopping over to the pitcher's mound, throwing a wad of paper to a whole line of batters.

From that day on, nobody ever made fun of Kyle again.

A month went by, and school started again. I was still volunteering at the Disability Center, but not as much as during the summer.

One day, Kyle's mother came to the Center and found me. She said, "I have something to tell you." She told me that Kyle had lost his real leg in an accident, and that his father had trouble dealing with it. His dad eventually decided to leave them. She'd been trying to raise him on her own the best that she could. But he was always sad because the other kids made fun of him.

And she said, "One day this summer, he came home from the Center and asked me if I wanted to play baseball. I asked him when, and he said, 'Now!' I told him it was raining outside. But he said that didn't matter. He said, 'We can play inside, Momma. Just watch me.' And I could tell he was so excited to show me something."

"Then he went into the kitchen and got a piece of paper and wadded it up. He came back in the living room and told me to stand in the corner. Then he unstrapped his leg and used it like a baseball bat to hit the wad of paper across the room. He had the biggest smile on his face. We spent the rest of that afternoon hitting that wad of paper all over the house."

"I asked him where he learned to do that, and he told me it was from you. You taught him that he had his own private baseball bat. He said all the guys were nice to him now and play with him. And ever since then, whether he's walking on two legs or on one leg, he walks with pride. And I just can't thank you enough."

Kenny's voice had started to crack a little, and his eyes had welled with tears. Usually when that happened in our interviews, I started having the same reaction. Either because the story warranted it, or as an empathetic response to Kenny.

But not this time.

This time I just smiled. I knew what those tears meant, and it wasn't sadness. It was pride. Pride humbling enough to bring a grown man to tears. It was the first time I'd seen that in Kenny Tedford. And, at that point in his life story, it was probably the first time he'd ever felt it.

I'd argue that Kenny had made a life-changing impact on several other people by that point in his life: the bullies he befriended with the nickel backs of candy, the prostitute he listened to instead of taking advantage of, maybe even the crabby psychiatrist touched by his butterfly story. But he probably never knew what a positive role he played in their lives.

But with Kyle, he did. For the first time in his life, Kenny Tedford realized that he could do exactly what he wanted to do since he was a child: To be Mighty Mouse and save the day for someone. To improve someone else's life immeasurably with his words and stories. Perhaps not quite the stick figure man on the podium just yet. But a critical first step on the journey to get there.

In February, I got a letter from the State of Tennessee Red Cross. It said I'd been nominated to be considered for an ambassadorship to represent the United States for people with disabilities. They said there were over a thousand nominations, and they would be talking to my foster parents, bosses, and the kids I work with. Based on that, they would narrow it down from 1,000 to 500, to 50, to 10. And then finally they would pick two ambassadors, one with disabilities and one without.

I didn't hear anything the rest of the month, or in March. But in April, I got a letter that said they wanted me to come to Nashville to the Red Cross Center as their guest. And that's all it said.

So I went to Nashville. When I got there, we were in a conference room with a long table and a bunch of people around it. Those were the Board of Directors of the Tennessee Red Cross. And one of the men there was from Washington, D.C.

And there was another guy there who came up to me and introduced himself and asked me who I was. I told him my name. And he asked me if I knew what was going on. He said he just got this letter to come to a meeting. I said, "Me, too."

Well, we sat down, and I noticed that my director was there, from the Center. And this other guy's director was there, too. The other guy worked with people with disabilities just like

I did. Then the guy from Washington D.C. got up and said that me and this other guy had been selected as the two ambassadors from the United States! And he said he hoped that we would accept this honor and a three-week trip to Oslo, Norway. All expenses paid.

He called it a "Friendship Tour." And we would be teaching about what we've learned about working with people with disabilities.

I thought this was the greatest honor of my life. But I looked at the guy next to me and he looked disappointed. I asked him what was wrong, and he said, "Aw, man! I was hoping we'd get to go to somewhere fun."

About that time, the man talking said, "And you'll also be going to London, Paris, and Switzerland." And then the guy next to me jumped out of his chair and yelled, "Yes!" So I guess he wasn't disappointed anymore. Then they introduced us to a woman who was gonna be our chaperone for the trip, since we were both under twenty-one. She helped make sure we got our tickets and passports and things like that.

I graduated in May. We left the first week of June, and flew to Norway. I'll never forget it as long as I live. We flew one of the brand new Boeing 747 airplanes. It was bigger than a house on the inside. When you go in, there's a staircase that goes up to a second floor. It was unbelievable!

When we landed and were getting off the plane, there was a line of people there waiting for us, and waving the American flag. I felt like a celebrity. The director of the camp we were going to stay at was at the front of the line. He greeted us and said, "Welcome to Oslo."

I told him, "Hi, I'm Kenneth and I'm from Tennessee." And he started giggling.

Then I went to the next person in line and I introduced myself again, and they started giggling, too. Everyone in line did the same thing and would laugh after I introduced myself. By the time I got to the fifth person, they were laughing before I even said anything.

Finally, I got to the end. And I was already disappointed. I'd been so excited to come to Europe. I thought I'd be away from people who make fun of me and laugh at me, but it wasn't any different here. The director was next to me at that point and he could tell I was disappointed. He said, "My sincerest apologies. They're not making fun of you. They think you're funny."

And then one of the people in line spoke up. He said, "I want to tell you, you funny. Funny man. You remind me, Gomer Pyle."

"What?"

"You know. Marine. TV. Singer."

Of course, I knew who Gomer Pyle was. I just didn't know I looked like him. And then another one said, "You remind me of Donald Duck." And another one said, "You walk like a penguin."

So I guess I really was a celebrity. It didn't get much more famous than Gomer Pyle and Donald Duck.

I didn't say anything. But I took some quiet satisfaction in the fact that it was Kenny who was the funny-sounding duck in this story instead of me.

Our first night in Oslo, all the ambassadors stayed with a different local family in their house. I got to the house I was staying at after dark, so I didn't notice. But the next morning, when I got up, I opened the window, looked out, and I could see grass hanging down off the roof.

About that time, the woman who lived there knocked on my door really loud and came in. She was carrying a metal bowl with handles on the sides. She walked over and put it into a hole in a table where it fit perfectly. And there was water in the bowl, fresh, clean, spring water. And then she said, "Wash up. Breakfast is waiting."

Before she turned around to leave, I said, "There's grass coming off your roof. How do you get a lawn mower up there?"

She laughed, and said, "Oh, no, we have several goats up there for that."

I thought she was just teasing me, so I said, "You don't really have goats on the roof."

She just smiled and said, "Finish washing up and come downstairs, and we'll show you."

So I finished up, and got dressed and closed the window and went downstairs. Her daughter met me and took me outside. We walked way out into the front yard and turned around, and she pointed up. And there they were, three goats! It was just like I'd seen on postcards and magazines. I never really thought it was real. But it was.

The next day, we all went to a campsite where we could all stay in cabins around a lake. It was beautiful. We had dinner in a big dining hall. They had the flags from each country spread out around the tables. And you sat by your flag with the other people from your country. Each night we had food from a different country. And whoever's country it was that night, the ambassadors from that country got to make a toast with their favorite drink. Most of them liked different kinds of wine. I never did like to drink alcohol. I saw what that did to my momma, so I would just ask for water or a soda.

The first night was Norway, since that's where we were. They had all kinds of cheese and a special kind of bread. And the meal was lunch meats. Only theirs wasn't processed like it was in Tennessee. You should have had the bologna. It was amazing! It wasn't anything like our bologna. And they had soup and some kind of dried fish that they're famous for. Oh, and goat cheese.

Three or four days later, we'd all gotten to know each other pretty well. At dinner that night, the country was Russia. When it was time for the toast, they brought everyone a glass of water and everyone stood up.

The ambassador from Russia said some words, and raised his glass. And then everyone was supposed to take a drink. Except, instead of drinking it, everyone turned to look at me. And they had big smiles on their faces.

I turned to the guy who came with me from America, and he said, "They're all waiting for you to drink."

"But, I didn't make the toast."

"It doesn't matter. Drink it."

"Sip it?"

"No, kill it."

I put it to my mouth and turned the glass up and swallowed the whole thing. . . and I thought my throat was on fire! It burned like I had just swallowed hot lava. I started to choke and cough. I put the glass down and leaned back to sit down in the chair. But I'd moved the chair back when we stood up for the toast, so I missed it and fell flat on the floor.

Most everyone was still laughing when they helped me up. They explained to me that in Russia the favorite drink is vodka, which is basically just alcohol made from potatoes. It looks just like water, and doesn't have much of a smell either. My mouth was still burning, so I asked for some water. Somebody brought me a glass and I took a big gulp. Only, it wasn't water . . . it was more vodka! Ugh! That made me choke and cough all over again.

Well, that sent everyone into a whole new round of laughter. Only this time, I didn't fall down. And when the laughing ended, I got a big round of applause, a standing ovation. I didn't think the vodka was that funny. But the standing ovation was pretty cool.

One day at the campsite, I was talking to a guy named Orin. And he said, "Hey, tomorrow I'm going to the steam room. Do you want to come with me?"

I'd never heard of that, so I said, "What's a steam room?"

"Oh, it's really hot, and you pour water on these rocks and it makes a bunch of steam, and the room looks like it's full of smoke."

And I go, "Don't you choke? Smoke makes me choke."

"No, no, no. It's not like smoke from a fire. It's more like fog. You're coming with me. I've got to show you. You'll like it."

Well, I told him I'd try it. The next day I met him at the locker room. When we got in there, I asked him what I should wear. He told me I could wear my shorts if I wanted. But that it was better to just go naked.

I said, "I'll just keep my shorts on."

"Oh, you Americans. There's nothin' to be ashamed of. These are just our bodies."

"Okay. Still, I'll just keep my shorts on."

"Fine, it's up to you."

He stripped naked right there and walked over to get some towels for us. And, it's not like I've never been around a naked man before. We all took showers together in high school when I played football. But you *had* to be naked to take a shower. And I knew those guys. I'd just met Orin. I guess people in Europe are just different that way. They're not embarrassed for people to see their bodies.

Orin wrapped himself up with a towel and said, "Hey I've got to go do something real quick. You go on in and I'll meet you in there."

Well, I thought about what he said while he was gone. And I wondered what it would be like to be in there naked. Maybe it would feel a lot better or something, so I took my towel and wrapped it around me. Then I reached underneath and took off my shorts. There wasn't anyone else in the room, but I guess even I didn't want to be naked in front of me.

Then I opened the door, and the steam just came rolling out. And it was hot. That really felt good, because even though it was summer, it was kind of cool in Norway.

I went in and sat down. And then I poured some water on the rocks and made more steam. And then, just about the time the steam settled down enough to see, somebody came in. I assumed it would be Orin, so I looked up. And standing right there in front of me was a stark-naked woman!

Kenny's eyes got as big as saucers, and he let out a muffled gasp.

I couldn't believe my eyes. And before I could say anything, I heard someone say, "Hi!" And I looked over and it was another woman, just as naked as the first one!

More gasps from Kenny. I chuckled to myself as I tried to imagine the scene. But just visualizing an 18-year-old male in a steam room confronted by two smiling nude women doesn't do the situation justice. You have to imagine him with an 18-year-old man's body, but with the mental and social development of a ten-year-old. Remember, this is the guy who couldn't, or wouldn't, even get to second base with a prostitute at a drive-in movie, so I had to ask myself, "How would a ten-year-old boy respond to a situation like that?"
I was about to find out.

They took one look at me and said, "What's wrong?"

I jumped up off the bench and ran out the door! And when I shoved the door open, it slammed right into Orin and knocked him to the ground. He yelled out, "Owww!" and was holding his head.

Kenny laughed at himself and the comical scene.

The door shut behind me, and I helped him up. I said, "I'm sorry. I'm sorry."

He just looked at me and said, "What's wrong with you?"

I shouted, "There's naked girls in there! They're naked!

"They're supposed to be naked, Kenneth!"

About that time the girls came out of the steam room with towels wrapped around them, saying, "We're sorry! We're sorry! Haven't you seen a woman naked before?"

I said, "Nooooah! I haven't even seen my sisters naked, and I've got four of 'em." But I ended up telling them it wasn't their fault. It was just me. I wasn't used to all that.

They suggested we all go swimming instead, so that I wouldn't feel bad. So we all went back to our cabins and put our swimsuits on and met down at the lake. When we got there, they said, "We're gonna have a contest. Last one to the island is a rotten egg. That's what you say in America, right?" There was a little man-made floating island in the lake with a ladder on the side of it and room to lay on top.

Orin said, "Everybody ready?" And then he started counting, "One, two. . ." And when he got to two, the girls just took off running. They were cheating! So I took off running. Well, they didn't seem to be giving it all they had, so I caught up pretty quick and passed them. When I got to the water, I dove out in the air and landed in the water. And it was like a million little knives poking me all over my body at the same time. The water was freezing! I came up and I was blue all over.

I stuck my head out and looked around and all three of them were just standing on the edge of the beach with a big smile on their faces. Orin yelled out, "Keep swimming, get your blood moving! You'll warm up!" And then I thought about how my dad taught me to swim and I started to swim out to the island. After they had a good laugh, they all jumped in, too. Orin actually beat me to the island. It turned out he was on the swim team.

When we all got to the island, the girls found some towels there and laid them out on the ground. They wanted to lay in the sun and warm up and get a suntan.

Kenny's face flushed a bit as he snickered sheepishly and paused. But this wasn't a feature of his performance. It was a genuinely embarrassed reaction to whatever he was about to tell me.

One of them looked at me and said, "Would you mind taking off my top?" She had on a two-piece bathing suit, and the top ties in the back, so I guess it's hard for her to reach it.

I'd never done that before, so I didn't know what to do. She said, "Just pull the string." I looked over at Orin and the other girl and they were just laughing their heads off.

I yelled, "It's not funny!" Then I pulled the string, and the whole thing just fell to the ground. She turned around to thank me. And then, there I was, for the second time in less than a half-hour, standing in front of a naked woman.

I'll never forget it, that's for sure. She was beautiful. And I had the urges of any man. I knew then I was normal that way, whatever that is.

About that time, the other woman took her top off and they both laid down on their towels to get some sun. I looked over at Orin and I said, "Well, I hope you're not gonna take off your swim trunks now."

"No!" he said. "We don't do that. I mean, I could. But I won't do that because you're here." I guess in some places in Europe people go to the beach *completely* naked. But this wasn't supposed to be one of them.

Anyway, I decided to just lay down on my towel and focus my attention on the beautiful land and scenery. It was already an exciting enough day. And besides, there was someone else there I had my eye on.

She worked at the Red Cross in Norway and helped with everything at the camp. She was the most beautiful woman I'd ever seen up to that point in my life. I was hoping I'd get a chance to spend some time with her alone before it was time to leave Norway.

On our last night in Oslo, I got my chance. They had horse-drawn carriage rides out in the woods that we could take. She knew I liked horses, and came up to me that day and asked me if I would take a ride with her that evening in the carriage, just the two of us. My dream came true. I couldn't think of anything I'd want to do more. But I told her, "It's gonna be dark. I won't be able to see your lips to tell what you're saying." But she told me it was supposed to be a full moon that night. So it would be bright enough to see her. And that made it nice and romantic for us, too.

It was beautiful that night. The man drove the carriage slow so we could see everything. It was kind of cold, so she put her head on my shoulder and kind of snuggled up a little. Then, she told me I was the funniest man she'd ever met. And that she loved listening to my stories. And then she put her hand on my chest.

Kenny turned from me and stared off into the distance. He let out a long, slow sigh.

I almost melted. I put my hand on top of her hand. And then she leaned over and gave me a kiss.

I never wanted to leave.

Kenny was still staring off in the distance as he talked. It was as if I'd left the room and he was just reminiscing out loud all alone. Or, maybe it was more like young Kenny was telling the story to old Kenny. Whatever the right metaphor, I didn't belong in it. I felt like a voyeur watching an intimate scene I wasn't a party to, equal parts guilty that I hadn't left, and privileged that I knew Kenny wanted me to stay.

And I felt young again.

Well, the next day was our last day. There was a closing ceremony at noon. We all got there and were having lunch. One of the guys at the table was gonna deliver a keynote address when we were done eating, you know, remind us what all we did and learned, and wish us all the best, and thank us for coming. That kind of thing.

While we were eating, about thirty minutes before his speech, he came up to me with someone else. He started talking. But there wasn't much sound coming out.

Kenny mimicked the garbled, raspy noises of someone with no voice struggling to speak.

The woman next to him said, "He got laryngitis last night. We were out riding the carriage in the cold." Then she said that he couldn't give the keynote address, and that he wanted me to do it for him!

I just said, "No. No, no, no, no."

More garbled, raspy noises.

I looked at the woman to understand.

"Please, Kenneth. Everybody loves you. They think you're so funny."

And I was at that point that I get to sometimes, when I'm tired of people thinking I'm funny when I don't mean to be. So I said, "I don't think so."

"Please! People love your stories. You've got to tell the one about the steam room."

"What? How did you know about that?"

"Oh, Orin's been tellin' everyone. He thinks it's hilarious."

I asked, "Is anything sacred around here?"

Well, I don't remember actually telling her I would do it. But a few minutes later she got up to introduce the speaker, and she said, "I'm sorry, Mr. So-and-so was gonna give the closing address. But he got laryngitis last night, so, instead, we've asked Mr. Kenneth Tedford from the United States to speak." And people just started clapping and whistling and yelling like a famous person was about to show up.

I stood up. And they had a podium there. And I was almost about to cry. But not because I was scared. I guess the truth was, I was so honored to be asked. My Aunt Jessie had just died last year. Of all the things in the world, I just wished that my parents and Aunt Jessie could have been there to see me. And my brothers and sisters, too, so they could finally see what I could do.

I talked a little about what we'd learned that week, and how happy I was to make friends with people from all over the world. But I mostly got to tell them stories about my life, stories like about my mom and dad and the tree dance. And I asked them how many of them had heard of Dale Evans and Roy Rogers. And, believe it or not, a lot of them love to watch American movies. Especially cowboy movies. They all cheered and said, "Yeah! Yeah!"

So I started to sing the song "Happy Trails". . . "Happy trails to you / until we meet again / Happy trails to you / keep smilin' until then . . ." I mean, I can't sing very well. And I didn't sing all of it. But I did it. And they clapped like crazy. And I told them, "Until we meet again, treasure what you've learned here from each other. Thank you for inviting us. It's been an honor to work with the Red Cross. If I had a hat on, I'd tip my hat to all of you. . . so a toast."

Then I looked at my chaperone, and I asked, "What are we drinking our toast with?"

She said, "Vodka," and everybody started laughing, so I knew it was just a joke.

Everybody raised their glass for a drink while they were still laughing. And then they took a drink and then gave me a big round of applause. It was one of the proudest moments of my life.

After it was over, they had a little dance for us. And I love to dance. The man who was supposed to give the speech came over with the lady again. He had tears in his eyes. He had a funny smile on his face and then as clear as day he said, "I love you, man."

"WHAT!? You can talk?"

I looked over at the lady, and she was all smiling and saying, "We did it! We did it!" like she was singing a song. I guess they really got me. But I'm glad they did.

And then I got to dance with the pretty girl.

~ ~

After I got back from Europe, I was about to start school at Memphis State University. Well, right before school started, Uncle Larry came into my bedroom. He had a clipboard with him. And it had some paper on it. Sticking out of the bottom sheet was a place for a signature and he wanted me to sign it.

I asked him what it was. He just said, "Oh, nothin'. Just rental insurance for the house."

"Why am I signing rental insurance? We've never done this before."

"Just sign it, Kenneth. Just sign it."

I got a little suspicious. I was nineteen years old then. I wasn't a dummy. I grabbed the clipboard out of his hand, and he reached to get it back. But I kept it. I pulled up the top page to see what I was signing underneath. It was a paper to give him the right to receive my father's social security payments. Aunt Jessie had been getting them to help feed us and put clothes on us. But now that she died and I was eighteen, that money was supposed to come directly to me. Unless I wanted Uncle Larry to have it, and that's what the paper was for.

I was really disappointed in Uncle Larry. That really made me angry. That he would stoop that low to try to trick me into signing it.

I called my cousin Jeff's father, Winston, to ask if I could stay with them. Jeff was away on a two-year Mormon mission. They said I could stay in his bedroom. So I packed my bags and left.

I never moved back.

FOUR DAYS WITH KENNY TEDFORD

We spent the entire day on the patio, recording story after story as I peppered Kenny with the dozens of questions I'd been outlining since our last meeting. As I listen to it now, I can hear the gurgling of a small water fountain and the chirping of birds in the background. Normally I find that soothing. But in this case they're a minor annoyance, because I have to listen through them to understand all of

Kenny's words clearly. The irony isn't lost on me that what I find to be an annoyance, Kenny couldn't hear at all, and no doubt wishes he could.

After dinner I asked Kenny if he would mind telling a couple of stories to Lisa and the boys. He'd been staring at me for an entire day. I wanted to give him a new audience. But I also wanted to give my family an opportunity to get to know Kenny better.

I knew Kenny would ask which stories he should tell, so in advance of sitting down for the show, I prompted my fourteen-year-old son Matthew with the name of two stories he should ask for. Once everyone was seated, Matthew stood up and announced with as straight a face as he could muster, "Would you please tell the ones about the night you lost your manhood in the haunted house, and the pussy story?"

It's impossible to know who was more shocked and embarrassed by that request. But everyone in the room, except for me, was definitely in the running.

My wife looked at me with that look that meant, "You better know what you're doing." For his part, Kenny laughed and said, "Why does everyone always want to hear those stories?" in a tone that suggested he had no need for a response.

Kenny told both stories in as unadulterated a manner as he could in mixed company. Everyone laughed in the right places. My wife's laughter grew as it became more obvious the stories were harmless. Ben, always fidgety, was oddly calm and able to listen without interrupting a single time or feeling the need to add his opinion to how the story should go. And Matthew didn't excuse himself to go play video games or even look longingly in that direction.

Kenny received as rousing an applause as you can get from four people. And then delighted us even further by showing us how deaf people applaud. Making noise by clapping obviously doesn't do much for deaf people. What you do instead is raise your hands above your head like someone was stealing your wallet at gunpoint, and then rotate your hands back and forth as fast as you can. Done properly, you look like a dancer doing jazz hands while surrendering to the audience.

I announced it was bedtime for Ben, and Matthew probably had homework, which drew a precious "Awwwww" from Ben and a grunt from my teenager. We all could have listened for hours. But Kenny had been talking all day, and I wanted him to be able to wind down and get a good night's sleep.

Kenny went downstairs and we all made preparation for bed or homework. But after a few minutes, Matthew came to me and asked if Kenny could come back up and tell more stories. It was a surprising request. My shy son, who hours earlier would have crawled out of his skin to avoid any of this, was now asking for more! I told him Kenny was tired and already in bed. But he was uncharacteristically insistent. And one thing I'd been trying for some time to impress upon him was that he needed to overcome his aversion to asking for what he wants, to advocate for himself. I wanted to reward what I saw as an attempt to do exactly that, so I agreed we could go down and ask. And by "we," of course, I meant "he."

We talked about how he might go about asking, including how to even enter the room. I'd learned from Kenny that you don't just walk into a room and start talking to a deaf person. It's too startling. What you do is to flick the light switch on and off a few times to announce your presence first. And so that's what we did.

When we walked all the way in, we found Kenny, not in bed as we'd expected, but sitting in a recliner wearing boxer shorts and a tank-top t-shirt, half-covered in a bedsheet. Apparently, Kenny's more comfortable sleeping in a chair that way, even at home.

Matthew repeated his practiced request, and much to everyone's satisfaction, Kenny accepted.

We went back upstairs, and I announced there would be an encore performance as soon as Kenny could get dressed. Ben celebrated with a "Yay!" and we all settled back on the couch for round two. Kenny regaled us again with stories of being bullied in grade school, and his own rendition of a story about why Abraham Lincoln grew a beard.

Part of what's so enchanting about listening to Kenny Tedford tell a story is the sound effects. When the story includes a horse-drawn carriage, Kenny mimics the clip-clop of the horse's hooves. When the story includes a windy storm, he'll make the whooshing sounds of the gale. And his delivery is always remarkably true despite his limited hearing. The result was a second act more mesmerizing than the first, despite the G-rated content.

We ended with the same "Awwwww" and grunt and the same tired storyteller. But somehow, something was different about Matthew. That visit to the basement marked a turning point for him. Prior to that, unfamiliar house guests made him uncomfortable. And his reaction was always the same: avoidance. Avoidance of prolonged eye contact, conversation, and even presence in the same room.

Kenny's visit changed that.

I can't say that he's now an extrovert, or that he's ever asked any other guest to stay or chat longer than planned. But the stress and anxiety seem to have dissipated. He actually enjoys our guests now, and will stay up late into the night talking to them.

Mighty Mouse had saved another day.

But not just anyone's day. This was my son we were talking about. And that made for something of a turning point for me, too. In the months since we'd started these interviews, I was documenting Kenny's impact on other people and their impact on him. But now he was starting to have a positive impact on me and my family, personally. I hadn't expected that.

I realized this was no longer just a business relationship. It was becoming a friendship.

Chapter 9: Going to College

I eventually got a real apartment of my own. But a few months later, I lost my job. I was doing contract work for the government, and the contract came to an end. I was living paycheck to paycheck, so I couldn't afford to have a month or two without work. My rent was $300 a month, and it was coming due in a few days.

That Friday I went by to see the office manager at my apartment to tell her that I got laid off and was going to be late on my rent. I had just enough money for food and utilities. And I needed gas money to get to interviews. But I hadn't planned my spending very well, and just didn't have enough for rent.

She felt really bad for me. But she said, "The rent is due on the 1st of the month. And the people who own this apartment say if you don't pay by the 5th you have to move out." There wasn't anything else I could do about it, so I just decided to give it to God and let Him figure it out.

Then Sunday morning I went to choir practice. And then at church service after that, we sang for the church. When we were done, the choir director came up to me and handed me an envelope. He said, "There's a couple who gave me this envelope to give to you. They pointed you out and said, 'We don't know who that guy is, the one with the thick glasses and the blonde hair.' I told them your name was Kenneth. Then they said, 'Please give this to him. The Lord told us to give this to him.'"

I opened it up and it was a check for $150. And on the place where it says what the check is for, it just said, "Love offering."

I asked, "Who are these people?"

He said, "I don't know. I've never seen them before. They said they were visiting."

I started feeling pretty good because that was half of what I needed for my rent. I thought maybe they would let me stay a couple of weeks so I could come up with the other half.

Well, that night the choir went to another church in another town to sing. It was about 35 or 40 minutes away. When we finished singing, the choir director came up to me and he looked like he was in shock. He handed me another envelope. Then he said, "You know the couple that gave you that other envelope this morning? They're here!"

"What?"

"They said that when they went home and were eating lunch they thought, 'We didn't do what God wanted us to do. We need to give that young man more.' They said they felt bad, so they called the church to find out where the choir would be performing next, and they came here to give you this."

I was just gonna put it in my pocket and leave, but the choir director said, "Whoa, whoa, whoa! Open that up. I want to see what's going on here."

I said, "Fine," and I opened it. It was another check for $150! Now I had my whole rent. I couldn't believe it. They even had an ice cream party at the church for the choir. They had cookies and pies and Dr. Pepper and Coca Colas. My belly was full. I stuffed my pockets with cookies. And I had two job interviews scheduled for the next week. I was so happy and bubbling that I went home and I cried.

I trusted God to make a plan for me. And He sure did. It was like learning from my father. Like when he was trying to teach me to swim and he had me on his shoulders in the lake and told me to jump. He just said "Jump" and then, "Trust me. . . do you really think I'd let you drown?" And that's what my God does. He says "jump" and "trust me." Sometimes He tells me to do things I'm not comfortable with. But I do it. And I trust Him. And it's always worked out. Just like with my daddy in the lake.

By Christmastime I was still doing odd jobs and struggling to pay my bills and save up to buy a car. I wanted to get a Volkswagen Super Beetle, just like my brother Terry used to come save us in.

But the most amazing thing was that Leawood Baptist church was only a few blocks away, so I could walk to church and back on Sundays.

I didn't share with anyone at church how much I was struggling with money. I was just grateful to be alive and have Christmas lights in the living room and on the door. But for the first time, I knew that I wasn't gonna be able to have a Christmas tree. And that really bothered me.

A Christmas tree is a big tradition for me. And they smell so good! I was getting pretty depressed about it, knowing I was gonna have a Christmas without a tree. I don't care if I have gifts. But I always want a tree to put lights and decorations on, like those little balls. And back in those days we had those little silver strips that look like tinfoil, and you just throw them on the tree and they hang down and look like icicles.

I thought to myself, "I remember those!" I hadn't seen them, or even thought about them, in decades. Like Kenny, I have such fond memories of throwing fistfuls of tinsel on the tree like confetti. My mother would pull them back off and tell me they were to be placed one at a time; and that they should be draped with care, so that they'd hang down straight. That way they'd actually resemble an icicle instead of a wad of tinfoil.

I'd follow her instructions for about two minutes, and then I'd heave another fistful up to the top of the tree like I was lobbing a hand grenade out of a foxhole.

These little reminders of my youth were like candy to me. And Kenny seemed to sprinkle them throughout our conversations like

unexpected gifts: TG&Y stores, Minute Man restaurants, little red
Bibles, the toy monkey playing drums, cane fishing poles, Thermos
bottles, knuckle sandwiches, and the dancing hot dog on the drive-in
movie screen, all ubiquitous parts of my youth that most kids today
would be completely unfamiliar with. And, were it not for these
interviews, all things I might not ever have occasion to consider again.

I savored this icicle memory like it was the nougat at the center of
a 100 Grand chocolate bar.

Well, the week went by and it was pretty tough. But I made
it. And then it was the day before Christmas Eve. I'd been out
looking for work, and applying for jobs. That evening I went
over to a friend's house for supper. So when I came home that
night, it was dark.

When I got back to my building, I had to walk down a long
hallway, and then turn down another short hall to my
apartment. And as I was walking down that long hallway, I
started to smell a pine tree. And I knew there weren't any pine
trees near our building. And I thought, "No way. I want a
Christmas tree so bad, now I'm starting to smell it!" I turned
around the corner, and there was a Christmas tree leaning
against my apartment door!

It was a beautiful tree. Thick. And next to it was a box. A
big box. And on the tree was a card that said, "Kenneth" on the
front of it. I opened the envelope, and the card was handmade!
There was a drawing of a Christmas tree and a log cabin on the
front. And there was a river running by the cabin and there was
a moose! And I love mooses. I guess somebody knew those are
three of my favorite things: Christmas trees, log cabins, and
mooses.

I turned the page, and on the next page was the writing. It
just said, "Merry Christmas and Happy New Year. You're a
blessing. We love you." And that's it. No signature. No name. I
looked all over the card. Nothing. And the handwriting was a

funny scribbling, like somebody wrote with the wrong hand so I couldn't tell whose it was.

I was so excited, I opened the box right there in the hallway. It was full of Christmas lights and balls and icicles! I got so excited I started crying. I got a little farther into the box and found a tree stand at the bottom. They really thought of everything.

So I took everything in and set it up. Got the tree decorated. Played Christmas music. I didn't have any presents under the tree that year. But the tree and lights were the greatest gift I could have asked for. I didn't need anything else. I treasure that Christmas.

To this day, I still don't know who did it. Even when I got to church or got around other friends, nobody said anything to me about it. Nobody said, "How'd you like the tree? Did you get the box?"

So I started telling people about it. "Guess what!? I got home the other day and there was a Christmas tree there! Did ya'll do it?"

But everybody just seemed surprised. "What? Did you need a tree? You get one every year, don't you?" And that's when I remembered that I didn't tell anybody about not having a tree. And I hadn't had anyone over to my apartment to visit. I was going to everyone else's house to visit. I don't know who did it or how they did it. But as a Christian, it just showed me how God provides. He knew that's what I wanted. And He took care of it.

And He knew what else I needed, too. Two days after Christmas, I got a call with a job offer. This time as a job coach for people with all kinds of disabilities, not just deaf people. And that was wonderful!

But, I was more excited about the Christmas tree.

~ ~

I found out the first semester I started classes at Memphis State that college was going to be hard for me. The classrooms are bigger than they are in high school. I couldn't see the board or the professor very well. And, of course, I couldn't hear very well either. So I was making Ds and Fs on my tests. And, eventually, I just stopped going to class.

After a few weeks, my advisor called me and asked me to come meet him in his office. He was a really big fella. And when I say 'big' I don't mean fat. He was really tall, and really muscular. He said, "What's this I hear about you quitting school?"

I told him why, and all the trouble I was having in class. He said, "That makes sense." And then he said he'd been thinking about me and what to do about it. And he said, "Why don't you go to Gallaudet University in D.C.?"

I said, "What's Gallaudet?"

He told me it was a university for deaf people. In fact, the only one in the world just for deaf people.

I told him, "I don't think so."

"Why not?"

I said, "I don't want to be like all those deaf people walkin' around like. . ."

Kenny wiggled his hands around incoherently like he thought deaf people looked when signing. And to add insult to injury, he delivered it with a disdainful look of stupidity on his face, the kind of face a ten-year-old boy makes while saying the word, "Duh!"

In fact, now that I think about it, I probably looked a lot like those bullies who made fun of me when I was a kid.

Well, he didn't like that very much. He got up out of his chair and walked around to my side, so I got up and started backing up toward the door because I was kind of scared. When

my butt hit the door, he got up real close to me and said, "My
sister is deaf. And she speaks sign language."

"Oh."

"So you wanna do that thing with your hands again and
tell me why you don't want to go to a school for the deaf?"

I said, "No, no, no, no."

"Good. Now, sit down and let's talk about this." So I sat
down. And he sat down. Then he said, "I think Gallaudet
would be great for you. But I think you'd be great for
Gallaudet, too. You're good with people. You've been traveling
all over Europe with the Red Cross. The other students there
could learn a lot from you. And you'd learn a lot better, too.
Plus, you need to learn sign language eventually, because you
told me that your hearing is getting worse."

Then he said, "I'll make a deal with you. I want you to go
to Gallaudet this summer, just for three months, and learn
sign language. And I'll pay for it myself. I'll pay all your
expenses. Then when you're done, if you like it, and you can
afford it, you can stay. But, if you don't, you can come back
here and start classes again, and we'll provide a sign-
language interpreter for you in class."

Well, that sounded like a pretty good deal to me. So I
went to Washington D.C. to go to Gallaudet.

It was like a scene right out of the movie Miracle on 34th
Street, *when the Macy's Santa starts sending kids to Gimbels if he
knows they'll find a better or cheaper option there. This MSU
counselor was sending Kenny to another university, at his own
personal expense, just because he thought Kenny would be better off
there.*

And who says there's no Santa?

That summer, the only class I took was sign language. It
was hard, just like learning any new language would be. I tried

to quit three times. But the teachers and students were really encouraging, so I stuck with it.

And my roommates helped a lot. They put me in a dorm with a couple of other deaf students who already knew sign language. That turned out to be pretty smart. They were also oralists, like me, so we could just talk and read lips in our dorm room. But they wouldn't let me. When we were having dinner, and I wanted them to pass me a fork, they wouldn't give it to me until I made the sign for fork.

Then, when one of them went to the kitchen, I asked him to bring me back some coffee. He just looked at me and signed, "What? What?"

I voiced again, "Coffee. Will you bring me some coffee?"

He just smiled and shrugged his shoulders like he didn't understand me. I looked over at my other roommate. He was holding his hands under the table, showing me the sign for 'coffee,' like he was telling me a secret, so then I could ask for coffee in sign.

At the end of the summer, I knew sign language pretty well. At first, I was afraid to do it in public. I thought it just called attention to the fact that I was deaf, and would get me labeled again. But I got over that pretty soon.

And I decided I liked Gallaudet pretty well, too. I found out it was the first place anyone ever used a huddle in football. It was all the way back in 1890. Their team played other deaf teams, so the other players all knew sign language. And you can't whisper in sign language. To keep the other team from seeing their signs, they had to stand around in a little circle with their backs facing out so nobody could see into the middle where the quarterback was signing the next play. Now all the football teams do it.

I thought I'd like to go to school there, but I knew I couldn't afford it. Then I found out the Tennessee State Vocational

Rehabilitation program would pay for it, because of my disability. So I decided to stay.

My first year at Gallaudet was the first time in my life I spent a lot of time around other deaf people. I went to classes with all deaf people and lived in the dorms with all deaf people.

One of the first things I learned was that it's hard for deaf people to say the 'th' sound. They usually try so hard to say it right that they end up spitting all over you. And when your name is 'Kenneth,' that's a problem. That's when I started going by "Kenny."

After a few weeks, I found out something else about being around a bunch of deaf people. I started finding notes on my door. They'd say things like, "Go home!" or "You don't belong here!" or even "You're not deaf."

I thought that was strange, since one of the reasons I came to a deaf school was because lots of people in the hearing world would tell me I didn't belong with them, either.

I went to my counselor and asked him why I was getting the notes. He said, "It's because you talk."

That's when I found out there was a problem in the deaf community. It wasn't anything about Gallaudet. Apparently, that's just the way it was in the whole deaf world, everywhere.

If you look at other disabled communities, I don't know if you'll see this. I haven't seen people who are blind or in a wheelchair do this to other people who are blind or in a wheelchair. Maybe they do.

But in the deaf community, it's definitely a problem. There are all these little groups. If you're hard of hearing, the people who are totally deaf might not accept you. If you're oral, someone who speaks only sign language might think you're a not one of them.

My last year at Gallaudet, they announced there would be three students who had cochlear implants coming in the Fall. A group of students made some signs to protest. They said, "This is a *deaf* school!" They didn't want cochlear-implant people to come and take over. I even know a lady who got a cochlear implant, and then her deaf friends stopped inviting her to parties. They thought she was ashamed to be deaf.

There's even trouble between the people who use ASL (American Sign Language) and the people who use Sign English.

"Really? So ASL and Sign English aren't the same thing?"

Oooh, noooOOOOoah!

The second half of the word "no" took on a sharp increase in both volume and pitch, as if Kenny suddenly realized, mid-word, the full ineptitude of my question.

If you use Sign English in front of some people who use ASL, they might flip you off! I mean, only some of them, but this stuff happens. Most of them learned ASL a long time ago, and they don't want to have to learn another way to sign.

"What's the difference between ASL and Sign English?"

ASL is kind of like shorthand. It's what I learned when I first learned sign. It's all there was then. If I wanted to ask you to go to the store with me tomorrow, I'd sign the words: 'you, me, store, tomorrow, question.' But if I was using Sign English, I'd sign all the words: 'do, you, want, to, go, to, the, store, with, me, tomorrow, question.' That came along later. The reason for learning Sign English is that it makes it easier to read and write like hearing people.

Can you imagine a person in a wheelchair saying, "I don't like the wheelchair you use" or "I saw your leg move a little, you're not crippled enough?" But that's what it was like in the deaf world I grew up in. And there are still people fighting about stuff like this today. Nowadays, two out of five kids born with deafness will get cochlear implants in the hospital. But sometimes you'll see lawsuits by people who want them to stop, and those people aren't even related to the child. They say the baby might not *want* the implant.

I thought about how tribal the human animal is. There seems to be no end to our ability to separate ourselves into "us" versus "them."

Chapter 10: Angela

My second year at Gallaudet, something amazing happened. I was having lunch in the cafeteria. And not too far from my table was the line where you would stand with a tray to get your food. But there was a little wall between the line and the tables. It wasn't much of a wall. It only went from about your knees to your shoulders, so you could see people's legs and feet underneath it and their heads over it.

I was just sitting and eating, watching all the legs go by. Sometimes they were pretty girl legs and sometimes they were big hairy boy legs. One time there was even some hairy legs that I thought was a guy and it turned out to be a girl.

Then, all of a sudden, I stopped eating. I just stared. It was the most beautiful legs you ever saw. I watched as she came around the corner, and her face matched her legs, gorgeous! She walked by me with a group of her girlfriends. I know she saw me, but she kept on going.

That night I went back to the cafeteria for dinner, hoping I'd see her. And, sure enough, there she was. She walked right by me again with her same girlfriends. But she didn't acknowledge me. Then I saw her staring in my direction, looking for another one of her friends. She was deaf, so I said to her in sign language, "Do you want to eat here?"

She just said, "No, thanks," and walked off.

Well, this happened every day for the next couple of days. Breakfast. Lunch. Dinner. Breakfast. Lunch. Dinner. I'd see her and ask if she wanted to sit and eat with me, and she'd say, "No, thanks." I thought, "If she wants to play hard-to-get, fine!" I even tried the next week a few times. But eventually I gave up. I guess I wasn't worth having such a beautiful woman.

Three days later it was Sunday. Not many kids eat in the cafeteria on Sunday, so there are a lot of empty tables. I was just sitting there, eating my food and reading the Sunday paper. And I noticed there was a shadow next to me. I turned to look, and it was her! She looked at me and asked, "Can I sit here?"

Then Kenny started laughing, as if that was the stupidest question he'd ever heard.

I said, "Sure! You can sit anywhere." She sat down, and we started signing to each other and introduced ourselves. Her name was Angela.

Then she said, "I'm sorry I made it hard for you to get me. I really did like you when I first saw you."

I asked her, "Well, then why didn't you sit down and eat with me?"

She said she had a bad experience in the past and didn't trust men. I just said, "Okay," and let it go.

But we just had the greatest talk. We talked about everything. And then she asked me, "What made you like me and want to talk to me? Was it my hair?"

"No."

"The way I dress?"

"No."

"Well, what was it then? Tell me!"

So I told her, "Your legs."

She said, "What? My legs?" I told her the whole story about me watching all the legs in the food line. When I finished, she just started cracking up. And she said, "Oh, I do like you!" I think Angela didn't think she had pretty legs. But I thought they were gorgeous.

After that day, we started dating, just like a typical couple. We started sharing more of our family life. I found out she wasn't American. She was Canadian. And she shared what happened to her when she was younger. She lived on the coast of Nova Scotia. And it was during the Korean War. The Navy ships from America would come into port and let the sailors off for shore leave.

Well, Angela happened to be at a bar one night and met one of the sailors and fell in love. He was in town for only a week, but they spent some of every day together. And, probably not too surprising, by the end of the week the sailor wanted to have sex with her. And he did all the kinds of things young men do to try to get young women to have sex with them. He said things like, "If you really loved me, you'd do it."

But she didn't want to do that. She wanted to save herself for marriage. So he told her that he loved her and he would marry her. But his ship was leaving the next day. So she did it. She had sex with him.

Two months later his ship came back through Nova Scotia and he looked her up. And he took one look at her and realized she was pregnant. They still went out for dinner at a nice restaurant, as they'd planned. But he was acting really different. After dinner, he said he was tired and wanted to go back to his hotel room to sleep. He was tired from the work on the ship. But he said he'd come back tomorrow and take her to the park and for a walk along the beach.

So, the next morning, no show. That afternoon, no show. So, she went to his hotel to find him. But they told her that he checked out that morning to go back to the ship. So, she went to the ship to find him there. But when she asked for him at the ship, they told her there was nobody on board that ship by that name.

She said she never trusted men again after that.

And in her little village, it was so small, everyone knew everyone else's business. Plus, she wasn't married, and she was too young to raise a baby by herself anyway. She was still living with her mother. So, she went off for the next several months to have the child. After that, her mother came to get them both, and she ended up adopting the baby herself. So Angela became "Aunt Angela" to the baby, even though it was her daughter.

Angela was worried that would scare me away, that she'd had a baby. But it didn't. I loved her by then and I'd told her so.

But for whatever reason, something did worry me about her story. But it wasn't the baby. I remember learning in school that girls mature faster than boys. And that they were basically a few years older, mentally, than boys. And somehow I understood that if a woman was a day older than me, I shouldn't be interested in her. I should be with a younger woman so we would be the same age mentally. And so that's what I'd always done. And Angela knew all that, my philosophy about age.

But I'd also been taught that I should never ask a woman her age or her weight. So, I never asked Angela those questions. But her story made me think maybe she was older than I assumed. Plus, her birthday was coming up. And I had great plans. We were going to have the time of our lives. Believe it or not, I'm very romantic. I found a restaurant that had candles. I took the roses there early. There was a man there that played the violin on Friday night. But I paid him to come in on Thursday night for her birthday.

And here it was, three months after we'd met and had been dating. And I still didn't know how old she was. So, I asked her at dinner. I said, "Look, I know I'm not supposed to ask this kind of question. But, I'm so in love with you. I'm basically gonna have to find out eventually. So . . . how old are you?"

And she just busted out crying. Very emotional.

I said, "What in the world is wrong?"

She said, "If I tell you, you'll break up with me."

"Are you crazy? We've come this far. I've told you personal things about me that I haven't told nobody."

"But, I'm older than you."

I said, "What, you're fifty-eight and had a face lift or something? So, you're a few years older. That's no big deal."

She started crying again.

I asked, "You're older than a few years?" She didn't answer. I was twenty-one at the time. So, I took her hand and I said, "Angela, I love you. I don't care if you are 58 with a facelift. You're the most beautiful fity-eight-year-old-woman I've ever seen." I thought that would make her laugh, but she just started to cry again.

So I just said, "Stop it. Just tell me."

And she said, "I'm twenty-nine today."

And somewhere in the back of my brain was saying, "No, no, no, no, no!" But my heart was saying, "Who cares?" So I gave her a kiss, and I said, "I got the most beautiful woman on campus. And she's twenty-nine!"

Then we went to the park and had a walk. We had a wonderful romantic evening. And my whole life changed. I realized what a fool I had been, all these years, to believe such stupid nonsense. So what if I'm with a woman who's older and wiser than me?

In fact, that might come in handy, since I'm not too smart on my own.

~ ~

By the end of my second year at Gallaudet, my grades were pretty bad. You had to maintain a C average to stay in school, and I was making Ds. So I got suspended. I guess I was having too much fun. Not just with Angela, but I spent a lot of time talking to other students and telling stories. I was pretty immature then, and I didn't spend enough quality time with my homework. By the end of that year, I had to leave campus. It was the summer of 1976.

I moved back to Memphis and got a job. But after two or three months, I really started to miss Angela. I decided to take a chance and go back to see her. I bought an airplane ticket. When I got to D.C. I had about $20 in my pocket, no place to live, and no job.

The good news is that I still had some friends at Gallaudet who said I could sleep on the floor in their dorm room until I found a place of my own. But when the R.A. (resident advisor) found out I was there, they said because of the insurance that I couldn't stay. I had to be gone by Monday when school started. I prayed about it and hoped it would all work out. I'd only bought a one-way ticket, since I was planning on staying.

Well, that Saturday night they had a party in their dorm. I got to see some of my old friends who were still at school there. But there were some other people there who had already graduated and had apartments off campus. Two of them found out I needed a place to live and asked me if I wanted to move in with them. I asked them if they were sure they had room for me, and one of them said, "Yeah, we just kicked out our other roommate this morning because he wasn't paying his rent. You can move in tonight."

I thought that was awesome. I moved in that night with Randy and David.

The next night, Sunday, I was having my first dinner with them. Spaghetti. Then somebody rang the doorbell. Except it was a deaf doorbell, which makes the lights flash a certain way so you'll know someone is at the door. When the phone rings, it's another light that flashes, so you'll know the difference.

They answered the door and a guy came in and they all hugged him. They introduced me as Kenny, and we shook hands.

Then the guy turns to my roommates and said, "Hey, I came over to borrow your vibrator."

Now, I had only heard about vibrators shortly before this. and I thought it was strange that a man was asking to borrow one from another man. I thought it was only something a woman would have. I just listened.

David said, "I've got one, but there's no battery in it."

Then Randy said, "I've got a vibrator. But it's really thick and big. You might not want it."

Kenny's face took on a look of shock and confusion, and he let out several short gasps. As I was learning, Kenny doesn't just tell his stories. He experiences them. And as the audience, I get to watch him experience those moments all over again.

And I was just watching this, and I couldn't believe it. They were making this conversation like it was no big deal! I was wondering, "Am I missing something?" I mean, I didn't *exactly* know what a vibrator was, but I *kind of* knew.

Eventually, Randy said, "Let me go get it," and he goes back into his bedroom. When he came back out, he was holding it in his hand. And it was huge!

Another gasp and look of disbelief from Kenny.

He handed it to the other guy, who said, "Thanks, man. I'll bring it back when I'm done using it this weekend."

Another gasp and befuddled look. Each somehow different from the ones before.

And then he left. I was just standing there in shock. My eyes were probably as big as saucers. I still couldn't believe they were just talking about it like this. And I guess Randy noticed, and asked me, "What's wrong, Kenny?"

"Oh, nothin'. Nothin'."

Then David said, "Aw, come on. Somethin's wrong. You look like you're sick or somethin'. We can't help you if you won't talk to us."

Kenny let out a long sigh, as if conceding under duress.

I didn't like talking about that kind of thing. But I told them what I thought and why I thought it was strange. And they both just started to crack up laughing. I didn't think it was that funny. But they just kept laughing and laughing.

Finally, David went into his bedroom and came out with his vibrator and put it on the table right in front of me.

A look of disgust washed across Kenny's face. His nose crinkled up, pulled his head back, and turned his face slightly to one side, as he let out a few incoherent sounds that I could only translate as "ick."

And then David said, "Kenny, it's not what you think it is."

And I said, "Well, what else are you gonna use a vibrator for?"

He said, "We use it to wake up."

The bewildered look on Kenny's face got an audible laugh from me.

"What!? You mean, you put that in there and just sleep with it inside you and then it wakes you up?"

"No, no, no. Look, you see this button? You set the time you want to wake up. Then you put it under your pillow. Then when it's time to get up, it vibrates and you wake up."

Well, then I felt pretty dumb. And I said, "Okay. But that one he borrowed from Randy was huge! What's that for?"

And Randy said, "That's because I'm a heavy sleeper. The bigger they are, the more they vibrate. Plus, I don't like them under the pillow because it's lumpy. I put mine under my mattress."

That turned out to be an embarrassing way to learn something. But I learned it.

I actually applauded as Kenny and I both shared a laugh at his expense. It was a great place to take a break from our interview, as we'd soon be turning to more serious topics. . .

Angela and I started dating again, and continued to date for the next several months. We spent most of our time together. One of our favorite things to do was to drive over to Harpers Ferry, West Virginia to have picnics. We'd put down a blanket. She'd bring a fabulous tuna salad or spaghetti, and I'd make a chocolate cake. We'd walk along the river, and play Frisbee in the park.

On May 21, 1977, Angela and I got married.

We decided to go to Destin, Florida for our honeymoon. We both liked the beach. And I'd been there before with some of the guys from school. We packed our bags and loaded up her car for the drive. It was a long drive from Alexandria, Virginia. When we got about halfway there, we had to stop for the night in a hotel.

Kenny turned his head and looked away. It was moments like these that I knew he wasn't just telling me a story. Or performing a story. But reliving a story.

So there I was, in bed on the first night of our honeymoon, just full of anxiety. I'd never done it, had sex. And Angela came into the room, and started to undress real slowly. She was so gorgeous! And then she got on top of me, and started smothering me with kisses.

Kenny paused. That gave me a few seconds to reflect on that particular turn of phrase, 'smothering me with kisses.' I couldn't imagine a more innocent or understated way to describe the passionate kiss a man might typically experience on his wedding night. But I wasn't listening to a typical man. I was listening to Kenny Tedford, so I knew it wasn't an attempt to describe Angela's affection as less than sensual. It was just his way of treating her and that moment with the tender respect that she, and it, deserved.

And, perhaps, it was his way of preparing me for what was about to happen next. . .

And all of a sudden, I started smelling that odor again, that one from my dream with the old man in the hat. It scared me so bad, I freaked out. I threw Angela off of me. She fell over against the wall and slid down beside the bed. She looked up at me in shock. And as I looked down past the end of the bed, the old man was standing there by the dresser, with his hat down over his face. I just froze.

Angela jumped back up on the bed and told me to "Breathe!" She said I wasn't breathing.

And then he disappeared.

Angela just laid down beside me. And I laid there beside her. Things didn't work out the way I thought they would that night. And probably not the way Angela thought they would, either.

We got in the car the next morning and drove back to Alexandria.

Well, I didn't know what was wrong with me. But I needed to find out, so I went to see a psychiatrist and a counselor.

I asked them why I couldn't constipate my marriage, or whatever ya'll call it. And why did I always smell that smell and see that old man? But neither of them seemed to be able to help me. I think they just thought I was crazy. But one of them suggested I go see a priest, because he said maybe I was gay. I was like, "No way! I don't have any interest in men. I know I don't." But he told me to go anyway.

So I went to see two preachers. One was a Mormon preacher and one was a Baptist preacher. They both asked me a lot of questions, and studied the psychiatrist's notes. They called the psychiatrist back and said, "Nope. He's not gay. Straight as an arrow." So that wasn't it.

I got advice from all kinds of people. And they had all kinds of ideas about what was wrong with me. Some said Angela and I just weren't meant to be together. Some said I should be a priest. Another one said there was a possibility I was raped as a child and just don't remember it. And I thought, "Yeah, right. I think I'd remember that." One of them even told me I never really loved her, and that made me angry. I knew I loved her.

We eventually decided we needed to split up for a while. We didn't make a big ca-boo about it, or however you say that. It was kind of just a trial period, to see if something could work out.

Our last night together, we had a wonderful meal. We went to the Friendly's Restaurant and had that ice cream that's big enough for eight people to eat it. I brought flowers. We talked about our lovely time together. But I was angry, and screwed up. I couldn't even make a marriage work.

She said she found a place to live and asked if I wanted to know where it would be. I told her, "No." It seemed like it would be better if I didn't know.

The next morning, she made me breakfast. While we were eating, she told me, "When you get home from work, I'll be gone." I was working at Sears at the time. I was a salesman in the shoe department.

Kenny let out a big sigh. He looked genuinely disappointed in himself as he relived the experience in front of me. I felt awful for making him go through this, because I was acutely aware of how uncomfortable it was for him. But I knew he wanted his story told, and told properly. I thought of myself as a dentist who had to pull a tooth with only a modicum of anesthesia. It would hurt a little, but the patient would be better off for it. Or at least that's what I told myself at these moments.

About a month later, I was at home at night. I was still in our apartment on the 15th floor of a high-rise apartment in Alexandria, Virginia. And someone started banging on the door. I opened the door, and standing there was the deacon of our church and his wife. They said, "Hi." And I said, "Hi." But I thought it was strange, because they never came to visit me before.

They asked if they could come in. I said, "Sure," and we all sat on the couch together. He told me that Angela had been staying in a spare bedroom in the back of their house. He said she'd been crying every night. And that she was very upset, and angry.

And then he told me that I was an evil man. He said I wasn't a real Christian and I never was. That I just used her, and that I was going to hell. And that I was worthless. Then his wife told me if she wasn't a good Christian, she would claw my eyes out, and I was the most evil man she'd ever met and I was definitely going to hell.

I couldn't believe what I was hearing. I didn't think Christian people said these kind of things. But it got worse. The deacon told me "it would be wise if you just killed yourself. You ruined this woman's life. And you don't deserve to be on this Earth."

Then they stood up. She got her purse, and said, "We can show ourselves out." And they walked to the door.

I was confused. The reaction just seemed so irrational, so I asked Kenny, "What on Earth could Angela have told them to make them think you were so evil? I mean, it's not like you did any of this on purpose, right?"

I can't explain it either, Paul. I just stood there in shock. I'd never heard anyone talk like that before, and certainly not a Christian. And I've met some pretty stupid Christians. I mean, I've had people tell me that I can't be a real Christian because I have a disability. And you remember there were people who'd meet me and ask, "Who sinned? You, or your parents?" They thought my disability was a punishment from God. Serious, they think that! That doesn't make any more sense than the deacon and his wife were making, does it?

It was really an eye opener for me. Just because someone calls themselves a Christian, doesn't mean they are. And just because you're a deacon, doesn't mean you can't be mean. It's just a word.

When the door closed, I just collapsed on the floor. I'd never felt so worthless in my whole life, and I'd felt pretty worthless before. I couldn't be a man. Couldn't give my wife what she needed. What she deserved.

I was right in front of the window. When I got up, I opened the window and looked out. I thought about what the deacon had said. And I thought maybe it would be best if I just jumped out. So I leaned my head out and looked down. Straight below me, fifteen floors down, was the entrance to the building. I thought that would be far enough to kill me. But I might land on someone coming in or out of the building, and I wouldn't want that to happen.

I decided it would be better if I just took a bunch of sleeping pills. I put my coat on and went down to the 7-Eleven. And I just love Dr. Pepper. I used to drink two liters of that stuff all the time before I quit drinking soda. I bought the sleeping pills and Dr. Pepper. I figured if I was gonna die, it's at least gonna be funny. I'll go out drinking a Dr. Pepper.

I got back to my apartment and turned all the lights off. I didn't want anyone to see the lights on and come in. I didn't want anyone to stop me. I sat down and prayed. Cried. Angry at myself.

And it made sense. They were right. I messed up a woman's life. I didn't deserve to live. I opened up the pills and started to take them.

And then, I don't know how to describe it any other way, but a miracle took place.

Somebody started banging on my door. And I thought, "My goodness! The Lord sent an angel, in person, to help me."

I put the pills back in the bottle and hid them under a cushion. I got up to answer the door, and it was my friend John from work. He reached out and grabbed both my shoulders. He looked behind me and said, "Kenny. Are you okay? You doin' anything?"

I just shook my head and said, "I'm fine."

He said, "You're lyin'. I can tell you been crying. Is this about Angela?"

I said, "What in the world are you doin' here?"

He said, "I was just in church with Momma, and the preacher said, 'Pray for someone who's hurting and you think needs help.' And Momma turned to me and said, 'Go get Kenny. He's in trouble.' So I left church and came straight here."

He came in and we sat down. I told him about the deacon and his wife and what they told me. He said, "Aw, they can go to hell! Pack your bags, you're comin' to my mom's. She's making spaghetti after church."

I just laughed. I mean, I love spaghetti. But I said, "Do you really think spaghetti's gonna fix me? No, thanks. I'm not goin' anywhere."

"But you need somebody to be with you."

"No, John. I can do this on my own. I need to be alone."

"You're not gonna do anything stupid, are you?"

"No, I'll be fine," I said. "Have I done anything stupid, yet?" I hadn't told him about the sleeping pills, so as far as he knew, I hadn't.

He said, "Well, okay. But if you need anything, you've got my number."

When he left, I went straight to the couch and got the pills out from under the cushion. I took them into the bathroom, and flushed them down the toilet. Then I got my bottle of Dr. Pepper and got in to bed and drank the whole thing.

Then I got up all night to pee.

Kenny and I both enjoyed the most welcomed laughter either of us had had all day.

A couple of months went by, and I got more and more depressed. Angela and I eventually decided to get an annulment. Obviously, something was really wrong with me.

The judge had made us each write letters explaining why we wanted the annulment, which we did. Then she scheduled the hearing where she would make her decision two months later. But whenever I'd see happy couples in restaurants or kissing in the park, I'd cry. I still hadn't figured out what was wrong with me.

Well, my buddy John told me I needed to go see a doctor about my depression. And he said go see a psychiatrist. So I saw another psychiatrist, and he told me I should go spend some time with someone I loved and looked up to. I decided to call my stepbrother, Terry, in Dallas. He's the one with the red Volkswagen who always used to save me as a kid.

I told him I couldn't discuss everything on the phone. But I need to stay with him a while, and I'd discuss it all when I see him. He said okay, so I drove to Dallas. I sat down at the table with him and his wife and told them everything. They said they hoped it would work out, but I was always welcome in their home.

Sears let me transfer to their store at the Red Bird Mall in Duncanville, TX, so at least I had a job.

About a month later, I got a call from my lawyer. He got a letter from the psychiatrist for the judge to say I didn't have to be at the annulment hearing because I was depressed and suicidal, so my lawyer went to represent me. Angela was there with her lawyer. The judge told all of them she was going to approve the annulment. But that she was confused. She said we wrote the most loving and beautiful letters she's ever seen, even from people who are happily married. She didn't understand why we couldn't work things out. But she asked if both sides were certain they wanted the annulment.

They all said yes, so she approved it. And she said all these documents will be sealed for ten years, and then they'll be destroyed. But if anybody ever asked, we don't ever have to tell anyone we were ever married. It's like it never happened.

A couple of months later it was Christmas. I was talking to a friend of ours, and asked if he'd seen Angela. He said, "As a matter of fact, I did. I saw her at the Mall last week. She had her hair cut short, just the way you like it."

"She did?"

"Yeah. She looked good."

"Great. I'm glad to hear that."

Then he said, "She told me she left the Deacon's house shortly after she heard about you trying to commit suicide. She found out what they said to you that night. Apparently, they were proud of it and told her that they'd really put you in your place and told you that you were going to hell, and all that stuff." So then she yelled at them and told them they were wrong about you, and that they misunderstood why she was upset. And she even told them they were wrong about me not being a real Christian, and that if anyone wasn't a real Christian, it was them.

Then he said she told him to give me a message. She said, "Tell Kenny he's the most loving man I ever met. And I doubt I'll ever, ever meet another man like him. He made me feel whole, like a beautiful person, a beautiful woman. And tell him I love him with all my heart. And I pray that eventually he'll figure out his problems."

And she said all that in a serious voice. But then she got a playful look on her face and smiled and said, "But! If I ever hear that he does this again to another woman, he'll have to deal with me!" And then they both laughed. And when I tell this story today, I laugh, too.

That message was the best Christmas gift I could imagine getting.

Chapter 11: Putting the Pieces Together

A couple of years went by. I woke up one morning, and sat up straight, just raised in the bed. I had this thought that I have to go see Uncle Larry. That was a strange thought, since I'd never really gotten along with Uncle Larry. I loved him, of course, for letting me live in his house. But he never wanted me there. And he never really played the role of a loving father the way I wanted him to.

So I just talked myself out of it. I thought, "I'll go see him Sunday afternoon after church. Or I'll see him this afternoon after rehearsal." I was an actor at the time and had to rehearse for a play. But after rehearsal, it was late and I was tired. So, I decided I would go see Uncle Larry the next day.

Well, the next day was Sunday. And early in the morning, around 5:00 a.m. I raised up out of the bed again, just sat straight up. "Go see Uncle Larry right now," was running through my head. And I thought, "This is crazy! It's five o'clock in the morning and I haven't seen Uncle Larry in years!" So I told myself I would go see him after church.

When church was over I went home. The phone rang and I answered it. I had an amplifier on the phone in those days. It was like a hearing aid for the phone, so I could hear pretty well.

It was my baby sister, Mary. She said, "Kenny, I thought you might want to know that Uncle Larry died an hour ago." He had a heart attack in the bathroom, getting ready to go fishing.

I was shocked. I couldn't believe it. Why didn't I listen to my feelings and my heart and go visit him yesterday or this morning before church? I felt so bad and surprised that I actually dropped the receiver. I picked it back up and my sister was yelling because I wasn't saying anything. I told her that I was just in shock.

Many in the family didn't like Uncle Larry. In fact, many of them hated him. But in my heart I loved him, because he was my foster father. But I'd never told him that. And that's when it hit me. Now I knew how all those people felt the day my daddy died. All those people standing around saying "I wish . . . I wish . . . I wish . . ." and "If only . . . If only . . . If only . . ."

A few days later I went to the funeral to see him. A woman came up to me in a black dress and a black veil. I figured she was his wife now. Found out it was his third wife. She came over, and I was a little defensive in a sense. I didn't know if she was gonna slap me or get mad at me because I never came to see Uncle Larry all these years.

But instead, she raised her veil and said, "You must be Kenny. You look exactly the way Larry described you."

I asked her what she meant. She said, "All these years, he's kept newspaper clippings about you. . . When you were a U.S. ambassador for the Red Cross. Your high school graduation. Sports clippings. He kept all those articles about you." I just stood there. I couldn't believe what I was hearing.

She went on, "I kept begging him to call you and have you over for dinner. I wanted him to tell you how much he really thought of you. He really loved you, you know. He felt so bad for how he treated you. He wanted a chance to ask you for your forgiveness."

She didn't say it, but I know he was probably ashamed of himself. And that's why he never called to tell me.

So it wasn't just me. Even Uncle Larry avoided the chance to say how much he loved me. Words that I'd wanted to hear so badly for so long. To know that I was okay. That I wasn't such a bad person. And to know that I was loved.

For him, I guess he was too embarrassed to tell me after all those years, and too ashamed to ask forgiveness. For me, I guess I was too afraid he wouldn't tell me he loved me back.

I guess we were both fools.

I promised myself I would never again let someone I love die without telling them that I loved them. Even if they didn't love me back.

~ ~

My cousin Jeff was like a brother to me. The closest I ever had. In some ways, even closer than my brother and three stepbrothers.

I should think so. This was the guy who explained words like "melons" and "pussy" when other people wouldn't. The kind of guy who'd draw a picture of a vagina on a Minute Man napkin if you needed him to.

He didn't call me names and treat me like other people. But he didn't show much affection either. It was just the way he was raised, I guess. I don't know. He never said the words, "I love you," on his own. Sometimes he would say it back to me when I said it. But it would only be when we were alone and nobody was around. I don't know if he just thought guys weren't supposed to tell each other, "I love you." But he did love me like a brother.

He had two other wonderful brothers that I dearly loved, too. And his mom and dad were actually more like parents to me.

That next year, I got an urge to visit Jeff one day. It was cold and raining off and on. So I just decided to call him on the phone. His son answered, and he said his dad was up on top of the house, fixing the roof. I told him I'd really like to talk to him.

He left for a few minutes. When he came back to the phone he said, "Dad said for you to come over. He thought you could come help him fix the leak in the roof."

I thought it was too wet and cold to be climbing around on the roof, so I told him no. I was just being lazy. And stupid. I'm not sure if that's the right word, but that's how I feel now. What kind of friend and cousin was I being? Jeff needed me to help fix his roof and I was too lazy to do it.

A couple of days later, I heard Jeff fell into a coma and was in the hospital. He'd always had headaches ever since he had a bicycle accident years ago. He got rear-ended by an old lady driving a car and hurt his head. They had to put in a metal plate. Ever since, he had headaches, and they assumed it was the plate causing the headaches.

But it turned out the headaches were because he had brain cancer. He just didn't know it. I went to the hospital every day. I held his hand. Talked to him. Helped the nurses do exercises with him. I don't know if he could hear me, but I told him lots of stories. It was a blessing. But at the same time, I was angry at myself because I did it again. Why didn't I go see Jeff when I could? I could have told him one more time how much he meant to me. How much I loved him. Not just as a cousin, but as a brother.

I went to the funeral, and I heard those same words again and again. "I wish I'd called him . . . I wish I'd told him I loved him . . . If only . . . If only . . . If only . . ." It's a lesson I've been learning since I was eight years old.

Jeff stayed in the coma for about a month before he died. He never woke up.

I was really torn by Jeff's death. I got depressed and started having thoughts about suicide again, so I went to a psychiatrist about that. And she was superb! She really listened to me. She took notes and started putting everything together like pieces of a puzzle.

We talked about my life and my family and growing up. And we talked about Angela and the problem on our honeymoon. And we talked about the old man in my dream.

And she asked me all kinds of questions. One of the questions she asked me was, "Do you blame yourself for your parents' death?"

So I said, "Yes! I do."

She asked me, "Why?"

I said, "I don't know, but I've always felt that way." And I told her I always thought maybe it was because I was the only handicapped child out of nine kids. But that didn't make any sense.

And then she asked me something nobody else ever had. She asked me about times that I felt nervous or scared.

I didn't like to talk about it, because it's embarrassing. But I told her anyway — about something weird that happened at school when I was thirteen. I had to go to the bathroom really bad, number two. I never liked going number two at school. I always tried to wait 'til I got home. I wasn't sure why. I'd just been that way as long as I could remember. But this day I couldn't wait. I ran to the bathroom and went into one of the stalls and closed the door. Then I pulled my pants down and sat down.

I felt really strange just being in there. I guess because I'm used to only using the ureene at school, or whatever you call that thing boys pee in while they're standing up.

"Urinal."

That's it. Anyway, I started feeling nervous and sweaty. Like someone was watching me. Then, somebody else came into the bathroom. I know because the door made a loud noise when it hit the back wall. Whoever it was had to do the same thing that I did, because he came down the row of stalls pulling on every door really hard and really loud.

When he got to mine, I could see his feet underneath the stall door. And that's when I really started to freak out. I started shaking and breathing really heavy, like I'd been running somewhere. Then, I just froze up. I couldn't move. I couldn't finish going to the bathroom either. I just sat there like a statue for a long time, and waited for him to leave. Then I got up and put my pants back on and left, as fast as I could.

I tried even harder after that to not have to go number two when I was at school or at work. But when I did, I'd go in and make sure nobody was in the bathroom. And if there was, I'd just turn around and go back out and wait for everyone to leave, and then hope nobody came in while I was there. Or I'd find a bathroom that had a door with a lock so I could be the only person in it. And that's just what I did from then on.

Then she said, "I want you to do something. Close your eyes. I'm not gonna talk, because I know you can't hear me. But just close your eyes and go back. Visualize the old man at the end of the bed. Visualize him. You can go back. There's something there. Hidden."

Kenny closed his eyes in front of me, and continued talking. . .

I sat there for a few minutes doing what she said. Visualizing the old man. Visualizing the old man. Visualizing the old man.

And then, all of a sudden. . .

Kenny jerked up straight in his chair and his eyes and mouth shot open. He held that shocked look for a brief second before continuing. . .

And she just said, "Talk."

"It was at the playground. When I was eight. The leaves were falling, with different colors."

She said, "So it was in the Fall?"

"Yes. In Dallas. A bunch of us kids were playing at the playground at the school. We just lived two blocks over. And we were all playing in the park. Swinging. Sliding. The merry-go-round. And then it was five o'clock. Everyone had to go home at five o'clock. That's the way it was back then.

"But in the last twenty minutes we were there, everyone kept asking, 'Who's that old man standing over by the tree with the hat?' He looked kind of like a homeless person. Everybody said, 'It's not my dad . . . Not mine either . . .Not mine . . .' He was just standing there, watching us. It was kind of spooky.

"So then, everyone left to go home. I was leaving, too. But I had to go to the bathroom, like really bad. I couldn't hold it. And I was always one of those kids that couldn't just go behind a tree. I always had to go in a bathroom. And as they all left, the old man took a few steps forward towards me, no farther than that chair. Then he started talking to me, but I couldn't understand him.

"So I said, 'I can't hear very well.'"

"And then he said it again, 'You look like you have to go to the bathroom.' I guess I was doing what I call the 'pee dance,' you know?"

"So I said, 'Yeah, I do. I have to go real bad.'"

"He said, 'Well, you can go in the school, on the second floor.'"

"I said, 'How do you know about the bathrooms?'"

"He said, 'Oh, I used to go to school here, too.'"

"Then I said, 'But this is Saturday. The doors are locked.'"

"He kind of grunted. And then walked over to the closest door. And I had to pee really bad, so I followed him. He pulled on the door really hard a few times and it opened up. I went inside but I closed the door behind me. And it was the kind with that handle that runs all the way across it. And if you pull it up, it locks it. So I pulled it up really hard.

"I ran to the second floor and went into the bathroom. I only had to pee, but I decided to go into one of the cubicles so I could lock the door behind me. And as I was standing there, I heard the door to my stall rattle really hard. I looked down behind my legs, and I saw a man's feet underneath the door. About that time, the door opened up. That's when he came up behind me and got me, he molested me. And that's when I smelled that smell the first time. That odor. It was awful. And I remember his hat and that coat."

I told the psychiatrist lady what all he did to me. But it's not the kind of thing I want to put in a book. But it was awful.

Then I told her, "He eventually let me go. And as I started to run away, he grabbed my arm, and he said, 'If you tell your parents, I'll kill 'em!' And then I left. So I couldn't tell anybody."

We talked a little more, but we didn't have to. It all came back to me and made sense. Two months after the old man got me, my father died. And now I remember thinking, "He did it. The old man got my daddy!" Even though I never told anyone. Six months later, he got my momma, too.

I finally understood why I felt responsible for my parents' death. And why I was having these dreams about the man with the hat. And probably why I had those problems with Angela years ago.

I wanted to find out what she was doing, what her life was like now. I needed to make a decision about what to do. Was it too late to fix our relationship?

I had enough money to get a one-way ticket to Canada. I wanted so much to take her out to dinner and tell her the whole story, now that I knew it. And I would ask for her forgiveness. If her love was really there, like she had said, then maybe we could get married again and start over. I'd even become Canadian if I had to.

But I decided it would be better if I found all that out before contacting her. I didn't want to interrupt her life if she'd moved on, so I hired a private eye to go to Canada to find her. When he finished the job, he reported back to me. She was already married again.

I let her go. I hoped she was happy, and that he was treating her like I wanted to. I never went to Canada. In fact, I never spoke to Angela again.

The good news is, I never felt nervous going into a bathroom stall again. And, hopefully, I'd stop having dreams about the old man.

~ ~

By the time I was thirty-five, I'd dated several women. But I'd never been able to make relations with them or let them come in very close. I was struggling with some of my family relationships. And deafness still wasn't accepted by the public. Even in the deaf community, I wasn't accepted because I talked. I tried to join a group for deaf people one time, and they told me I couldn't join because I was oral. I guess I still didn't know who I was. Didn't feel like I fit in anywhere.

It's also hard when you're not part of the conversation. Ask any deaf person, and you'll hear the same thing. You're constantly left out. Somebody will be talking, and you can't follow all of it. Then everyone will start laughing, and you missed it. And before someone can explain it to you, they've moved on. Someone else is talking now. Eventually, you just learn to give up.

Or sometimes with family, some of my nieces and nephews would run up to me and just look at me funny. They'd say, "How come you talk funny?" And I would start to answer them.

But then my sister or brother would run over and grab them and say, "Tell him you're sorry." And then shoo them away. They thought they were protecting me, because they loved me. But what they were doing was teaching their kids to be afraid to talk to Uncle Kenny.

I'd tell them, "Let them ask questions. How else are they gonna learn?"

But that never seemed to work. Sometimes they'd say things like, "Oh, you're not really deaf," or "There's nothin' wrong with you." And again, they did that because they loved me and wanted me to feel normal and part of the family. But it's hard for someone who doesn't have a disability to understand this. At home, they tell me there's nothing wrong with me. But in public, people remind me of it every day.

I'd heard this from Kenny several times, that family members would say, "You're not really deaf . . . there's nothing wrong with you." For the longest time, it confused me. Were they really doing it, as Kenny thought, to make him feel normal and a part of the family? Perhaps, I thought. But now that I'd spent dozens of hours with Kenny, I had a different explanation: Because he's so good at reading lips, it's easy to forget that he's deaf. But just cover your mouth when you talk to him, and you'll find out quickly how deaf he really is.

I thought that was quite a testament to his skill as an oralist. But it was also an unfortunate situation for him, in that it leads to people taking his lip reading for granted. I took a moment to remind myself how much harder he has to work just to have a simple conversation than I do.

I made a mental note to never forget that. But I was still struggling with how to navigate this awkward territory between recognizing someone's disability and treating them the way they want to be treated. And then in his next breath, Kenny gave me the words I was looking for. . .

Yes, I wanted to be treated like everyone else. But not by pretending that I wasn't different. Being deaf and having brain damage and bad vision, that's all part of who I am. I don't want to pretend none of it happened. I want people to love me and accept me and include me for who I am.

There is was. That was the distinction I was looking for. Don't pretend it didn't happen. Love him for who he is. I wondered if he'd ever used words like that with his family. And then as quickly as those enlightening words came, the conversation turned dark again . . .

But a lot of it was my fault, too. I kept looking at the negatives of all those things in my life instead of looking at the positive. I kept focusing on things like the fact that I couldn't save my marriage, and I had to always be looking for a job, and the old man who molested me. And I looked at all the people around me my age, the people I went to high school with. They were all married, with kids, and a house. A nice job and a two-car garage. I kept stirring it all up, like a kettle of awful things. Stirring and stirring.

So I decided to end my life, for a second time.

I bought a ticket and flew from Dallas to D.C., and then drove out to Harpers Ferry, West Virginia. That's where Angela and I used to have picnics.

I stayed the night in a wonderful hotel with a view of the river. The next morning, I had a nice breakfast. But I knew I was gonna end my life that night. I wrote a letter to all my brothers and sisters, individually. Eight letters. I folded them all up, sealed them, and put them in envelopes.

I put on my coat and took the letters with me. I went to a grocery store and bought a bottle of sleeping pills and a two-liter Dr. Pepper, like last time.

Kenny laughed at himself. I wanted to join him but I couldn't manage it.

I had dinner at the hotel. The walls were glass and you could see out over the river. It was beautiful.

Then I went for a walk around the old town. I love history, and I love Harpers Ferry. It started getting dark, and I walked over to Harper Cemetery. It's kind of an old Civil War cemetery. It's up on a hill by the river.

There was an old tree stump where they cut down a tree. I sat down on the stump. I had all the letters in my coat pocket.

I had the pills in my hand and I was crying. I didn't want to die. I wanted to do something with my life. But I just didn't know how. I was ready to take the pills. And then, I heard a voice. It wasn't like someone was really there. And it wasn't like some big booming voice from the sky. But I heard a voice in my head say, "You need to forgive yourself." And then it said, "And when you do, forgive the old man. Then, after you've forgiven yourself and the old man, I want you to forgive your family." And all this I'm hearing in my head. It said, "I'll take care of the old man. You take care of you."

After that, I felt good.

I felt warm.

And I felt peace.

I got up from the stump, and I walked back to the hotel. I tore up all the letters.

The next day, I flew back to Tennessee. I made plans to go visit my family. Over the next several weeks, I got to visit a lot of them. At dinner, I told each one of them about what I'd learned about what happened to me as a child, about being raped by the old man at the school. I guess I thought, if they knew, they'd at least understand part of why my life had worked out the way it did.

By the end of my story, some of them were in tears. They'd stand up and walk around the table and hug me. Some of the others were just like, "Oh, grow a backbone. Pass me the salt."

I thought about laughing. But, Kenny wasn't. That didn't so much convince me to stifle my laugh as it did diffuse the humor. That moment still stung Kenny, which made it sting me.

But there was something else about that moment that bothered me. And it bothered me again the next time the topic of the old man came up. And the next time.

Something about that story that was nagging at me and I wanted to ask Kenny about it. But each time, I couldn't find the right words. The last thing in the world I wanted to do was to insult Kenny. And I was pretty sure the question rolling around in the back of my mind would do that.

But eventually, I found the right time and the right words. Or, at least I found a time, and some words.

I told Kenny that it was, of course, common knowledge that people often suppress the memory of traumatic events, especially when they happen as children. And that they can often find those memories through psychiatric therapy or hypnosis.

But after decades of research on many of those repressed memories, it's been discovered that, sometimes, just sometimes, those re-found memories turn out to be false. The brain sometimes fools itself and invents memories of things that never happened, simply as a way to fill in the missing details, or as a way to explain something unexplainable, or even to hide an even more painful memory.

After sheepishly stumbling through my setup, I asked Kenny if he had heard of that, and if he had ever considered if that's what was happening to him with this memory?

As soon as the words finished fumbling awkwardly out of my mouth, I felt a twinge of remorse.

Most of the other significant events in his life, I'd been able to corroborate somehow. I'd seen transcripts or diplomas from all the schools he attended. Found pictures of his childhood friends online in yearbook pictures that Kenny doesn't even have himself. I have his wedding photos. I've seen the gravestones where his parents are buried, letters of appointment from the Governor of Tennessee, and obituaries. I've spoken to family members and college friends to confirm shared memories, used Google Maps to find his old homes to confirm the exact distance of his morning walk to school, and watched every minute of the Billy Graham movie that changed Kenny's life to verify the major plot points. I've even seen his surgical scars.

But I knew there wasn't a single thing he could do to prove to me that he was molested as a child. There were no witnesses. And by his own admission, he hadn't told anyone about it when it happened.

So how did I expect him to respond?

I didn't really know. But the question was on the table.

He answered in the humblest terms. Yes, he'd heard about false memory retrieval before. And yes, of course it's possible that's what happened here. But he told me that the memory of what happened is as crystal clear to him as any other memories he has of that time in his life: going to the Dallas Symphony Orchestra, buying his bullies a nickel-bag of candy, the fat woman in the 7-Eleven, the magic crayon, the loud yellow coat, the death of his parents, all of it. It isn't some distant memory shrouded in a fog of vagueness and ambiguity. It simply happened.

I had my answer.

"I believe you."

I felt like I'd just given my wife a polygraph test to ask if she'd ever cheated on me. Yes, I felt some degree of satisfaction with the answer. But I think I felt even more remorse for having asked. After all, what else could explain decades of nightmares, panic attacks in bathrooms, and intimacy failure? It would have to be this, or something equally horrific, right? Was it really that important that I probe to make sure this particular horrific memory was the correct one?

Maybe not. But it was done. I'd have to live with it.

Later that year, I was invited to speak at a counselor's convention in Gatlinburg, Tennessee. There were about five- or six hundred people there, and I was set to speak over lunch. It was in a beautiful ballroom. And all the tables were set real nice.

I started telling stories counselors would appreciate, about my mom being an alcoholic, and my brother being an alcoholic. I even shared how they could be abusive when they were drunk. And I shared other stories about me and my problems. But I always end them with how I go home and look in the mirror and realize that I am important. I am somebody. I'm not just the "deaf guy," just the "retard," just the "fat man." I'm actually Kenny Lee Tedford, Jr. I was born that way and I'll die that way.

I only had about forty-five minutes, but I told as many stories as I could. When I was done, I got a standing ovation! I was really proud. But I was shocked, too. I wasn't used to that. And I was also exhausted. You can get really tired when you're performing, even if it's only forty-five minutes. I went back to my hotel room and took a nap. I got up later, and around 5:30 or 6, I met some friends and went to dinner.

After dinner, I came back to the hotel. I opened my door with a cup of coffee in my hand, and my newspaper. I walked in and there was an envelope that had been pushed under the door. It was really thick. And in the bottom corner, there was something really hard, and about two inches long. Well, I didn't know what it was, so I just threw the envelope on my bed. I went and took a shower and got ready for bed. I got my coffee and my newspaper ready. Got into bed. Put all the pillows behind me. And I was ready to start reading.

And then I remembered, *Oh, the letter!* I looked at the front of it and started laughing. Because the person who wrote it spelled my name "K-i-n-n-e-y." And that's not how you spell my name. But that's how it sounds, I guess. So I thought it must be from a kid. I went ahead and opened it. And when I did, that hard thing that was about two inches long fell out, landed on the ground, and started rolling across the carpet. It was shiny. And I thought, "What's that?"

I got out of bed and went over and picked it up. And it was a bullet! A real bullet that hadn't been used. And I thought, "My gosh, I must be a bad speaker. Now I got the Mafia after me!" I thought it was a warning of some kind.

So I started . . .

As an experienced researcher and writer, I pride myself on being able to patiently listen to people's stories. But this is one of the times my curiosity got the best of me. I blurted out in a desperate tone, "But what was the bullet for!? What did it mean?"

Kenny calmly responded, "Yes, I'm about to explain that."

I felt like a five-year-old begging the kindergarten teacher to skip to the end of the book.

I just nodded sheepishly.

It said, "Dear Kinney, there aren't words for what I want to say to you. I've never, ever shared my life story with anyone. But this is what I want you to know. My name is so-and-so, and I saw you speak today at lunch. I'm one of the counselors. I listened to your stories about abuse, and hardship, and your alcoholic mother and brother. And yet, you're up there with grace and love and hope. It's exactly what I needed to hear today. You'll understand when you hear my story. . ."

The letter went on to describe how she was molested and raped as a little girl. When she grew up, she became a prostitute. She eventually got married, but her husband beat her and abused her. She felt like she was worthless, like I felt many times in my life.

Then she said, "But when you talk about your life, born with brain damage, and deaf, and all these other things you had to put up with. But you're up there on stage and you seem like you're dancing in the rain! It really inspired me. In fact, I'm giving you my bullet. I brought it with me today to commit suicide. I don't need it anymore. . ."

Kenny wasn't done telling his story. But this is where everything came to an abrupt stop for me. I would have never started this project if I didn't think Kenny's life story could change people's lives for the better. But this was just further evidence that his stories already have, and in a more tangible and significant way than I had even imagined.

I was humbled to even be listening to these stories. It was a strange combination of feeling honored and unworthy at the same time.

He went on with the letter. . .

". . . Thank you. You saved my life. Please don't ever quit telling your stories. There are plenty of people out there like me who need to hear them. . . I love you with all my heart."

She closed the letter with, "P.S. When I go home tonight, I'm gonna kick my husband's ass!"

That made us both laugh.

What I think she really meant was that she was going to stand up to him and not let nobody ever mistreat her again.

I asked Kenny if he ever got to meet that woman. He said he didn't, but those were the sort of letters that let him know he was doing something right. A remarkable understatement, I thought.

Chapter 12: Marty

In 1993, I started a new job as a counselor at the Memphis Center for Independent Living. We helped people with disabilities find jobs, or get into school, or find a place to live. Things like that. I worked mostly as a job coach for people who were deaf.

About a week after I started, my boss, Deborah, came into my office. She has a wheelchair. It was the same size as normal wheelchairs. But it was one of the motorized kind that you operate with your hand. She said, "Hey, Kenny, we have a new employee starting today. His name's Marty. Marty Walker."

"Okay."

"Well, you're gonna train him. You're gonna help him learn the ropes."

Kenny's eyes got as big as saucers and he shook his head.

"What? Why not?"

"I don't like people."

"Oh, please. I know better than that, Kenny. You'll do fine. But I need to tell you something about him. He's a quadriplegic. He can't use his arms or his legs. He uses a straw that he blows into and it controls his wheelchair."

Well, that made me more nervous. I said, "I can't do that. What if he's always got the straw in his mouth? I won't be able to read his lips."

She just said, "You can do it. He's gonna like you. Besides, I think you two need each other."

And I was thinking, "But I don't like him already, and I haven't even met him yet." But she told me I had to do it anyway.

Well, later that morning, I was standing at the copy machine making copies, when, all of a sudden, the floor started shaking. We had all wooden floors in our office, so you could feel even little vibrations. But this was big. I turned to the other employees and asked, "Did ya'll feel that?"

"Yeah." They did.

And then the shaking started getting bigger. I thought we were having an earthquake! I turned around slowly. And around the corner came a guy in the biggest wheelchair I'd ever seen! He was sitting way up tall, with his hands just lying flat on the arms of the chair. And there was a tube running up to his mouth that he was blowing into.

The floor kept shaking more and more, as he wheeled right up to me. He looked up and said, "Hey, man, I'm Marty Walker."

I just stood there, kind of in shock. He said, "Do you always stand there with your mouth open?"

"No."

"What do you normally do when you meet people?"

"I usually shake their hand."

"Well, don't just stand there. . ."

I'd never met anyone who was a quadriplegic before. I didn't really know what to do, so I reached down and scooped up his right hand with mine. It just kind of laid there like a dead fish. And, since I didn't really know what to do, I just patted it a little, and then put it back down.

He said, "Jeez, I'm not a dog. Do you always pat people's hand when you meet 'em?"

Oh, I just wanted to smack him! I kind of grimaced and picked up his hand again. Then I squeezed it and shook it as hard as I could like a rag doll, then slapped it back down on the chair.

He just smiled and looked up at me and said in a nice voice, "That's better."

I probably didn't realize it at the time. But I'd just done the same thing to Marty that Uncle Larry did to me thirty years ago, the day he met me. And I'm not proud of it. I think that's what Deborah meant when she said we needed each other.

I wiped the grimace off my face and said, "Hi. I'm Kenny."

He said, "Oh, you're the deaf one, aren't you?"

Well, I couldn't believe he said that. I mean, I felt bad for patting his hand, but I was still as much of a smart aleck as I was when I was a kid. And he was kind of being a jerk. So I said, "Yeah, I'm the deaf one. You must be the crippled one. We're gonna be great friends, aren't we?"

I didn't think this was a great way to start a relationship. I looked over at my boss. She just smiled and held up two thumbs-up. Then she spun around and rolled back into her office.

I looked back at Marty, and he said, "Well, where's my desk?"

I pointed and told him, "Over there."

My mouth must have been hanging open again, because he said, "Why're you lookin' at me so funny?"

All I could manage was, "Uhhhh. . ."

He said, "Close your mouth. Your drawin' flies."

"Bite me!"

"I would if you get closer."

I'd just met Marty (in a literary sense), but I already liked him. Or maybe what I liked was the irreverent humor that he and Kenny seemed to share. I was waiting for Kenny to make a snide remark about the irony of a quadriplegic whose last name was "Walker," but it never happened. I got the impression they both knew where the boundaries were in their game of one-upmanship, and were careful not to cross it.

I didn't know what to think. Here we were, a quadriplegic and a deaf man with brain damage, trying to communicate. It didn't seem like the best beginning.

Then Marty started blowing in his straw and his wheelchair turned and rolled over toward his desk. The floor felt like an earthquake again. I followed him over. When he got there, he turned to me and said, "We're gonna be best friends."

I just smiled. But that didn't seem very likely to me. And then he said, "I guess you're wonderin' why I'm in a wheelchair."

Kenny shrugged, as if saying, "I guess so."

He said, "Well, I'm wondering why you're deaf. You talk pretty good for a deaf man."

So I said, "Well, you look pretty good for a man in a wheelchair." I thought that was a pretty good comeback.

He said, "I know. I used to be a football player." And he had a big smile on his face, like being a football player was something special. Then he went on to tell me about his accident. When he was seventeen years old, he was working on a construction site, up on the second floor. They hadn't put in the walls or handrails yet. He got dizzy and fell off and landed on his head on the concrete. Shattered his backbone at his neck. That's how he became a quadriplegic.

Then he said, "Now, tell me how you became deaf."

I said, "I was born immature."

He laughed and said, "I'll say."

I didn't get the joke. He said, "Kenny. You weren't born *immature*."

"Yes, I was."

"Well, you're acting like it." Then he laughed some more. "You were born *premature*."

I said, "Oh." And then I just laughed. I guess I'd been saying that wrong my whole life.

It was good to know I wasn't the only one who noticed Kenny's occasional malaprop. What I found insightful was how directly and unapologetically Marty corrected him. Up to now, I'd been largely letting those kind of things pass without comment, as long as I thought I knew what he really meant. I suppose I thought pointing them out might be insulting or disrespectful. Or maybe I thought he'd become self-conscious and scrutinize his words more closely, and those endearing moments would become less frequent.

But Marty's reaction made me realize that by not pointing them out, I was actually doing Kenny a disservice. Not pointing out the errors meant he'd continue to make them. Apparently, Kenny had been telling people his whole life that he was born "immature." And everyone he'd said that to had just let it pass without comment, just like I'd been doing. That, of course, is why he kept using the wrong word. Marty put an end to that. And he did so without making Kenny feel disrespected or insulted. Kenny actually welcomed the correction.

Kenny told me countless times that he wanted to be treated like anyone else. If anyone else used the wrong word in a conversation, I'd point it out, wouldn't I? Especially if it was funny? Of course, I would. Well, why wasn't I doing that with Kenny?

I was immediately embarrassed at my own lack of candor in those moments up to now. And it definitely changed the way I would think about such moments in the future, with Kenny, or anyone else, for that matter.

Well, when it got to be lunchtime, Marty and I agreed to go together. I'd never been with a quadriplegic before, so this was all new to me. We went outside and I saw that he had his own van. I helped him unlock the back doors and get the ramp down so he could ride up and into the back of the van. Then I closed the doors behind him and I went and got in the passenger side. I buckled my seatbelt and got comfortable.

A few seconds later, I heard Marty yelling from the back of the van, "Kenny!"

I turned and said, "What?"

"Who's gonna drive?"

"Oh," I said. "I guess that's me."

"Of course it's you. I can't move my arms."

So I got out. He told me where the keys were and I got in the other side. When I started to drive off, I could tell he was saying something to me. So I said, "Marty, you can't just talk to me while I'm driving. I can't see you behind me. I have to read your lips."

He said, "Take the mirror and move it. You read lips backwards, don't ya?"

And I said, "Oh right, I'm gonna be watching your lips move in the mirror and run right into a tree."

He said, "What if I holler?"

"I'm still deaf, Marty. Just like you'll still be in the wheelchair when we get to the restaurant."

He said, "I like you, Kenny. You're a funny man."

I just said, "Bite me."

Well, we got to the restaurant and went in. They showed us a table and I sat down. Marty rolled over to the table and just sat there a few feet away and stared at me. I finally pointed to the place across from me and asked him, "Well, are you gonna join me?"

"Move the chair, genius."

"Ohhh! Okay." So I got up and moved the chair. He blew in his straw and rolled up to the table, and I sat back down.

We both ordered a nice steak and after a little while they brought our food.

Kenny shifted into a mime-like performance mode that would make Marcel Marceau proud. He sat up tall in his chair, and pretended to unfold a napkin and place it in his lap. He picked up an imaginary knife and fork and proceeded to cut a single piece of steak and place it in his mouth. Then he said,

Mmmmmmm, this is delicious!

. . . as he continued to chew. Then he quickly cut another piece of steak and hurriedly put it in his mouth, then savored it with his eyes closed and a huge grin on his face before cutting another piece. Then another.

"This is really good. I like this restaurant."

Marty just sat there and stared at me. Then he said, "Yeah, I'm hungry, too."

"Oh, okay. Well, go ahead, take a bite."

Kenny cut another imaginary bite and began chewing it.

Marty watched me for a couple of more bites and then said, "You really are deaf and dumb, aren't you?"

"Yeah? Well, you're ugly."

Then Marty said, "How am I supposed to eat my meat?"

"Ohhh! You want *me* to cut it."

"No, I'm gonna use my toe. Of course I want *you* to cut it!"

So I cut some bites off his steak for him. But I decided I was gonna get even with him for trying to make me look stupid. So I put the first bite on the fork and held it up in front of his mouth. But when he leaned in to take a bite, I pulled it back just a little. He kept trying and I did the same thing again and again. He looked like a chicken walking around with his head bobbing in and out.

Of course, Kenny did his best to reproduce Marty's bobbing for steak, which was flawless.

I had a good laugh until the man at the next table came over and yelled at me. "Hey, you, stop bein' mean to him!" Then he asked Marty, "Sir, do you want me to feed you?"

"No, no, no. That's okay." Then he turned to me and said, "Kenny, you're embarrassing me."

I just said, "Well, you're out with me, what can I say?"

By then, Marty was getting kind of mad. He was gritting his teeth and said, "Just cut the meat and give it to me, will you?"

So I said, "Okay, okay." I held another bite up to his mouth. And when I did, he leaned in all the way to my hand and bit my finger! He actually bit it! "Owwww!"

He smiled like he was really proud of himself and said, "You told me to bite you."

It may not sound like it, but that was the beginning of a famous friendship. As much as I had to do to help take care of him (like driving his van and cutting his steak), he did lots of things for me that I would have never thought he could do. One day, he helped me work on my resume. When it was ready to type, he said, "I'll do it." I let him do it, even though watching him gives me a headache. He'd put a stick in his mouth and poke the keys on the keyboard really fast. He looked like a woodpecker and sounded like one, too.

I told him to just stop, because it was bothering me.

He said, "But, I'm doing your resume."

"I know. But you're making my head hurt just watching you."

"Kenny, go in the next room. I'll have your resume done in three minutes."

"Yeah, right," I said. Even people with their hands would take ten or fifteen minutes to do that.

He said, "I'll make you a bet, a steak dinner tonight."

"Fine. I'll give you five minutes."

So I went in the living room and started reading the paper. Four minutes later, the floor started shaking and Marty's wheelchair came rumbling in. He had a big grin on his face like he was about to get a free steak dinner, and said, "Finished."

"Right."

"I am. It's in the backpack."

I said, "Oh yeah? How did you get that paper from the printer into your backpack?"

He said, "Come watch." And then I followed him into the other room. He showed me a special kind of stick he held in his mouth that had grabbers on one end. He could pick things up with it and turn his head and drop it into his backpack.

I learned there were a lot of things Marty could do better than me, and he couldn't move from the neck down. More importantly, we found out we could do a lot more together than we could do apart. I had skills he didn't have, and he had skills I didn't have. We made a great team.

Eventually, we even went into business together. We did stage performances and workshops. We were like Laurel and Hardy, him and I. He was the serious one, what they called the "straight man," always making fun of me. I was supposed to be the funny one, which was strange because the more serious I try to be, the more people laughed. We had a great time doing shows together. We went to New Jersey and Mississippi and lots of other places.

But hanging out with Marty was good for me personally, too. Especially when I would get depressed. One day I was really down about things and started crying. As soon as he saw me start to cry, he started blowing into his straw and ran his wheelchair right into me! Busted my knees!

I yelled, "Ooowww!"

Then he looked up and said, "Stop. Pity. Party."

"I can pity party if I want!" I told him.

Boom! He ran into me again!

"Ooowww! What's wrong with you!"

He just said, "I'll keep hittin' you until you stop the pity party." Then we kind of stared at each other like we were playing a game of chicken to see who would quit first. Then he took in a deep breath and leaned up to his straw and just waited to see what I would do. So real quick I reached out and grabbed his straw and moved it so far away from his mouth that he couldn't reach it. I just laughed and laughed. I really got him with that one.

Or at least I thought. . . until he spit at me, right in my face!

He told me to put it back, so I did. I guess that was kind of mean.

Then he told me I should be ashamed of myself.

I said, "Me? Ashamed of myself? Why? Because I moved your straw? You spit on me!"

"No, not for that. Look at me, Kenny." Then he blew in his straw and pulled back away from me. "Take a goooood, hard look."

So I did.

Then, he said, "You wanna trade places?"

That's when I decided to stop my pity party.

I could tell that Marty was an amazing man, and that theirs was a beautiful friendship. I definitely wanted to know more about him. But there was something else we needed to talk about before we got back to Marty. "Tell me about the witch who became your angel."

Oh, that, Kenny laughed.

Well, I met her in 1996. I was working as a job coach in Memphis. I was in theater. I had a beautiful apartment. I was doing fine. Then one week, I started getting a lot of text messages. Actually, back then we called them "relay messages." Deaf people had things called TTY machines that would print out messages other people typed to you.

Back then, I also had a hearing aid before I stopped using it. And I could understand some people on the phone.

Anyway, I started getting all these people telling me, "You've got to apply for the State Director position for the Deaf and Hard of Hearing in Nashville." That's part of what they called TCHI, Tennessee Council for the Hearing Impaired. And I just laughed it off, because I thought, "Man, you gotta be smart for that. You know, college degrees and certificates. And I ain't got none of that!"

Plus, I was happy. I was in a great play, *Children of a Lesser God*, playing a major role, in a big theater in Memphis. And I loved working as a job coach. What more could a person want, you know?

But I kept getting bombarded all that week with people telling me I should apply. So a friend of mine got me a copy of the requirements, and I checked it out. I had none! You had to have a master's degree. You had to have five years' experience fund raising. And you had to have five years of experience working on political issues. And I thought, "Well, that takes care of that. I'm not qualified."

But I had one friend who sat down with me and really encouraged me to apply for the job anyway. So I went and talked to Winston. He was my cousin Jeff's father that I lived with after I moved out of Uncle Larry's house. He was like a dad to me, a wise man. And he was dying of cancer. He was very sick. He listened to me explain everything about the job. Then he told me, "What could it hurt to go for it? The worst they could do is say no. But from what I'm seein' here, I think you could convince them you could do the job."

And he even told me I could take his pickup truck, because he knew my car was pretty bad, and Nashville was over 200 miles away. I said, "Are you sure?"

"Take the pickup truck, Kenny."

So I sent in my resume and all the information they asked for, and I ended up being one of the five finalists they wanted to interview in Nashville. I drove Winston's truck to Nashville, and I went into the main office. They put me in a room with seven people around the table who were going to interview me. Apparently, they were the board members. One of them was Jack, the commissioner. I've known him for years. And they were all men, except for one woman, sitting just to my left. They all introduced themselves. The woman's name turned out to be Sandy. She was the executive director for the Library for the Deaf.

I shook her hand when she introduced herself. But she was very standoffish. Very tough.

Then Jack started asking questions. "What are you gonna do for us? . . . Why do you want this job? . . . What's your goal in five years?" Things like that. And after I answered all of his questions, he asked, "Does anyone else have any questions for Mr. Tedford?"

Some of the others asked questions like, "Your hearing and speech is better than a lot of deaf people. How do you think you'll be able to get them to accept you?"

I did my best to answer all their questions. Then Jack stood up and said, "Well, I'm satisfied. I really enjoyed this interview. I haven't laughed so hard in a long time."

Everyone started laughing and said, "Me too! . . . You're really funny!"

But Sandy never moved. She just sat there with her hand on top of my resume on the table in front of her. Then when Jack started to tell me I could go, she raised her hand and said, "I have a question for this man."

And in my head I was like, "Uh. Okay. That's weird." But what I said out loud was, "Yes ma'am?"

Sandy looked down at my resume and read through some of my jobs out loud. Then she said, "It looks like you can't keep a job more than two years. Why is that? Does that mean if we hire you, you're gonna leave us in two years?"

I said no, and I reminded her what I'd said earlier, that all of my other jobs weren't regular employment. They were all job contracts that only lasted two years. When the contract was up, the job was over. Unless they came up with money for another two years. And sometimes they did.

Sandy said, "Oh. Okay." Then after she thought for a little bit, she said, "You don't even have a degree."

I said, "Yes, that's right. That was established before the interview."

She said, "I know. I'm just not that comfortable with that."

I could tell she didn't like me very much. And I've always been a smart aleck, so I said, "Does that mean this job requires that you have to be a genius?"

She said, "Excuse me?"

So I said, "I'm just sayin'. You know people, like doctors, with Ph.D.'s, five of 'em . . . and they suck. They're not a people person. They don't know anything about kindness when they come to the office. They don't know how to work with other people."

Sandy went on to ask a bunch of other question that I don't remember. But I was starting to get stirred up. I never liked it when people questioned me like that, especially if it was a woman. I don't know why. Maybe it seemed too much like I was getting in trouble with my momma.

Then, as she was talking, the sound of her voice just started to echo around in my head and get lost. And as I was looking at her, it looked like she started to turn into a witch right there in front of me. A black dress. A big pointed hat. Her nails started to grow. Her face started to turn green like on *The Wizard of Oz*. And then her nose started to bend, and a wart popped up right on the end of it! And then, all of a sudden, I saw her petting a black cat. I couldn't even see the real Sandy anymore. It was just a witch in front of me!

We both let out a laugh at that point; for Kenny, out of embarrassment at the absurdity of a grown man having to admit to these childish hallucinations. For me, mostly from my own amusement watching Kenny relive such a fanciful experience. Seeing the reactions on his face and eyes and body as he told it was like watching a child first experience a Disney movie at the most whimsical moments.

Eventually she said, "I'm finished. Thank you."

I got up, and they got up. And we all shook hands. I even shook Sandy's hand even though it was green and ugly. Then I walked out the door. I was so mad, I started walking faster and faster out to the parking lot. Got in the pickup truck. Started it up. Then started driving out of the lot. But there was a crosswalk with people in it. So I had to wait. And I'm looking at all those people, looking for Sandy. "I'm gonna run her down!" I was thinking. But then I thought, "That's silly. She won't be walking. She'll be flyin' her broom!"

Well, all the way home from Nashville to Memphis, about a three-and-a-half-hour drive, I could not get her out of my skull! I was thinking of all the things I could do to her. I could burn her broom, and then she couldn't fly anymore. Or maybe I could steal her black cat. It was awful! I don't usually think like this. But she just really got on my nerves.

By the time I got back to Memphis I decided I didn't even want the job. I just wanted to go back to my peace and quiet. I pulled up to Winston's house and parked the truck. Got out.

Walked in the house, and there he was, sitting on the couch. I threw the keys at him and said, "There's your keys! Thanks for letting me take the truck."

I started to turn around to leave, and he said, "Whoa, whoa, whoa. Where you going? And what's wrong with you?"

I was so mad, I just said, "Nuthin'."

He said, "You're gonna tell a seventy-seven-year-old man, who's dyin' of cancer, that nuthin's wrong? You're a liar, Kenny Tedford." Then he smiled at me. And before I could say another word, he said, "What, did somebody question you 'bout you can't keep a job more'n two years?"

My eyes must have gotten as big as plates. "How could he know that?"

Then he goes, "Did somebody question your past and you didn't like it?"

I just stood there and stared at him. I couldn't believe what I was hearing.

Then he said, "And was it a woman?"

"Whaaaaat!!?? She called you! The witch called you! The evil witch called you! She flew here on her broom, didn't she?" And he looked at me and started giggling like a baby.

Then he said, "We need to talk. Help me up."

I pulled him up off the couch and we walked out to the pasture on his farm. But he couldn't walk very well. So he was holding onto a fence post. And we were looking at each other. And he looked at me real serious and goes, "Now, you listen to me. I don't know who this woman is who you called a witch. But that stops now." Then his eyes smiled a little and he said, "And I can't wait to meet her. What's her name?"

So I said, "She didn't call you?"

"Why? What makes you think that?"

"Because everything you said, she said!"

"I know you like a book, Kenny. You remember how I always got onto you 'cause you quit your jobs all the time? I know those were contracts, you told me that. But I tried to get you to work for my company, the power company. You could have had a career there for the rest of your life. But you wouldn't do it. I know you, Kenny. You are amazing."

He'd never talked to me like that before. So I asked, him, "What're you talkin' about?"

"Just like the witch prolly saw in you today. It's what I've known since you were a baby. You're adventurous. You can't stay in one place. You're always goin' and comin'. But you change lives. You make a difference. Me and Johnnie," that was his wife, "and some of the family always talked about you. What it was like for you growin' up. All the things that happened to you. The struggles. But I think all of that made you what you are today, a fine man. You're gonna get the job, Kenny."

"Why do you say that? Did the commissioner call you, too?"

"Nobody called me, Kenny. You don't think good of yourself. But you should. And you *will* get that job. And that witch, she'll be your best friend."

I just said, "Tthhhppt!"

He said, "You're not like this. You've never been like this to people, all the time I've known you."

I said, "Well, she got under my skin."

"What, because she questioned you? She's just makin' you think." And I knew he was right. Then he said, "And when you do get that job, and you will, I'm takin' her to dinner."

I started to say, "Over my dead bo—," but he cut me off. He didn't want to hear me say that, and he had something more important to tell me.

He said, "I never told you this. But you're like my fourth son. When you lived with us after your foster mother died, I saw the boy grow into the man your father wanted you to be."

Well, then he started crying and I started crying. We hugged each other. And he kissed me on the cheek. He'd never done that before. He kissed me like a father would his own son. And then I walked him back into the house.

Two days later, I got a call. A man on the other end of the phone said he was the commissioner. And he said, "Congratulations. You got the job!"

I said, "You're joking, right?"

"No. You got it!"

But I knew better. I'd told all my friends about the job and then about the witch, so I knew it must be one of them playing a joke on me. So I just hung up.

Well, he called right back and asked me why I hung up on him. I told him I knew it was just a joke. It's easy to play a joke like that on a deaf man, since I can't tell who it really is on the phone. So he said, "It's really me. Jack. And I can prove it. Remember in the interview when we said . . ." And sure enough, he said something that really happened in the interview! Well, I was pretty embarrassed. But I was more happy that I'd gotten the job.

Then he said, "I need to meet you in Nashville. We need to go over some paperwork and discuss your salary." So we made an appointment for me to see him in Nashville in a couple of days.

Well, I called Winston right away to let him know I got the job. He didn't answer the phone, so I left a message. I called back a few more times that day and the next day. But he never answered.

The next day I went to Nashville to meet with Jack. When I got there, he said, "I'm looking forward to working with you. Everybody on the board is excited. And I think you're gonna do great working with Sandy."

"What? Sandy! No, no, no, no, no. I don't want the job."

"I don't understand. Why not?"

"I can't work with Sandy."

"Why not? She's a wonderful lady."

"She's a witch!"

"Kenny! What do you mean, 'She's a witch'?"

So I told him. I reminded him about all the questions she asked me, and how she'd turned into a witch in my head right there in the conference room. He just cracked up laughing. I still didn't think it was funny. Then he said, "Look, you were honest with me, so I'll do the same. Sandy didn't really want you for the job. She was concerned that you don't have a degree. And Sandy's big on degrees. That's her big thing. 'You don't have a degree, you can't do anything.' But it's too late. You already signed the papers and accepted the salary. You're mine!"

Then he laughed a little. And he goes, "You're a good man, Kenny. I could even see you makin' friends with the devil. Or, a witch, in this case."

"Thanks a lot, Jack."

I went home. He only gave me a week to get ready. Apparently, they needed somebody fast, so I needed to pack my bags and get ready to move to Nashville.

I kept calling Winston but he never called me back. Then a few days later I got a call from one of his sons. He told me he'd relapsed and fallen into a coma a few days ago.

Winston died later that night.

He never got to find out that I got the job. Or have dinner with Sandy.

The next week I went to Nashville and started the new job. Pretty soon, I had my first board meeting, and Sandy was coming in for it. And as people were coming into the meeting, I saw this woman coming in. And she was dressed in black. Of course, it was Sandy. I thought, "Perfect! Matches her character."

And it was soooo hard. I had to go up to her with a smile. This universal smile. And say, "Welcome, Sandy. It's good to have you in my meeting."

Kenny forced an awkward smile.

And she says, "I'm looking forward to working with you."

All I could say back was, "Good." I couldn't even say, "Me too." I'd be lying!

So we had the meeting, and right after it was over, Sandy says, "Let's have lunch."

I said, "Sure." But I wasn't sure if I was going to have to ride on the broom or if I could ride in my car. I still couldn't get the witch thing out of my head.

We went to lunch, and the most amazing thing happened; she told me how much she respected me as a person, and that she was really looking forward to my ideas. She even repeated some of the things I said, and I didn't even think she was listening. She said, "Nobody ever said the kind of things you said before. And you said it with heartfelt meaning."

Then later she said, "Most people in those interviews just told us about their credits." Or however you say it.

"Credentials?"

That's it.

"But," she said, "you told us stories. And that's what we needed to hear most."

Well, that made me like her a little better. But she still looked like a witch in my head. And I still didn't think I was going to like working with her. And I knew she didn't want to work with me. So I asked her if it was permissible for us to have dinner one night, to get to know each other a little better. She said, "Sure."

I took her to dinner the following Saturday night. Just me and the witch. It was a really nice restaurant, with chandeliers. And I got to know her much better. Turned out she was actually a human being. And as they were clearing off the dinner plates for dessert, I started to notice something. The wart on the end of her nose fell off. Her green face looked normal, and her black dress turned to white. And then her pointed hat turned into a halo. And then, instead of a broom leaning up against her chair, I saw wings popping out behind her. And all the way home that night, I could imagine her flying over my car on her wings instead of on a broom.

It's easy to not like people you don't know. But once you get to know them, even a little, it's pretty hard not to like them.

After that night, Sandy and I became the greatest of friends. She was the witch who became my angel.

Those words stuck in my ear. "It's easy to not like people you don't know. But once you get to know them, even a little, it's pretty hard not to like them."

Not very helpful in a family, where everyone already knows everybody else. But at work, this must be the single biggest barrier to productive working relationships: People just don't know each other, at least not on anything more than a superficial level. And when that's all you have, even the littlest annoyances get magnified and sour the relationship. Like Sandy asking Kenny about his past jobs.

But little annoyances get lost like a rounding error when you have deeper, more meaningful relationships. Kenny solved that problem with one mid-week lunch and one Saturday night dinner. Two meals! That's it. Plus all the conversations you can have in that two- or three-hour period of time.

Having attended countless expensive and professionally facilitated team-building events in my career, I was impressed at the simplicity (and affordability) of Kenny's solution. But mostly it just reinforced the legitimate need for getting to know your coworkers better, no matter how you do it. It's time, and money, well spent.

~ ~

My new office was in downtown Nashville, so you had to park a long way away and walk, or take a shuttle. But I liked the exercise, so I always walked. I wore a tie and carried my briefcase like everyone else. I was proud of what I was doing. But I was under a lot of stress, and the work took a lot out of me. I had to go to different cities across the state and talk to deaf people. Some of them didn't like the fact that I wasn't completely deaf, or that I wasn't sign-only. It made me relive some of my life as a boy when I was told that I was no-good or not worthy.

Then, on February 14, Valentine's Day, I was walking from the parking lot to the office as usual. I had some candy in my briefcase to give out to the people at work. And I was planning on having dinner with Sandy that night, so I was really looking forward to a nice day. Well, there's one place where I was walking up a hill from the parking lot where I started having chest pain. It wasn't that bad, so I kept walking. But then it started getting worse, to the point that I couldn't breathe. And the pain started going down my left arm.

Kenny grabbed his left arm just below the shoulder and grimaced, the same way I imagine he did when it happened.

There was a short wall nearby so I sat down, and put my briefcase down. I was breathing really heavy. And there were a lot of people walking by. Some of them stopped and said, "Sir, are you okay?" or "You're really sweating. Are you having a heart attack?"

"No, no. I'm fine. I've been walking a long way."

"Are you sure?"

I told them all, "Yeah, yeah. I'm fine. Thank you." And they kept walking.

I finally got tired of people asking, so I stood up. It wasn't hurting anymore, so I just took baby steps the rest of the way to work.

Kenny laughed at his own stupidity. Or, perhaps it was at the thought of a 270-pound man in a suit and tie toddling along the street with baby steps. Either way, I returned a smile.

When I got there, I started sweating again. More chest pains. But I smiled and got on the elevator. I had to go to the 15th floor, so I was on the elevator for a while. And some of the people knew me. One of them said, "Kenny, are you okay? You look pale."

"I'm fine. It's a long walk from the parking lot."

When I got to my office, I started feeling faint, so I put my hand on the wall and took a deep breath. It just so happened that somebody saw me. They ran over and said, "Kenny, you're having a heart attack!"

I said, "Get away from me! I'm fine." And I shut the door. I sat down at my desk and the pain was continuous at this point. The next thing I knew, the door flew open and it was my boss. He looked at me and said, "What in the hell is wrong with you? You're having a heart attack!"

"No, I'm not! Would everyone just leave me alone?"

"Of course you are. Look at you. You're pale. You're sweating. Your breathing is irregular. And you look like you're in pain."

I just shrugged my shoulders.

Then he said, "If you don't go to the hospital right now, I'm gonna fire you."

"No you're not."

"I will. I'll fire you."

"You told me I was the best employee you ever had. You're not gonna fire me."

He yelled, "You're so stubborn!" Then he turned and waved to someone. And then two guys came in. Really big guys. Then he said, "Okay, you have two choices. Either get up off your ass and let one of these guys take you to the hospital, or we're gonna call an ambulance."

I said, "I can't take an ambulance. I don't have insurance yet. That doesn't kick in for another month."

"Fine. One of these guys will drive you."

"No. I'm not going."

He turned to the guys and said, "Pick him up." They walked over to me, and the chair has wheels, so I pushed and rolled back a little. One of them grabbed my arm and the boss said, "Make a decision. Walk to the car, or they're gonna carry you to the car. I can be just as stubborn as you."

I decided to get up. He told them to take me to the hospital. And they drove me to the emergency room. When we got inside, they told them they thought I was having a heart attack, so they popped me in a wheelchair and took me to the back. The nurse had my shirt unbuttoned when the doctor came in. He said, "I'm doctor so-and-so. We don't have time to chat." And he put his stethoscope on my chest and listened. He got a real serious look on his face and looked up and said, "You're having a heart attack."

He turned and said some things to the nurse. And she ran to get a big machine and rolled it into the room. And while they were getting it all set up, I just stood up and started buttoning up my shirt. When he turned around and saw me, he shouted, "What the hell is wrong with you? Did you hear what I said? You're having a heart attack!"

I said, "I know, but I got a new job and I can't lose it."

"Would you rather lose your life?"

And I didn't want to die, but I didn't want to lose my job either, so I kept buttoning my shirt. About that time, the nurse came in with one of those gullies that they lay you on.

Yes, I noticed his use of the word "gulley" instead of "gurney." And given my newfound wisdom from Marty, I should have stopped him and said something. But, Kenny was on a roll.

The doctor turned and said some things to her. And then she pushed it along the wall behind me and was doing something back there, so I didn't pay any attention to her.

The doctor looked at me and just held up his hand to get me to stop for a second. And that's when I felt it. "Owww!" It was like a bee had stung me right on my butt! And then it was the greatest feeling. Like I was floating. And I started to tip over, and the doctor and nurse put me on the gulley. And to be honest, I don't remember anything else until the next day.

When I woke up, I was in the ICU. Machines all around me. A tube down my throat. A machine breathing for me. And the walls in the room were all made of glass, because, apparently, they had to watch me really close. Someone told me they lost me twice during the surgery and had to revive me with the little paddles.

They said I had a quadruple bypass and that my arteries were almost 100% clogged. I was in ICU for three days.

Having that tube down my throat was horrible. Finally, they took it out and moved me to a private room. I stayed there for about two weeks recovering. When they let me go home, they told me I should stay home on bed rest for three months. But I would need my roommate to watch after me. When I told them I didn't have a roommate, they told me I would have to stay in the hospital and that would cost a lot of money. When I told them I didn't have insurance and couldn't afford that, they said, "Well, I don't know what to tell you. If you don't have someone who can stay with you, you can't go home. You're weak and you'll need help. Plus, you're stubborn. I have the feeling that you might not take the medicine you need unless someone is there to make you take it."

Good thing for me, I had some friends come to visit me in the hospital. Four of them. Each of them said they would stay with me and take turns. "I'll stay a week, he'll stay a week, she'll stay a week. We can take care of you."

But I told them, "No. That's nice, but I don't want ya'll in my house. I don't even know you that well." And they just looked at me like I was crazy. Then they went through my pants and found my keys. Two of them went to my apartment. They took the bed out of the bedroom, which was upstairs, and moved it downstairs into the living room. That way, I wouldn't have to walk up and down stairs every day. Somebody else brought over a single bed to put upstairs for someone to sleep in while they were staying to take care of me.

A male nurse from the hospital came in every day and checked on me. Sometimes he would help give me a bath.

I was really enjoying the freedom of being back home. But nobody trusted me. One day, one of them was waiting for someone else to show up before they left. John called her and told her he was on his way, but stuck in traffic. But it was eight o'clock in the morning, and she had to go to work. I told her to go ahead. I'd be fine until he got there.

Kenny laughed in a mischievous way I hadn't heard before. Despite his innocent and charming persona, it suited him quite well.

Well, I really wanted to get out of there and smell the fresh air. So as soon as she left, I put some clothes on and got in my car. I wanted to go to McDonald's and have some coffee. And what I wasn't thinking about was all the pain medication they had me on. It made me feel really good. But probably made it hard for me to drive well. I got in the car and started to back out. But when I tried to push on the brake, it just didn't feel right. I wasn't pushing hard enough, so I kept going backwards into traffic. I ended up slamming on the brakes and making a bunch of other cars skid to a stop.

I started to sweat. And I looked down at my chest, and I had blood all over my shirt. One of my stitches had come out. And I thought, "Great! I can't go to McDonald's like this." So I pulled back into the driveway and went into the apartment.

About that time, John got there and came in. When he saw blood on my shirt, he made me get in his car and drove me back to the hospital. The doctor was mad at me for not staying in bed. But he sewed me up anyway. And even today, there's a little white soft spot on my chest where that stitch came out. It's a constant reminder to me of what happens when you make stupid decisions.

Kenny laughed in his more familiar, self-deprecating way. But I was too lost in thought this time to laugh with him, or even return a smile.

I was thinking about how grateful I was that most of my bad decisions in life didn't leave visible signs. But a part of me wondered how many fewer such bad decisions I might make if they had. A constant reminder a few inches below my chin might keep me from all kinds of foolish mistakes.

After that, I decided to not be so stubborn. I had all these people around me — friends, strangers, doctors, nurses — all trying to help me. And I kept pushing them away. It took me a month longer to recover because of that. And it almost killed me. Letting other people help me meant that I had to admit that I had a heart problem. And I didn't want to do that. Just like when I was a kid and I didn't want to wear a hearing aid because I didn't want to admit I was deaf. It's just stupid.

And especially with doctors, you have to respect their advice and let them do their job. When you're sick, especially having surgery, you're in the hands of a doctor. And for me, I'm in a doctor's hands with the Lord guiding them, so I always pray that an angel will guide my doctor's hands so that they'll do the right thing and not slip up or clip the wrong thing.

"Do you think you learned your lesson?"

Kenny thought about that for a moment and then laughed. And the slight pause between my question and his answer told me he wasn't laughing at the question, but at the story he was about to tell me.

Well, the next time I had chest pains, I didn't ignore it.

About eight months later, I was out hiking in the woods. I love the outdoors. I got halfway through the hike and I started having chest pains, so I got right in my car and went straight to the hospital. And one thing you learn is that once you've had heart surgery, they treat you different at hospitals. Any time I go in and tell them I'm having a problem, they take me to the back right away. I don't have to wait in the waiting room like everyone else.

Well, I was in there for six hours that day. They did all kinds of tests on me. And it cost over a thousand dollars. And at the end of it they came to me and said, "Congratulations, Mr. Tedford. You have gas."

I about fell out of my chair. All that worry, and time, and money, and all I needed to do was fart.

About fifteen months later, I got a phone call. My friend Marty had been in an accident. The van he was in flipped over. So they told me to "get to the hospital. He wants to see you."

I was still living in Nashville, so I drove to Memphis. When I got there, Marty had tubes coming out from all over him. His head was shaved and all swollen up. And he had stitches going from the top of his head all the way to the back. He'd had a TV in the back of his van mounted to the ceiling. He even had closed captioning put on it for me. That's how good of friends we were. When the van flipped, the TV came off and hit him in the head. That's why his head was all swollen with stitches.

I went over to his bed and whispered in his hear, "You're gonna be okay." Then I hugged him. Marty loves to get hugged, just like everyone else. But he can't feel it like most people. So when I hug Marty, I reach up to the back of his neck and squeeze it. That way he knows he's getting hugged.

I was sorry about the accident. But I was glad Marty was still alive. I stayed with him a couple of days before I went home.

Every few sentences, Kenny would break eye contact with me and look away for a few seconds. It was the now familiar sign that he was reliving the story, and not just performing it. And it was normally a foreboding sign.

I didn't like where things were going.

A month later, they called me again. He'd gotten worse, so I drove back to Memphis. When I got there, other people were in the room. But he was asleep.

I said, "Look! He's handsome again! But I still look like me." Everybody laughed. But I meant it. All his hair had grown back. You couldn't see the stitches any more. And his head wasn't swollen either.

When he woke up, I found out he couldn't make any sounds because he was breathing through a tube coming out of his neck. But he could still move his mouth. And that's the beauty of being able to read lips. He couldn't talk or write. But

I could still understand him. And I saw him mouth the words, "I love you, brother." I guess anyone could understand those words. You don't have to read lips to know those wonderful words.

But then he said, "Thanks for coming. I want you to tell my mom and dad something."

I said, "Sure." And I called them over.

"What is it, Kenny?" his mom asked.

"Marty has something to tell you." And then Marty told me what to say, and I wrote it down for his parents. It was a beautiful letter. A love letter to his mom and dad to tell them he was proud of them. And how he was so glad to be their son. And how grateful he was that they stood by him all those years after he broke his neck and ended up in the wheelchair. He was only seventeen when it happened. And he was twenty-seven now. They read the letter out loud to everyone in the room. They laughed and they cried.

I stayed a few days with Marty again.

A month later, I got another phone call. Marty's kidneys were failing, and they couldn't get them to work right. And he was tired of fighting. Marty told them to call me and other close friends and asked us to come to Memphis to say goodbye.

I said, "Say goodbye? Where's he going?"

"Kenny, he wants your permission to go home. He said you'd understand, because you believe so strongly in God." Then they asked me again to come to Memphis. They said I had to come today because they were gonna pull the plug that night around 10:30.

So I drove back to Memphis a third time. Along the way, I thought about all the great times Marty and I had together. Like the time his wheelchair got stuck in the mud and I had to pull him out. I never told you about that one.

And I thought about the question he asked me one time, "Do you want to trade places with me, Kenny?" Remember, that's how he taught me to stop having a pity party for myself. At the time, that made me happy to be me. But now, I wanted to change my answer.

Kenny was sobbing by this point.

I prayed to God to let me trade places with Marty so He would take me instead. He was so young. And he had a girlfriend and was engaged to be married. I was older, and still single. I'm ready to go see my mom and dad, anyway.

In between sobs, Kenny yelled, "Take me, Lord!"
And then paused to compose himself.

When I got to the hospital, there were so many family and friends waiting out in the hallway. When I got up close to the door to his room, Marty's mom and dad came up and hugged me. They said, "Marty is so looking forward to seeing you. Every time he hears your name, he smiles." Then they told me I could go in right away to see him. "Are you ready?"

I took a deep breath and let it out. Then I said, "Yes."

We walked in, and there was Marty. He had all the tubes coming out of him. Next to his bed were all the machines that were keeping him alive. And there were some nurses there working the machines. He saw me walk in, and his eyes got really big. He looked good. But really tired.

I walked up to the bed. Then he mouthed, "Can I go home?"

"Of course."

Then I asked him if he wanted a hug. He mouthed, "Yes." Everybody looked at me like I was crazy, since there were even more wires and tubes all over him than there were last time. But

I just leaned over and reached behind his neck and gave it a big, long squeeze. I saw a tear go down Marty's face. He probably saw a tear go down mine. He looked up at me and mouthed, "Thanks."

I stood up and wiped my face. Then I said, "Wait a minute. Wait a cotton-pickin' minute!" Everybody started looking at me funny. Marty just smiled because he knew I was gonna say something silly. I said, "You listen to me. This ain't right."

And Marty said, "Why?"

I said, "In the last seven days, Princess Diana died. And then Mother Theresa died, and now you want to pull the plug so that you can get Princess Diana and I get stuck with Mother Theresa." Marty started laughing so hard his tubes were wiggling all over the place like a plate full of spaghetti.

I looked over at his mom and she was smiling, but crying at the same time. She said, "Thank you," to me.

I said, "What for?"

"He hasn't laughed like that since the accident."

Marty said, "Thanks. I needed that. Now quit your long face. I'll let you have Princess Diana."

Then he said, "I love you, brother."

"I love you too, Marty."

I turned around to leave. But felt something pull me back towards the room, so I turned around and looked at Marty from across the room. He looked at me and mouthed the words, "I'll see you again on the other side. And if you quit performing and telling stories, I will kick your butt at night in your dreams!"

I smiled and turned to leave again. I walked over and put my hands on the steel door. It was cold. I couldn't believe that in three hours, my best friend Marty would be gone. I wondered if I would ever have a best friend like that again. I thought I would lose it right there at the door. But I didn't want Marty to see me bawling.

Deborah was right all along. Marty and I did need each other.

I pushed the doors open, and they swung closed behind me. I leaned up against the wall outside his room and had a good long cry.

They called me that night to tell me that Marty was gone.

And I was sad. But I was also excited to get to the other side myself someday. I'm looking forward to going places with Marty without him having to blow through a straw. And maybe having a nice steak dinner with him without having to cut his meat.

After Marty died, I had the dream about the old man again. I was really hoping that would stop, once I remembered what happened. I went back to my psychiatrist again to see what I could do.

The good news was, she said, "There might be a way to stop this dream. Next time you dream it, tell yourself to not wake up. Finish the dream. Let him stab you in the dream if you have to. Let him know that you know who he is."

"How do I do that?"

"You'll just have to try it," she said. "Just don't wake up. Finish the dream."

Well, it seems like I had that dream every time something bad happened in my life. Somebody died, or there was a trauma. So I just had to wait.

It had been a couple of years since my bypass surgery. My doctor said my heart was doing very good, which was awesome! Plus, it was just a beautiful day and I was in a really good mood, so I decided to go out on a long drive. At one point, I started seeing signs for Fall Creek Falls State Park. My daddy took me there when I was a little boy, and I thought, "I wanna see Fall Creek again." I parked the car. And the thing is, if you've never been, when you parked your car, the waterfall was right there. All you have to do is look down. Whoa! Waaaaay down! And it's a beautiful waterfall.

Then I saw this sign that says: "Trail to the bottom of the waterfall." And it had a fence, an old wooden fence, like in Colonial days. And it switched back and forth down the side of the mountain. You know, go down, you turn, you go down, you turn, you go down, you turn. By the time I got to the fourth turn, I was getting bored. I knew I could get to the bottom a lot faster if I just went straight down. And I knew the trail was for old farts, and I wasn't old.

I looked over the rail, and I could see the waterfall. I looked around to see if anyone was watching . . . and then I climbed over the fence! Then I started to climb down the mountain backwards, on my hands and knees. But the grass and bushes were wet from the spray off the waterfall. Then, all of a sudden, I started to fall over backwards. I went, "Whooaaaa!" and I grabbed a bush. But it came out of the ground, root and all! Then I grabbed another bush with my other hand, but it came out, too!

One thing I learned about falling off a mountain: The best way to do it is to put one arm in front of your head, and the other arm behind your head. That way the rocks and things mostly hit your arms instead of your brain.

But I must not have done it completely right, because the first thing I remember was hitting my head on the side of a rock. Then I started tumbling down the mountain, bouncing off one rock and onto another one. Through one bush and over another.

I finally got to the bottom of the waterfall. My leg was over here, my hand right over there, one of my eyeballs over here. Nah, I'm just kidding.

But my glasses were crooked and broken. And I had grass and mud all over me. And I was bleeding.

There were people down there taking pictures. And other people: hikers and swimmers. They all ran over to me.

They said, "Don't move, don't move! We're gonna call the park ranger. We gotta get you to a hospital. You might have a broken neck. You might have a broken back!"

I got up and said, "No, I'm fine. I'm fine." I was thinking "I'm a big guy, I'm tough."

"Are you sure?" they said.

"Yes, I'm sure. I'll go see the doctor tomorrow," I said. But I figured it couldn't be that bad. I mean, I've already got brain damage. There's not much more you can do to me, right?

So I started walking back up the hill. What took me ten minutes to get down took me about two hours to walk up. By the time I got to the car, my left arm was just kind of dangling at my side. Remember, when I was born, the brain damage made my left side not work very well. But now there was hardly any feeling left in it at all. And my neck was killing me. So I got in the car and drove the best way I could to go to Walgreens to get a bottle of aspirin.

I got home, and I had a major headache. I got all the blood wiped off and made sure I was okay. But I knew I had to get some rest. Because the next morning, I had kickboxing! I'd been working out for three weeks. I love kickboxing. And a friend of mine was coming over the next morning to give me another lesson.

The next morning, I got in my little shorts and my T-shirt, put the mat out. My friend comes in and says, "What in the world happened to you? You're cut all over!"

"Oh, I'm fine. I'm fine."

"You sure? We don't need to be doin' this today."

"No, I'm fine. I'm fine. I only fell down a hill."

"A hill? Hell, it looks like you fell off a cliff."

"Okay, it was a big hill. Look, are we gonna do this or not?" You know, I always was a bit of a smart aleck.

And he goes, "All right." But then when I turned to pick up a boxing glove, my friend took his leg and started to kick me in the head. Now, I don't mean he actually tried to kick my head. He was just testing my reflexes. Well, believe me, he tested me well. When he came around, I jumped this way, and we both heard a crack! It was my neck. It just snapped! Apparently, when I went home the night before, it was already cracked from falling down the mountain. All I had to do was turn it hard and the bone just broke. I just fell to the floor, shaking.

Well, good thing for me, my friend was a muscular guy. He picked me up and put me in the car. We got to the hospital and they rolled me in. They laid me on the gulley.

"The gurney?"

Oh, is that it?

I nodded. And he nodded back.

Well, I couldn't move. I was paralyzed from the neck down.

They put that angel halo thing on my head and screwed it tight, and I knew right then I was screwed for life. I was having a hard time breathing, too, so they put me on a thing called a ventilator to help me breathe. They said they had to go to the bone bank to see if they could find a bone the right size and shape to replace the one I'd broken. And they weren't sure they'd find a match.

Well, sometime that night, when the nurse came in to check on me, I told her I just wanted her to pull the plug and let me die. I didn't want to live like this. She said, "Oh, lots of people say that after surgery. But tomorrow, you'll be glad I didn't."

Only I didn't. The next day I felt the same way. I asked one of my deaf friends to take me off the oxygen and let me die. They said, "No, no. You don't know what you're saying. You'll walk again. You need to get the old Kenny back."

Then they told me to just think of Marty. Think of how much he could do, and how many lives he'd touched. And he was paralyzed from the neck down. So that's what I thought about all that night and the next day. And it kept me going.

I guess the nurse was right after all.

The next day, my doctor, the one who did my heart surgery, was in the hospital. He came in and he looked me over and yells, "Why in the hell did I put you back together? I did a four by-pass surgery just two years ago, and you go and jump off a cliff. You're an idiot, Kenny Tedford!"

And everybody around me was shocked and saying, "Be nice to him. He just broke his neck!"

So he yells at them, "You don't know this man like I do. He loves danger!" And they're all just thinking he's the meanest doctor in the whole world. Then, all of a sudden, he looks at me and winks and says, "Whaddya think?!"

He knew he was just playing with me. And I knew he was just playing with me. But nobody else did. And I guess I've always been a smart aleck, so I just looked sad and said, "Huh?" Because they all felt bad for me, because the doctor was yelling at me. But to me, he was just talkin' to me. See what's good about being deaf? "BLAH! BLAH! BLAH! BLAH!" That's what they heard. Just screaming and yelling. But all I heard was a nice quiet voice.

And everybody said, "Stop bein' mean to him! You get out of here!" And they shooed him away. I couldn't move or I would have done a little happy dance that I'd fooled everyone.

Well, they eventually found the right bone. But they still had to put a little triangular piece of metal in my neck with three screws. Now I joke and tell people that my doctor screwed me over three times. So now when I go to the airport, I set off the alarms. And when I get an X-ray, you can see the little triangle! It's so cool!

Anyway, it must have worked, because about four days later, I started feeling the bottom of my foot. They take that scraper thing and scrape it across your foot. The first three days I couldn't feel a thing. But now I could. The doctor said, "Your feelings are coming back. That's great!"

But he was also honest with me. He said there's still a possibility that you'll never walk again. And if I wanted to walk, it would be a lot of work in therapy.

And it sure was. I couldn't do anything for the first week. But then I started to be able to feed myself. Then after another week, I started to be able to stand up as long as someone held onto me.

Pretty soon, they had these two big guys hold my arms on both sides and they taught me how to take little steps again. One time I just pulled my legs up off the ground and made them hold me in the air like a kid, swinging his legs. They didn't think that was nearly as funny as I did.

But it was depressing, too. It was really hard, and I didn't know if I'd ever be able to walk on my own. They had me go to group therapy to talk about depression. I guess a lot of people want to commit suicide when they can't walk anymore. Anyway, I suppose that group therapy helps some people. But it just seemed to make me more depressed, listening to all these other people moaning and groaning about never walking again, so I stopped going to that. But I still needed something to help me stay motivated.

And then I had a dream one night about Marty.

He was in his wheelchair, and rolled right to the side of my bed. He told me, "It's going to be okay, Kenny." He said he wanted me to keep doing the walking therapy, and said, "Don't make me run over you with my wheelchair!" He would do that kind of thing, remember?

I smiled and nodded.

And then the most amazing thing happened. Marty stood up! Right out of his wheelchair! He looked right at me and said, "All things are possible, Kenny." And that's when the dream ended.

I stayed in therapy the whole six months after that; as long as the insurance company would let me. And at home, I had friends come over and help take me for walks in the back yard. I used a cane for a while, but eventually I didn't even need that. I was walking all on my own.

Kenny had accomplished all kinds of impressive things in his life. But this one seemed more instructive than most. Something about the combination of things needed to succeed that I thought might apply to all kinds of situations at home or work. It took 1) hard work and dedication on Kenny's part, 2) support and assistance of others along the way (doctors, therapists, friends), and finally, 3) someone or something to inspire and motivate him (Marty).

I thought about how many difficult and worthy goals failed because of a lack of one of those three things. Laziness robs people of the first one. Pride gets in the way of the second one. And apathy destroys the third.

I'd thought a lot about those first two before, and how to combat them. But I hadn't spent much time thinking about apathy, and how to avoid it. And Kenny's dream had just solved that riddle for me. It was easy for Marty (even though in a dream) to make Kenny care enough to try hard at learning to walk again because Kenny cared enough about Marty to be motivated by him.

If we don't love anyone other than ourselves, there won't be anyone capable of inspiring us.

Chapter 13: Moving On

A couple of years went by. It was 1999. And I got a phone call. It was about my baby brother, Robert.

I hadn't seen Robert in years. He started drinking when he was fourteen. By the time he grew up, he'd become a chronic alcoholic. When it was really bad, he would drink heavy liquor like water. That ruined his liver and probably his marriage. It also made it hard for him to keep a job. In fact, there were times he didn't have a place to live. And I guess when you're an alcoholic and homeless, you sometimes start doing all kinds of things that aren't good for you.

By the time I found out, he was near death, so I drove to Nashville. I was praying on the way there I could just see him alone, without all the doctors and nurses in the room.

When I got to the hospital, there was a sign on his door that said, "Contagious Patient." They told me I had to wear a gown and those gloves and mask you see doctors wearing when they operate on someone. I guess so I didn't catch whatever he had.

But I told them, "There's no way I'm gonna hug Robert like a plastic man." You know? So I just didn't wear any of that. They made me sign a release form that said if I got sick that I couldn't sue the hospital.

I went into the room. Robert just started crying as soon as I walked in. I went over to hug him. But he stopped me and told me I couldn't hug him because I might get sick. I said, "Well, I'm already sick of you, so what's the difference?"

Well, that made him laugh, so I gave him a hug. And then he started crying again. I asked him why, and he said, "You're the first person to give me a hug since I got sick."

"Well, you're my little brother, big guy!"

I sat down and we talked. I told him stories about when we were little. Funny stuff. Sad stuff.

And he asked me to forgive him for his drinking. But I told him, "Robert, I forgave you a long, long time ago. I wouldn't trade you for any brother in the world."

He told me that a couple of years ago he'd been saved. And he wanted me to reassure him he'd be in Heaven. He asked me if God would take him even though he'd been a bad person. I told him I was sure of it, and that I planned on seeing him in Heaven one day.

We talked for about an hour and a half. Then the nurse came in and told me it was time for me to leave. She said he needed his rest. I thought that was kind of weird. I was thinking, "He's gonna die in the next 24 hours and you're tellin' me he's gotta rest?" But I did what they said and left anyway.

Robert died the next day. He was 43 years old.

Sometime that week, I had the dream again. The one about the old man. And just like every time, I'm always just an eight-year-old boy again. I never grew. And I always woke up soaking wet. Of course, as I got older I didn't wake up crying so much. But my chest hurt.

Anyway, I had the dream again: I wake up, nobody is home, go into my parents' bedroom, close the window, turn around and see the old man, try to run out, he grabs my hair, the knife comes up . . . only this time I didn't wake up! Like my psychiatrist told me.

I raised my hand up over my head to keep him from stabbing me. And when I did, I saw his face! I saw him. And he knew I saw him. I didn't recognize him. But I'd finally caught him, and he knew it! I could see it in his eyes. He was shocked that I'd finally caught him!

I never had the dream about the old man again.

"Did you forgive him like you promised yourself you would?"

Oh, of course! I did that while I was still sitting on the tree stump in Harpers Ferry. Why would I want to hold a grudge and get depressed over a stranger I never even knew?

"That's a good point. Do you think you'd feel differently if it was someone you knew personally?" Kenny thought about that a minute before replying.

No, I don't think so. I had a good friend steal $1,500 from me one time and that was about all the money I had in the world. But I forgave him.

"Did he ever pay you back?"

No, I never got the money back.

"Do you ever see him anymore?"

Oh sure, he's still one of the closest friends I have.

"Really? Even after he stole from you?" That seemed odd to me. Or maybe just foolish.

Well, sure. Forgiving him didn't mean I forgot what he did. I can't trust him around my credit cards anymore. I mean, I'm not stupid. But that doesn't mean I have to stop being friends with him. Imagine if you forgave someone for doing something bad to you, and then you never spoke to them again because you were so mad. That's not how it works. That's not forgiving.

I'll never forget what he did. But I don't think about it every day. When I look at him, I think that it's a friend I'm looking at. I don't think, "That's the guy who stole $1,500 from me." That's what it means to forgive.

I smiled. I thought that was about as fine an answer as I could imagine. And one perfectly fitting of the man I'd come to know and love as Kenny Tedford.

Suddenly, keeping his friendship didn't seem so odd. Or foolish. Once again, the teacher had taught the student.

I thought about the old expression to "forgive and forget." I wondered how many people equated those two things and avoided forgiving because they just couldn't forget. And I wondered how different the world would be if we could all learn to forgive without having to forget.

I still wonder.

~ ~

A few years later, I went back to Gallaudet to finish my degree. I was a lot more serious than I was the first time, so I knew I could make better grades this time.

In early December that year, I went to the mall to do some Christmas shopping with my friends Jeff and Chris. At one point, we went into a toy store that had a bunch of animals, and I saw this moose. A giant, stuffed moose! Real soft. You could cuddle it and hold it. And I'm a moose collector. I'm crazy about mooses, so I picked it up and hugged it. I said, "Isn't this cute? Look at these big ears!"

Jeff and Chris just rolled their eyes at me. I guess they thought I was acting like a kid instead of a grown man. But so what? Life is short. I fell in love with that moose.

Anyway, a few weeks later, when it was getting close to time for Christmas break, they told all the students that we couldn't stay on campus. We had to leave for the whole break. And that was unusual. I don't remember if they were doing some kind of restoration, or plumbing work, or they had to turn off the electricity. But whatever it was, we had to find somewhere else to live for three weeks.

Well, I couldn't afford to go all the way back to Tennessee because I didn't have a car at the time. So I contacted Jeff. He and Chris had an apartment off campus. I knew Jeff would be going to stay with his parents in Maryland over the break, and Chris would be going to his parents' house in Savannah. So I asked, and they told me I could stay in their apartment while they were gone.

On the last day of class, before I left to go to their apartment, I planned to go to the campus post office to get my mail. I had a $400 check that was there waiting for me. And I had to have that check, because all I had in my pocket was 17 cents.

When class was over that day, I started walking across campus to the post office. It was cold outside, because Christmas was coming. And I love that time of year. But I was running a little late. When I got there, the door didn't open. I tried the other door, and it didn't open either. Then I looked up, and there was a sign. It said, "Closed for Christmas".

I was like, "This can't be happening. This can't be happening! I have to be off campus by the next day at noon, and all I've got is 17 cents in my pocket." Fortunately, I already had a subway and bus pass. So I went back to my dorm room and packed my bag. I went to the bus stop and used my pass, and made it all the way to Jeff and Chris' apartment.

They were gone when I got there, but they said the key would be under the mat. I looked, and it was. So I was safe. I got in. I still didn't have any money. But I was still excited. I made it to their apartment, and Christmas was coming. And I knew they'd have some food in the kitchen. Plus, they'd be back in about four days anyway. So I didn't really have anything to worry about. I was gonna be alone for Christmas Eve and Christmas Day. But I love that. I've grown used to that over the years.

When I got in, I put my bag in the bedroom, and walked into the living room. They had a Christmas tree with lights on it, which made me really happy, even though it wasn't a real tree. I was already thinking about and praying for snow in two days, since that was Christmas Eve. And I love snow on Christmas Eve.

Then I went into the kitchen. I thought I'd make myself a sandwich or something. I opened the refrigerator, and it was . . . empty. Empty! All I saw were some crackers in the corner, a jar of mayonnaise, and some pickle relish.

I looked in the drawer for fruits and vegetables, and the only thing in it was green. But it was the kind of green that doesn't look like the color it was supposed to be, whatever it was. And I thought it might start moving. Then I looked in the freezer. Ice! That's it.

Well, I wasn't gonna give up. Water's still good for you, so I got a glass. Then I went to the cabinet. I thought I might find some soup and other things that could last me. I found more crackers, and two cans of tuna. I thought, "Well, that's good. That's all I need for a nice tuna salad sandwich." I love tuna salad.

I was feeling so good. I went and turned on the Christmas tree lights. It was getting dark outside now, so they looked nice. Then I went back in the kitchen and I got out one can of tuna, the mayonnaise, and the pickle relish. They didn't have any bread, but I figured I could just put it on the crackers. I looked at the can of tuna just to check the date, and it had expired 6 months ago. Ugh. I knew tuna lasted about two years. So I knew this was really old tuna. I thought, "This is not happening." But I didn't really have any other options.

So I opened the can and smelled it. It smelled funny, and I figured it would probably taste funny, too. But it looked okay. And I was starving by that point. Starving! I thought, "Maybe if I put the mayonnaise in it, it'll make it taste better, like it's supposed to." So I opened the jar. Apparently, it was out of date, too, because it had separated. It looked like water on the top, and then brown mayonnaise underneath.

Just the thought of rotten tuna and spoiled mayonnaise gave me a gag reflex. The only relief I had was the hope that Kenny's own gag reflex and sensibilities would encourage him to abandon the project.

But it didn't smell bad. So I just stirred it up really good so it was all mixed back together. I just told myself by whipping it up it would taste fine.

So much for abandoning the project. I closed my eyes and stifled another gag.

So I dumped the tuna in a bowl, and put the mayonnaise in. Then I thought, "Ah! The pickle relish!" I could eat pickle relish on crackers all by itself. I love pickle relish.

So I opened the pickle relish. And right on the top were a bunch of little grey spots. I knew that was bad, so I just threw it away. I wasn't gonna take any chances.

Right. Not taking any chances with the spotty relish. But the stinky tuna and the brown mayo, that's no problem. . .

Well, then I got out the box of crackers and opened it up. The two crackers on top crumbled, just crumbled into tiny pieces! Then I picked up the third one and it just didn't look right. I looked at the box, and it was four months out of date! And I just looked up and said, "Lord, you think I could get out on probation if I murdered Jeff and Chris when they get back? If not, how bad could it be? Even in prison you get three square meals a day, and that's more than I'm gonna get this week."

At this point, I couldn't decide if I was angry with Jeff and Chris and sorry for Kenny, or if I was angry at Kenny and sorry for Jeff and Chris. Either way, I knew nothing good was about to happen unless Kenny abandoned this meal idea.

So I went ahead and made tuna salad with what I had.

No! Kenny. No!

I put a little bit lightly on a cracker.

Abort! Abort!

Prayed with all my heart.

For a stomach pump and a shot of penicillin, I hope!

And then I ate it.

Dammit, Kenny! That thought was followed by the biggest gag reflex yet.

Tasted really funny.

Ewwww. . .

So I put some salt and pepper on it.

Of course you did.

I even found some paprika to put on it and that made it spicy! That killed a lot of the bad taste.

Not enough for me.

Well, I ate seven crackers with all of that on there. Then I went into the living room and sat down. Felt pretty good. And I started watching a movie.

An hour later, I started to get cramps in my stomach.

And, so it begins. At this point I decided I was angrier at Kenny than at Jeff and Chris, because I knew what was coming next. And I knew that Kenny Tedford was going to make me live through every nasty, nauseating detail with him before this story was through.

Then my throat started getting tight. I started thinking, "No, no, no, no," because I knew what was coming next. I ran into the bathroom just in time to throw up. And that's what I spent the rest of the night doing, vomiting.

By the next morning, I was pretty dehydrated. So I drank a lot of water. And periodically, here and there, I threw up. But I was still really hungry. And that's when I started making plans for how I could kill Jeff and Chris without getting caught.

Eventually I realized I'd better think about something else. I thought, "Tomorrow is Christmas Eve." I looked under the tree and I saw two Christmas presents and they had my name on them! And they were wrapped really nice. One was about the size of a box that a dress shirt would come in. It said, "To Kenny, From Chris." And the other one was really big. I had no idea what that one would be. And it said, "To Kenny, From Santa." So I might die before Christmas, but at least I got one last present from Santa.

Well, I made it through the day. Kept drinking water. Peeing a lot. And I was tempted to eat that other can of tuna. I was so hungry. I thought, "What if I just eat three crackers with tuna instead of seven?" That seemed a little safer.

Seriously?

So I made the tuna the same way as last time and put it on three crackers.

Apparently, so. Cue another gag reflex. . .

But this time I put them in the microwave for a while since I know microwaves kill germs.

Well, Lord and behold! I learned my lesson the hard way again. I went through another night of throwing up. But this time I also had diarrhea. I had it coming out of both ends! It was awful. It felt like I was dying. But I asked the Lord to please let me live long enough to kill Jeff and Chris.

Somehow I made it to Christmas Eve, still alive. I got up that morning. Felt pretty good, but dehydrated again. I walked toward the kitchen to get some water, and as I was going through the living room, I could see out the back patio through the sliding glass door, it was snowing!

I was so excited! I opened the door and walked out onto the patio, still just wearing my shorts that I slept in, and no shirt. The cold air hit my chest, and the snow landed on my shoulders. I tilted my head back, opened my mouth, and stuck out my tongue. The snowflakes fell on my tongue. And I started to cry. It was beautiful. And I knew I was going to be okay.

When I came back in, I decided to take a shower and get dressed and go for a walk. I was still a little nauseated. But after two days inside, I started to get a little depressed. I knew there was a McDonald's about a mile away. And I just love

McDonald's coffee. I knew I only had 17 cents, but I decided to go anyway. So I just started walking.

As I was walking I just focused on the snow and how beautiful it was. I didn't focus on what I didn't have. Just on what I appreciated that I did have. Plus, I still had a chance to kill Jeff and Chris when they got back.

Kenny and I both shared a laugh every time he made these empty threats. Plus, it took my mind off his unfortunate decision to give himself food poisoning. Twice.

Pretty soon, I passed a bus stop, the kind with the Plexiglas walls that you can see through. And as I was right in front of it, I looked down and I saw something shiny. I bent down to look at it, and it was a quarter! Nobody else was there, so I picked it up and put it in my pocket. I thought, "All right! This is great! Now I have 42 cents!"

When I got to the next bus stop, I decided to look around some more. People have to pull out the right change for the bus, so maybe lots of people drop coins here. And since there weren't any sidewalks in front of the bus stops, just grass, they wouldn't hear anything hit the ground. I looked around and found a nickel! Then I looked some more, and I found four pennies by the curb.

By the time I got to McDonald's, I had 79 cents in my pocket. I knew a small cup of coffee only cost 59 cents, and you get free refills. So I was in good shape. It was perfect! It was snowing. I love McDonald's. I love coffee. And it was Christmas Eve.

And one other thing. One of the things I love about Christmas is that the Friday before Christmas, they always have a big giant newspaper. Every city I've ever lived in does it the same. It's got everything about all the sales they're gonna have after Christmas, 50% off this, and 75% off that, plus all the news.

And I just love reading a real newspaper. I don't like technical newspapers. I like how it feels in my hands, especially when it's big and heavy. And especially when I have a cup of coffee in my hands when I read it.

Well, I started to think about how nice it would be to have a newspaper . . . and some food. But I didn't have enough money for either of them. So I was getting kind of negative. But the thing is, God allowed me to find 79 cents so I could afford coffee. And He knows I love coffee. I could drink coffee all day on a normal day and not even be hungry. But this wasn't a normal day.

I walked up to the counter anyway and ordered my small coffee. When the guy brought it and put it on the counter, it wasn't a small coffee. It was huge! The largest they had. I said, "Oh no, I just asked for a small coffee."

He just smiled and said, "Merry Christmas." So I thanked him and I took it. But then he didn't charge me for it at all. So then I still had my 79 cents. It wasn't enough to get any food, but I still had my coffee, and it was snowing, and I was in my favorite place.

I sat down and started drinking my coffee. I watched the other people eating and talking. Some of them were whole families with kids, and they were talking about Christmas and Santa Claus and presents. All very excited, like they were having a party. I thought I could get depressed pretty quickly, so I tried to focus on where I'm at and the opportunities I have. I thought about the fact that I've still got a chance to kill Jeff and Chris. That made me laugh. And then it hit me. Tomorrow is Christmas and I have two Christmas presents waiting for me back at the apartment! And one of them is from Santa! I guess I'm still just a kid at heart, because that made me really happy. Plus, it was still snowing.

So I sat there and drank my coffee and tried not to focus on my hunger pangs. I tried to focus on just being alive. And the snow. And my present from Santa. By the time I was on my third cup of coffee, someone came up and tapped me on the shoulder. I looked up and this old man looked at me and said, "You want this?" I looked down in his hand and he had an Egg McMuffin, with bacon and cheese.

I go, "Oh, no thank you."

He said, "Please. I got two of them and I'm already full. I just feel like you need it."

I couldn't believe it. I stood up and gave him a hug and he said, "Merry Christmas."

I go, "You, too." We smiled at each other and he walked away.

Now, over by the coffee is the condominium stand, where they have things like pickle relish and mayonnaise that aren't expired.

"You mean the condiments?"

"Yes, that's the word."

So I took my Egg McMuffin over there, and I made a big sandwich out of that thing, I really did! And I ate it slowly! Bite by bite, and treasuring it every time I bit into it.

And the next thing I knew, somebody else tapped me on the shoulder and said, "You want this?" And it was a newspaper! And not just any newspaper. It was the big, heavy, Friday-before-Christmas kind of newspaper! And he wasn't trying to sell it to me either. He gave it to me. I just wanted to cry!

Everything I dreamed to do on Christmas Eve was coming true. I really don't have words for it. Just the joy of being alive. I was so happy. Even though for most people, that would all seem little. But once you've been starving, broke, throwing up for two nights, and alone, you learn to appreciate what you have.

And I did.

Kenny kept talking. But I'd stopped listening. Those last few words rang in my ear and set off an avalanche of thoughts and feelings.

I'd been poor. But never homeless.

I'd lived on Ramen noodles and cereal in college. But never hungry.

I'd bounced a few checks out of carelessness. But never had only seventeen cents to my name.

I'd even gotten food poisoning from eating expired food before. But I never had to go back for seconds.

Being happy with what you have isn't the most revolutionary insight. We've all heard it. We've all given it. But being happy that you've got a cup of coffee and a newspaper and that you're not currently vomiting out of both ends of your body was a reality check for me. As he sat in front of me and told me that his happiness was so overwhelming that it drove him to tears, I knew he meant that quite literally. I thought about how easy it was for me now to be unhappy if I don't get an aisle seat on an airplane, instead of thinking, "Oh my God, I'm flying!"

I decided to savor a few such thoughts and reset my own happiness threshold.

So I sat there and read the paper, got more coffee, watched the snow, read the paper, got more coffee. I didn't leave McDonald's until 4:30 that afternoon, and I'd been there since 9 o'clock in the morning. It was beautiful.

When I stood up to leave, I got one last refill on my coffee. I put a few packages of creamer and sugar in my pocket. And then I left to walk home. When I got there, I slowly drank my coffee. I still had a half a cup left when it got cold. Thank the Lord the microwave worked, so I could heat it up.

Then the Christmas movies came on, so I laid down on the couch and watched TV and drank my coffee. Then, when it was getting close to midnight, I remembered the tradition we had as kids. We got to open one present on Christmas Eve. And for a few more minutes, it was still Christmas Eve! I picked the smaller box from Chris. I opened it up, and it was a T-shirt, called Crappy. It had the words "I'm Crappy" on the front , C-R-A-P-P-Y.

I thought that was an odd thing to put on a shirt, but I kept listening.

It had pictures of lobsters and crabs on the front. That's what Maryland and Maine are known for.

Kenny must have seen the now-common mixture of confusion and amusement on my face that I got when he said something that wasn't quite right. I could tell he wanted an explanation, so I said, "Well, crappie is a type of fish. Could that be it?"

No, crappy. Like, 'you're just being crappy.'

And that's when it hit me. "Oh, crabby! You mean crabby, like a crab, right? Crabby is another way of saying grumpy or irritated. Crappy's another way of saying shitty."
Kenny erupted in laughter. It was part of what I was learning to love about him. Instead of getting frustrated or embarrassed over his verbal miscues, he laughs at them, honestly enjoying the almost slapstick humor the same way an audience to them would.
Kenny answered, still laughing,

Yes, that's it. CraBBy, like a crab. Of course.
Anyway, I loved it. It was so funny. I put it on to watch the rest of my Christmas movies. I watched until about 3 o'clock in the morning, till I fell asleep right there on the couch.
I woke up just before the sun came up. At dusk. Or dawn, whatever you call it. It wasn't very bright out yet. But it was still snowing. Everything was covered with snow. And the Christmas

tree lights were still on. I love Christmas. I love lights. I was so excited. I felt like a little kid again.

I went out onto the patio and scooped up some fresh snow in a big cup and took it into the kitchen. Then I got the packages of creamer and sugar that I brought back from McDonald's. I opened them up one at a time and poured them in the bowl. And if you've ever done it before, you know what that makes — snow cream!

"Snow ice cream?"

That's it! That's what I had for breakfast. This really was turning into the perfect Christmas.

I took my snow ice cream back into the living room and picked up the big present. I took my time opening it, while I ate my snow ice cream. When I finally got the wrapping paper and the lid off, it was amazing. It was the giant stuffed moose from the mall that I fell in love with! How did Santa ever know?

I laid back on the couch and played with the moose. Next thing I know, I fell asleep again. When I woke up, the moose was on my chest, staring at me. I just laughed. I said to it, "I guess I need to give you a name."

So I thought about it for a while. And that's when I thought about Marty. Marty was my best friend. And Marty is a good name for a moose. Plus, Marty always said that one of the things he missed the most after he became a quadriplegic was being able to feel what it was like to be hugged.

Well, this moose was gonna get a lot of hugs. So I named him Marty. And now I can hug Marty again, any time I want. And so I did.

In fact, sometimes when I travel now and give speeches, I bring Marty with me and put him on a stool next to me. Little kids sometimes come up afterwards to give Marty a hug.

And that's the story about 17 cents and Marty the Moose.

I laughed and applauded at the same time. "Did you ever kill Jeff and Chris?"

Ha! Not actually. They both came back at almost the same time the next day, because they had to go to work. When they came in, I was sitting on the couch with Marty. (I had to keep Marty away from them. I was afraid he'd rip their heads off because he was upset with them.)

They came in and looked at me. They said, "What's wrong? What's wrong?"

I said, "I almost starved to death because of you two. And I was planning on killing you both. But, because of Marty the Moose and you guys being nice to me for Christmas, I'm not gonna kill you."

And they go, "What happened? What happened?" So I told them the story I just told you. They started looking at each other and started blaming each other.

Chris said, "I thought you got food! You were supposed to go to the store before we left!"

And Jeff said, "No! I said I was going to my mother's. You said you were gonna go to the store!"

I just said, "Stop!" I could have just let them go and kill each other. Might have been nice. I'd just make myself another snow cream thing and watch.

Well, they felt so bad, they grabbed their coats and said, "We're takin' you do Denny's! You can eat all you want!" And we did.

I guess I learned my lesson. I never leave home without money. At least more than 17 cents.

And never eat expired food.

~~~

June 2002, I transferred from Gallaudet to the University of Tennessee in Knoxville (UTK) to get a degree in counseling. I loved helping people, but my teacher and psychiatrist told me that I could do more good for more people on stage than in one-on-one counseling. So I changed my major to theater.

One of the first things I had to remember was how different it was to be in a class with mostly hearing people. It's a lot harder. The professors aren't used to having deaf people in their class. When they go to the board to write something on it, I can't see their lips. But I know they're still talking. And even when they're facing the class, sometimes I have to look down at my paper to write things down properly. But when I do that, I can't see what they're saying, so that puts me behind. And sometimes these professors would have big, bushy beards. And back in those days, they were allowed to smoke a pipe in class. But with all that stuff in their face, it's hard to see their lips moving.

Anyway, at some point, I got a D on a research paper. I was starting to wonder if I made a good decision. UTK is really strict. If you want to get an A on a paper, it had better be good. Top notch! And I was feeling depressed about my grade, so I got on the bus to go downtown. I wanted to go to my favorite coffee shop and think. I didn't even bring my laptop. I just wanted to be alone. Just me and my God.

While I was on the bus, an old lady got on and sat right across from me. She kind of reminded me of my grandmother. And she started staring at me. Then she said, "Are you okay?"

"Yeah, I'm fine."

"Now, you cain't lie to an old woman," she said.

I told her, "You don't know me."

She said, "I don't have to know you. I have seven kids and fifteen grandkids. I know when someone is upset. Now . . . spit it up."

So I told her that I'd made a D on my paper. And she said, "So what? You made a D. It's just a letter. Is that who you are?"

"No."

"Do you feel dumb?"

"Well, yeah."

"But it's just a letter," she said. Then she asked me, "Two days ago, did you feel dumb?"

"No, ma'am."

"Are you any more dumb today than you were two days ago?"

"I guess not."

Then she paused for a minute. "You have a hearing problem, don't you?"

"How do you know that?"

"Your speech. And because you pay attention really well. I can see you looking at my lips when I talk. If I could get you to teach my grandkids to do that, I'd take you home with me right now."

And that made me smile. Then she said, "So about this D. What are you gonna do next time?"

"Study harder? Make a B next time?"

"That's the idea. Or maybe just shoot for a C. Something better. But remember, it's just a letter."

I talked to that old lady all the way downtown. And when I got off the bus, I wasn't dumb anymore.

~ ~

Ever since my heart bypass, I have to have a heart checkup every six months to make sure I'm okay. One day when I was in to see my doctor, he said, "Hey, Kenny, your heart's lookin' pretty good, but I need to ask you something. You're over 45."

"And?"

"When's the last time you had a colonoscopy"?

I said, "A what?"

"A colonoscopy, Kenny."

"A colo . . . a cococucu . . ."

"Co-lon-o-sco-py."

"A colocucu . . . A what?"

"Oh, good grief. A 'butt check', Kenny. When's the last time you had a butt check?"

"Ohhhh, a *butt* check," I said. "What are you gonna do?"

He said, "See that long hose over there. It's got a camera in it. I'm gonna stick it up your butt, and I'm gonna take pictures. I'm gonna look for polyps."

And I said, "I don't think I want that to happen."

Something about the way Kenny said that last sentence made me laugh out loud. Partly because of the turned-up nose and nasally tone he said it with. And partly just because I found that statement itself absolutely droll, both matter-of-factly dry and witty in understatement. I now use it myself when confronted with the prospect of something unpleasant.

"You won't feel a thing, Kenny. I'll give you a shot. We need to check because a lot of men over 40 get colon cancer, but it doesn't run in your family. You ain't got a thing to worry about. Most of your family has heart conditions."

I thought, "Okay. As long as I don't feel a thing up my butt, I'm okay." So I made an appointment and came back a few days later to have it done.

Now, once I learned sign language at Gallaudet, I could get a sign language interpreter to come with me for important things, like classes at school or going to the doctor, so I had an interpreter with me when I went back. I didn't mind being in the hospital gown in front of her. But they had a big mirror next to the table, and then another one over the bed. That's so you can watch the procedure they're doing on you. I guess some people want to do that. I don't know why. I don't even want to see my own butt naked at home. And I sure didn't want my interpreter to see it with a tube up it, so I asked them to move the mirror, and they moved it before I laid down.

They gave me the shot so I wouldn't feel anything. I didn't even know he was doing it. I was just talking to my interpreter the whole time. The doctor told me to talk to her since I wasn't gonna watch. At one point, he had to tell me not to move, so he told my interpreter and she signed that to me. Sometimes he told her to tell me to take a deep breath.

Then, after a few minutes, he tapped me on the shoulder and said, "We're finished." My interpreter started laughing when she told the next thing they said. She signed, "They say you have to go in the other room and fart."

I said, "Noooah. I'm not gonna do that. It'll stink."

The nurse said, "Well, everyone else is doin' it." And about that time, they rolled me past all these people lined up in a room. She said, "All these people are farting. They had the same butt check that you had."

I said, "But, it doesn't stink."

And she said, "No. That's because it's just the air that gets pushed in during the procedure. You can't leave until you get it all out."

So I laid there and I'm talking to my interpreter, and she just started laughing. I asked her what was so funny, and she said, "You're lucky you're deaf."

"Why's that?"

"Because you can't hear all these people farting right now and I can. I'm just glad it doesn't stink."

Well, that made me laugh. And the next thing I know, thhhhhhppttt! I let out the biggest fart! Oh, it was so embarrassing. A few minutes later, the nurse came in. And she didn't even ask me. She turned to my interpreter and said, "Did he fart?"

"Yeah, he sure did."

Then the nurse said, "Well, good, I don't trust him," and she smiled at me.

I had to go into another room to get dressed to leave. When I got done I opened the door and there was a nurse standing there waiting for me. She had a sad face and said, "The doctor wants you to stay. He wants to see you."

I asked, "Why?"

She said something, and I looked at my interpreter and she said, "You just need to go to his office. He wants to see you." So I went to his office. As I was sitting there, the doctor comes around the corner, and that's the same doctor who took care of me when I had heart problems, when I broke my neck, and now he had to come around the desk with red eyes. I could tell he'd been crying. He wasn't just like a doctor; he was my friend. He put his hands on my shoulders. He said, "You been through hell, left and right, Kenny. It hurts me to tell you this. You have cancer. Stage three. And unless you have surgery right away, I think you probably have six months to live."

I was just shocked. Absolutely shocked. I'm sure I sat there for a few minutes without saying anything. I was thinking, "My God, where is this gonna stop?! When?!" I didn't know what to do, so I just got up and put on my coat and started to walk out.

He stopped me and said, "Where are you going?" Then he turned to my interpreter and asked, "Does he understand what I just said?"

I said, "Yes. You can talk to me. I've got cancer."

"Well, where the hell are you going? What do you want to do about this?"

I said, "I'm goin' home. And I'm not doin' anything about this!"

He said, "You can't just walk out. You have to have the surgery. Why would you not want the surgery?"

"Because I'm just screwed, doc! I'm tired. I'm angry. Look at me! I've got scars all over me. I just got done recuperating from heart surgery and I went out and broke my neck falling off a cliff. I spent the last year in therapy for that. Now I'm done with that, and you tell me I have cancer."

I saw my interpreter crying, so I told her to shut up. At least that made her laugh. I figured if she was gonna be making useless noises, it might as well be laughter.

Then the doctor said, "Look at it like this. You're not afraid of death. I know you're a Christian believer."

"Okay."

"So let me open you up, and see if we can get all the cancer out. If it works, you'll wake up and you'll be alive. Now, there's a possibility you'll have to wear a bag for the rest of your life. But you'll live. And if it doesn't work, you'll wake up and see Jesus, you've gone to heaven. But if you wake up and see me, you've died and gone to Hell."

Everybody had a good laugh at that; me, Kenny, and the good doctor in the story.

I told him I still needed to think about it, so I asked him if I could go to the mountains and spend two months with my God to think about it. He said, "Sure . . . I'll give you two days."

I left his office and I was crying. And cussing. And that's a big deal because I never cuss. I was angry at the world and angry at God. "How could He let all these bad things happen to me?"

I went home and packed a bag and drove up to the mountains in North Carolina, where I like to go and be alone with God.

There's a place where the highway runs along the side of a cliff. I pulled the car over and got out. I walked over to the cliff and looked out over the edge. Still crying. Still angry.

I kicked some dirt and watched it go over the side. And I thought about if I should just go over with it.

I was just so tired and so angry.

The thought of another surgery was just more than I could stand. The scars on my neck were still pink. And I've heard stories about people who had radiation and chemotherapy. I've seen my cousin go through that. So thin and in pain. They give them as much morphine as they can, but it's not enough. Barely breathing at the end. I didn't want to die like that.

And even if the surgery worked, what if I had to wear that bag? The butt check bag. They said I might have to wear that thing the rest of my life. And all my poop and pee would go in there, and then I'd go to the bathroom and pour it out.

All that made jumping off the cliff look like a pretty good deal. But then, I thought, with my luck, I'd just break my neck again and have to have someone wipe my butt the rest of my life.

And then I started to think about what the doctor said, that I have a Higher Being I can believe in, and so it doesn't matter if I wake up to see the face of Jesus or the doctor's face. Either way, I'll be okay. I mean, it's not that I want to die and go to heaven right now. But if it happened, I'd be okay with it.

And then I thought this might just be another stepping stone in my life that I had to overcome in order to pursue my dream of being a storyteller. In my mind I thought, "Maybe this will give me stories to tell."

And I thought about how grateful I was that the doctor found this when he did. I mean, I had cancer. What if he didn't do that test and we just found out six months later, when I was dying and it was too late? So I was grateful to the doctor, and glad that I had the butt check.

And then I thought about Marty, and all he suffered through. I thought, if he could do it, so could I.

It all made me realize there was a purpose to all this. There was a plan. Just like there always was in my life since I've been walking with Christ.

And I just had peace.

I sat and looked out at the mountains a while. Then I got back in my car and drove home. I tossed and turned a lot that night, thinking about things. The next day, I drove around and walked around. I walked around a lot. Crying. Still a little angry. Still questioning God, "Why me?" Still thinking, "This is not happening." But I had a peace about it that I didn't have the first day.

The next day, I went to the doctor's office. I walked up to the nurse at the desk, and she looked up at me and smiled. She said, "They're ready for you, now."

I said, "Who is?"

She said, "The hospital. The doctor knew you'd come back a day early. Your room is ready." So I went home and packed a bag and came back to the hospital to check in.

The surgery was the next morning. Six of my friends came to the hospital to see me off. They all knew I might not make it through the surgery. After my heart surgery, the doctors had told us it was risky.

They wheeled me into the operating room. And once the doors are closed, all you can see through is this little square window at the top of the doors into the waiting room. And this is one of those times it's great to speak sign language. As the doors were closed, and I couldn't see their faces anymore, I saw six hands reaching up to the little window. All of them had their little finger, index finger, and thumb sticking up, and their other fingers down. That's sign language for "I love you."

Awesome!

When I woke up, I didn't see Jesus's face, so I figured I either lived or I was in Hell. One or the other. I was in a lot of pain and had tubes all over me. And because of the metal pins in my neck, I can't turn my head very well to see if anyone was in the room with me. That made it seem like I was alone. So it was looking more like Hell.

But then the doctor came over. And my interpreter was with him. And I could see some of my friends from work. I figured I must have made it. I looked down and I didn't have a shirt on. There was a big Band-Aid on my stomach and I could tell it was bloody underneath. I guess they needed to let it air out.

The doctor told me they had to take out a lot more colon than they expected, and there was a chance it could come back. But, in general, he said I came out of it okay. Only that didn't sound okay to me. He said I had 120 staples on my skin where they went in. And he said not to take off the bandage or look at it. They would change it later at the right time. He said, "Right now you're still drowsy, so we'll come back a little later."

Then he asked me if I was feeling okay. And I really wasn't. But I told him, "Sure. But I wish everyone would leave. I want to get some sleep."

He said, "Okay, but are you sure you're all right?"

"I'm fine. I'm fine."

After everyone left, I started looking around the room. They have this tray on wheels. The wheels roll under the bed and the tray sticks out over the bed on top of you. I pulled that over a little closer to have a look at what was on it. I knew there was a mirror on it. I raised the bed a little. I couldn't go far because I was in pain.

And, I guess like a little kid, when they tell you not to do something, it makes you want to do it more. I didn't understand why the doctor didn't want me to look under the bandage. It's my body. Why can't I look at it? So I grabbed the corner of the tape and just ripped it off. And I started cussing. It really hurt!

As the pain went down a little, I held up the mirror so I could see all the way down my stomach where they did the surgery. And there it was, all those 120 staples. It was all bloody. You could see the cut in the skin, and where it was all wrinkled where they had it stapled together. It was really gross. And I could still see the scars from my heart surgery. I looked like a monster, like Frankenstein.

I put the mirror down. And on the corner of the tray, there was a pair of scissors, the kind they use to cut the bandages off, I guess. And I'd just had it. I didn't want to live looking like a monster. And maybe I was still too drowsy to think straight. But I picked up the pair of scissors, and opened them up. One side was more pointed than the other. I grabbed it so the sharpest end was pointed at my chest. I closed my eyes, and I thought, "I'm just gonna do it, before anyone comes back." And I plunged the scissors at my chest, towards my heart.

I felt an awful pain! I opened my eyes and looked down. There was blood everywhere. But instead of going straight down into my chest, the scissors went sideways a little and ran into one of the staples. I always think of that day like I had an angel watching over me, moving the scissors just enough to save me from myself. That staple kept the scissors from going in too deep. But it popped out when the scissors hit it, which is why there was so much blood.

It hurt so much, I couldn't even think about trying again. Plus, as a faithful man, I really felt like God had sent that angel to keep me safe. And I had to respect His wishes.

So I just pushed the button to call the nurse in. They cleaned me up and put in another staple.

I didn't tell anyone I'd done it on purpose.

They made me take chemo pills for a while. And I had to go get X-rays every few weeks. But that was all fifteen years ago, and the cancer hasn't come back yet.

Months later, during one of our video calls, I asked Kenny if I could see his scars.

He laughed and told me lots of people have asked to see his scars. He told me one woman even came up to him after a show and ripped his shirt open to see them! She said, "There's no way someone who's been through all that could be as happy as you are. I had to see for myself."

There was an awkward pause. Then Kenny looked at me and said,

Oh, you're serious?

"Well, yeah, if that's all right? You've just talked about them so much. . . I mean, if you don't mind." It wasn't as uncomfortable a request as me asking about the old man in the bathroom. But it was still awkward. Especially because we were having the conversation over Facetime.

Kenny put his phone on the table in front of him. While he unbuttoned his shirt, I got to stare at the ceiling of his living room. The longer I had to wait, the more awkward the moment felt.

He picked up his phone and held it up to his neck. He moved the phone around until I had a clear view of the scars from his neck surgery. He explained again how they had to put in new bone and three screws after he broke his neck. The scar ran diagonally from the left side of his neck towards the front, just above his sternum.

Then he started moving the camera down his chest until a bright vertical scar in the middle of his sternum appeared. It began only an inch or two below where the neck scar ended and extended all the way down to the middle of his chest where it opened up into a wide, football-shaped pattern before returning to a thin, bright line. "That's from my open-heart surgery," *he explained.*

Kenny continued panning down. A few inches below the last scar, another bright vertical scar began that continued all the way down to where it disappeared behind the waist of his pants, which is where the tour appropriately ended. That was from his colon cancer surgery.

In all, he has a nearly continuous set of scars running from the side of his neck, all the way down to below his belly button. A permanent record of surgery and trauma. Of life and near death. Of pain and suffering and healing.

It was the most intimate moment of any we'd spent together before or since. And we weren't even in the same state.

~ ~

Most of the work I'd ever done was contract work and the contracts were always ending. Plus, I was in and out of school a lot. So, I was always looking for a job for one reason or another. It's hard not to feel worthless when you're always having to look for work.

I woke up one morning early and decided to go to Pigeon Forge. It was summer and classes were out. I just love the Gatlinburg area. I went to the McDonald's, because I love McDonald's, and I especially love the McDonald's in Pigeon Forge. One of the walls there is all glass, so you can see the mountains. It's beautiful.

I ordered coffee and sat down with the newspaper to look for a job. I guess I was feeling pretty sorry for myself. I looked up and the sun was rising. It was purple and pink, like looking at heaven.

I noticed the manager was walking around talking to people, asking them where they were from, things like that. At most restaurants, you'll see the manager in the back telling all the employees what to do, or in their office on the computer. But this guy was out walking around, and I thought that was really cool.

When he got over to my table, he looked down and noticed I had the paper open to the job section. He said, "Lookin' for work?"

"Yeah."

"We're doin' some hiring. You interested?"

I didn't expect that, so I just said, "Uhhh . . . nah. I don't think so."

"Oh. You too good for McDonald's?"

Well, I really didn't expect that. And I felt so embarrassed I couldn't even think of what to say, so I didn't say anything.

He said, "I had two people quit on me this morning. One of them just didn't show up." Then, it was the weirdest thing. He just said, "What size shirt do you wear?" And I hadn't even said anything. Then he goes, "You look like you could use a job." And then he smiled and kind of whispered, "Besides, McDonald's isn't that bad."

He asked me what kind of work I liked to do. I told him I didn't think I could work in the kitchen because I was deaf. "What if I turn around and walk into someone carrying a hot pan or something because I don't hear them coming? I could hurt someone."

He goes, "I tell you what. How about you just work out front?" He told me I could clean the floors, take care of the bathroom, make sure the coffee and all the condomin, uh, I mean the condiments are stocked up.

I smiled. And I imagine Marty did, too.

Anyway, I started feeling better right then. Someone believed in me and that felt good. So I told him I wore a large, and he went into the back and got me a hat and shirt. He said, "You go ahead and get changed. We'll do the paperwork later." I went to the bathroom and changed, and started work.

He turned out to be one of the greatest managers I ever worked for, anywhere. But I still felt a little strange taking a job at McDonald's, like I should be ashamed of it. But it didn't make any sense. If you told someone you worked at a bank or a grocery store, well that's okay. But if you tell them you work at McDonald's they might laugh or make you feel like you should be embarrassed.

Yet, McDonald's is one of the biggest charities for children in the world. They make sure kids all over the world get to see doctors and dentists. They help sick kids stay with their families while they're in the hospital. They give scholarships to kids that can't afford college. They probably do a lot more of that than other fast-food restaurants. So I don't understand why people thought it was so bad to work at McDonald's. But they did. And that made me feel that way, too, I suppose.

Anyway, when he gave me my McDonald's hat, I asked for the biggest size they had. And I wore it pulled way down over my face so you couldn't see who I was. That way, when I had to go outside to pick up trash, and my friends from school would drive through, they couldn't tell it was me. I didn't want anyone to know that I worked there.

Then, one day, I was sitting at a table taking my break, eating. But I still had my hat on. And all of a sudden, this man was standing next to my table. A big man, but older. Maybe in his seventies. A little grey on the side of his head. And I looked up, and he said, "May I sit?"

"Sure," I said.

He said, "Pull your hat up. I can't see your eyes."

I pulled it up a little, but not much.

Then he said, "Are you ashamed of your job?"

"Noooah."

"Well, why do you keep your hat so low? And why is it bigger than your head?"

"I guess I just like big hats."

He must have been a wise man, because he just looked at me and said, "Are you telling me the truth?"

And I'm thinking, "Who is this guy!?" But I didn't say anything.

He kept talking and said, "Why are you ashamed of working at McDonald's?"

I probably stuttered a little, but I told him about my friends from school that come by and how I didn't want to be embarrassed.

Then he said, "Let me tell you a story."

I said, "Sure."

He said, "Long ago, when I was a young man, a lot younger than you, and you know I'm black, right?"

If you saw how thick Kenny's glasses are, you'd know that wasn't a stupid question. Plus, it's hard to see through the brim of a hat.

"Yes."

"Well, we couldn't find jobs. Just mediocre labor. . ."

I knew Kenny meant "menial" labor.

". . . mostly garbage. Cleaning out the bathroom. Pickin' up after people. Pickin' up, pickin' up, pickin' up. That's all we did. So if anyone should ever be ashamed of what they did, it would be me."

And then he asked me, "Do you have a dollar bill?"

Oooohhhh, I thought. "Now I get it. This guy is a bum! He's just trying to get me to give him some money."

I said, "Yes, I've got a dollar." And so I took it out.

Then he reached in his pocket and pulled out a dollar. He looked at both bills. Then he looked at me. And he said, "Now, which one of these dollar bills is the oldest and dirtiest?"

And I said, "Well, looks like mine."

He said, "Okay. Just go with me on this. Let's switch. You give me your dollar and I'll give you mine."

So I did. Then he said, "Now, I want you to take your dollar, and go up there to the counter. What do you like to drink?"

I said, "I like coffee."

"Okay, you go up there and get yourself a coffee."

I told him I didn't have to pay for my coffee because I worked there. But he told me to pay for it instead. "Use that dollar in your hand."

So I went and asked the guy behind the counter to charge me for a coffee. He did, and then gave me my change and I got a fresh coffee. I went back and sat down with my coffee and the man said, "Okay. You got that with your dollar. Actually, it was my dollar. But we switched. Now here's my dollar. I want a Coke. Would you go up there and buy me a Coke with this?" And he handed me his dollar.

I played along. I went to the counter and bought him a Coke and got the change. Then I brought it back and sat down and handed it to him with his change.

Then he said, "Now, did you have any trouble buying that coffee or Coke?"

"No, sir."

"And you bought them both with a dollar. One was dirty and ugly, and the other one was pretty new."

"Yeah, I guess."

"This is the point of my story. When I was younger than you, I did all the dirty parts of labor. I also worked for McDonald's. Back when it first began. I worked there for seven years. And I was also ashamed. My friends would come in and see me there pickin' up the trash and sweeping the floors. Other people would come in and tell me I was in the right place doin' the right job because I was black.

"But I was worth more than that. My father and grandfather taught me to be a man, to be proud of wherever I worked, and to put every effort into whatever it was that I was doing." And then he said, "Just remember the dollar bill, and I'll make my point."

I sat and drank my coffee and just listened to him. He took a drink of his Coke. Then he said "Through the years, I did what you're doing, cleaned the floors, bathroom, kitchen. Even on the bad, stormy nights when the trash blew all over the place. Who do you think they sent out to clean the parking lot? Me! I knew from the day I started there who was gonna clean the parking lot, me. If the trash can falls over, all the white folks stayed inside. I went out to pick it all up. And I cleaned that parkin' lot like my daddy was watchin' me."

Well, I was already starting to feel a little more pumped up about my job. But he went on. He said, "I did that for about seven years."

I said, "The same position?"

"Yes. And then, they promoted me!"

"They did?"

"Yep. I got on line. I got to greet customers. Take orders. They trusted me with the money! I was a cashier, but back then they called it 'on-line.' And I did that job to the best of my ability. Like my daddy was watchin'. If somebody wasn't happy with their order, I got 'em a new one."

I was getting even more pumped up, listening to him. This was getting interesting. He had a job like me, and then they promoted him!

Then he said, "But I didn't stay in that job long. Six months later, they promoted me again. Assistant manager!"

And my eyes got really big. I couldn't believe it. I said, "This back in the 60s? And they made *you* an assistant manager?"

"Yes, they did. In fact, I was one of the first black assistant managers in that area. Not just at McDonald's, but in any restaurant! I worked hard and they believed in me."

"Good for you!"

"But that didn't come lightly. Remember, I'd already worked there seven and a half years. And then I was assistant manager for about two years. And guess what my next promotion was."

I just said, "Manager, I guess."

He goes, "Sure was. I became the manager of that McDonald's. Made good money, too." And then he said, "You still remember the dollar bill?"

"Yes, sir."

"Good. Keep that in mind. Now, I worked that job as a manager for several years. Then they offered me another promotion."

"They did?" I didn't even know what the next position would be. But it had to be important.

He said, "Yep. I became a district manager. For five McDonald's in the area."

"Wow. That's great!"

"Made really good money then. And, I didn't tell you I was married, did I?"

"No, sir."

"I had four children. Three boys and one girl. My girl is a doctor. She has a Ph.D. One of my boys is a lawyer. Another one is an engineer. And my last son, he's the manager of three hotels. And you know what? They all went to college and got their master's or Ph.D. But you remember that dollar bill?"

"Yes, sir."

"Well, who do you think paid for all those college degrees?"

"I don't know. College loans? That's a lot of college."

"Nope. I paid for it. All of it. I paid for all of it with money I earned working at McDonald's. I just retired a few years ago. I'm living a wonderful life. I have my own house, and a boat I go fishing on. Me and my wife travel all over the country having the time of our lives."

I just smiled. On the outside, and on the inside.

"Now, remember the dollar bill?"

"Yes, sir."

"You see what those dollars are worth? I doesn't matter if I'm black or white. Or if I earned that money as a doctor, or lawyer, or pickin' up trash at McDonald's. All those dollars are the same. Never be ashamed of where you work or what you do. How honestly you worked to earn that money, and what you do with that money, will say everything that needs to be said about who you are as a person."

"And there's no reason why you can't do all the same things I've done. You don't know it, but I come in here all the time. I've seen you before. I say 'hello' to you, but you just keep walking and don't look up and don't say anything to me." (I hadn't told him I was deaf, yet.)

He stopped talking for a minute while I thought about that. Then we both stood up and he shook my hand. He said, "So what do you think?"

I smiled and told him, "I think I'm gonna go get a smaller hat."

Kenny never got the man's name. In fact, he never saw him again. But Kenny still carries a piece of that man with him everywhere he goes. Any job he does, Kenny does it like his Daddy was watching him.

Like that old woman on the bus, the fat lady in the 7-Eleven, and the unfamiliar teacher who gave Kenny a bigger box of crayons, that man became one of those rare strangers who come in and out of life, only for an instant, but make an enormous impact on who we are.

We expect that of our parents, our bosses, family, and friends. We spend most of our lives with those people. And Kenny certainly had his share of those: his father, his mother, Aunt Jessie, cousin Jeff, Winston, Angela, and Marty, just to name a few. But it was the unexpected impact of these random strangers that was just dawning on me.

I tried to think of times I'd had a similar experience and was changed by a stranger. Nothing came immediately to mind. But then I had a more interesting thought. I wondered if I'd ever been that random stranger who made a difference in someone's life. Well, that seemed like too self-serving of a question to dwell on, so I quickly turned my thoughts to an even more important question, which was this: What kind of life would one need to live in order to be that random stranger all the time?

What kind of character or personality traits does it take? What kind of observational skills does it take to see that sad little boy among the hundreds walking down the hallway at school? What kind of wisdom does one need to have to meet a dumb kid on a bus and send him away a confident student? What kind of leader does one need to be to inspire a perfect stranger to pull his hat up and do his job with pride and confidence?

I didn't know the answer to any of those questions. But I was pretty sure they were worth spending time considering, and that anyone who did so, would surely make the world a better place.

~ ~

Now, if you know anything about Pigeon Forge, you know that's where Dollywood is. I'd been working at the school for the deaf as a counselor. But it was summertime now, and my job at McDonald's was only part time. I had a lot of people tell me I should apply for a job at Dollywood, so one day I decided to give it a try.

I went there and waited in the lobby. You had to take a number; and when they say your number, you could go in the back and have an interview.

But it was a slow day. They didn't have that many people there.

I saw there was a list of jobs on the wall, so I went and looked at it. One of them said, "groundskeeper." I went up to the lady at the front desk and asked her what that was. She said that was basically picking up trash, riding around on a little golf cart and pulling out the bag from the garbage cans and putting in a fresh bag. And you got to pick up cigarette butts with a long stick with a nail at the end of it!

And I said, "Oh, that sounds fun." I just wanted to be like a kid, enjoy my summer, see all the rides at Dollywood. And I don't know if you've ever been to Dollywood. But there's really good music and it's everywhere! They've got these big speakers. And they've got this little white church, and that's where Dolly Parton was baptized. It's a real church. They picked it up and brought it there. Her parents even got married in that church.

Anyway, they called my number, so I went to the back and met the guy. And he said, "I see here on your application that you're interested in being a groundskeeper. What brought you to Dollywood?" So I told him about my job at the school and what my friends said. And we talked a while. Then he said, "How would you like to be a street character?"

I said, "What's a street character?"

He said, "You'd be on the streets in different costumes, depending on what season it is. And you'd be greeting guests."

"Naw, I don't think so."

He said, "You're a people person. I can see it. You're funny. You're vibrant."

I didn't see that, but I didn't say anything. I just looked at him kind of weird. Then I said, "Naw . . . groundskeeper."

"Why do you want to be groundskeeper so bad?"

I said, "Because I don't like people."

He started laughing. "You *are* funny." Then he said, "You know, I'm a 'people'."

I said, "Well, that's debatable," and we both had a good laugh.

I didn't really know why we were even having this conversation. I just wanted to be a groundskeeper, and they obviously needed one. So I told him I could be friendly and say 'hi' to people. But I didn't want to be a street character.

"Why not?" I interrupted. I tried not to do that often. But clearly he was leaving something out. Something important.

Hmm?

He said that as if he didn't hear me properly. But I knew that he had. He was avoiding answering me. Or, at least buying himself a little more time to answer.
"Why didn't you want to be a street character? Most of your life you've loved working with people. But at that point in your life, you obviously didn't. Why?"

A pained look crossed his face. He was quiet for an unusually long time. His eyes got watery. And when he finally spoke, his voice was shaky.

Oh, boy. . .

More silence.

I don't know how to tell you this, Paul. 'Cause I'm still wrestlin' with it.
I was thirty years old . . . Every job I'd had was contract work, and the contracts ran out after two years . . . I felt like a failure . . . I guess I always felt worthless . . .

Kenny paused and shifted in his chair.

It's amazing. You'll be at a party, and you're the only deaf. . .

Another pause and shift. All of his words now, what few there were, came out through muffled sobs.

And . . . a lot of people I loved had died . . .

He was clearly searching for an answer that would satisfy my question. But perhaps more importantly, one that would satisfy him. He made a few more attempts, each similarly cut off in the first sentence or two. But I got enough to know that he had obviously been depressed. And with good reason.

After a few more starts and stops, he continued . . .

I guess one of the mistakes I made in life more than any other was feeling sorry for myself. And that made me push people away. Probably not the smartest thing to do, since that's when you need people the most.

I don't know if you've ever felt like that before. But sometimes when you get kind of depressed, you just don't feel like being around people. You just want to be a loner. It's like when you're in school and you go to the cafeteria. You see a table where all the football players are sitting. Another table with the cheerleaders. One with the rich kids. One with the nerds. Another has the ones with disabilities. Then, way over on the other side, are the tables for the loners. Usually just one or two people at a table. That's where I felt like sitting that day.

I waited for a while to make sure he didn't have any more to say about that. Then I said, "Thank you, Kenny. Now, what happened next?"

Well, at one point the man held his finger up to get me to stop talking, and said, "Wait right here." He went into the other room and came back a few minutes later with another man. He pointed at me and said, "This is him." Then he looked at me and said, "Tell him what you just told me. About why you don't want to work with people."

So I said it again, "I don't like people."

They looked at each other, and the second man said, "He'll be perfect!"

I thought, "Is he even listening to me?"

Then the first guy looked at me and said, "Did you know we have a new addition to the park? Up on the top of the hill, with the water fountains the kids can play in, and the ropes, and the water slide?"

I nodded.

He said, "I'd like you to go up there and just look at it. You'd be great with the kids as a park ranger."

Ugh. I didn't want to work with people, and especially kids! So I told them, "Look, I can't hear so well."

They said, "That's okay. You don't need to. We're talkin' to you and you're doin' fine. As a matter of fact, you'd be a bonus. Do you know sign language?"

"Yes."

"Great! When deaf people come in you can greet them and make them feel welcome."

I said, "You're supposed to be doing that already."

He said, "I know, but you'd be even better at it."

I still didn't want the job, but he said, "Just go look at the park. They haven't opened for the season yet, but you can go look at it." So I went to look at the park. It was really nice. But I still didn't want to be a character. I just wanted to pick up trash.

When I got back to the office he asked me, "Well, what did you think?"

I said, "It's nice. But I still want to be a groundskeeper."

Then he said, "Well, I've got bad news. That job's already been taken." So I looked up on the board where the jobs are written in chalk. And it had been erased.

I said, "It's only been ten minutes!"

He said, "Yeah, but someone else just finished an interview who'd be better for that job. You'd still make a great street character, though. Plus, you'd make more money."

I said, "I'm not here to make a lot of money. I just want to work and keep busy."

He said, "Well, if you want the job, you've got twenty minutes to make it to the costume trailer."

"What are you talking about?"

"You've got to be measured for your costume, the one you'll be wearing next week when we open the park."

Well, I wanted a job, so I walked over to the costume trailer. When I got there, three ladies looked up and said, "You must be the funny guy. You're Kenny, aren't you?"

"Yes, ma'am."

"Well, come on over here," they said. Then they measured every part of me, my neck, my head, my arms, my legs, my waist. Then they told me to come back Tuesday to pick up my park ranger outfit.

So Tuesday I went back and got my outfit. And then we did training for three days straight, to get ready for the park to open on Friday. We learned how to greet people, and how to look after rowdy kids. Things like that.

When I started on Friday, I began to think about other theme parks or fair grounds I'd been to. I remembered back to when I was little and we would go to those places as a family. Once the greeter found out I was deaf they just ignored me and talked to my mom or dad. And that really hurt, especially for a little kid. I thought, "What did I do wrong? Why won't they talk to me?"

But it didn't just happen at theme parks with deaf kids. I noticed it happened to people in wheelchairs, too. Like at a hotel. I was checking into a hotel one time, and I saw a woman and her husband come in and go up to the front desk. The woman was walking but the man was in a wheelchair. And the person behind the desk asked all their questions to the woman who was standing. "Does he need anything special for the room . . . Would he like someone to carry his bags up to his room?"

Things like that. And the guy is sitting right there! Why don't they ask him?

I didn't want Dollywood to be the same as all those other places. So that all gave me an idea. I told all the other greeters to let me know when someone came into the park with some kind of disability—in a wheelchair, cerebral palsy, Downs syndrome, deaf, blind, mentally challenged—whatever. And I wore this pager. So if they saw someone who was blind come in, they would text me 999. And if they were deaf, it was 888, and so on.

When I would get a page, I'd go to their area and they would point me to the person and I would go greet them personally.

My first one was a little girl with cerebral palsy in a wheelchair. When I got there, I said a big 'hello' to the whole family. Then I got down on one knee right in front of the girl and said, "And how are you doin' today, little angel? My, aren't you a pretty thing?"

And the little girl started shaking and making a funny noise. I thought maybe I'd scared her or made her mad. So I stood up and looked at her mother, and said, "What did I do? What did I do?"

She had a sweet smile on her face and her eyes looked watery. She said, "Oh, you didn't do anything wrong. That's how she laughs. You made her happy. Most people don't talk to her. And nobody has ever called her an angel except for me. Thank you."

And that's when I knew I was doing something right.

Another time an older man came in with some other people. He was probably in his sixties, and he was deaf and blind.

I got the 999 page, and I went to the front to meet him.

He was standing with his family and had one arm laying on top of the arm of the woman standing next to him, so she could help lead him around. I walked up and said hello to all of them. Then I turned to him and put my hand out and said, "Welcome to Dollywood, sir." But he just stood there and didn't move. I looked over at the other people and they said, "He can't hear you. He's blind and deaf."

I said, "Ohhhhh." Then I reached out and tapped him on the front of his other arm. When I did, he reached up like he was trying to grab something, so I held out my hands under his and I started to talk to him in sign language. Well, you'd have thought he turned into a kid again. He took his other arm off the woman and reached out with both hands to read my signs. He had a huge smile, and we talked for quite a while. It seemed like he didn't get to talk to people very much. That happens a lot to deaf people. Most of the time people don't learn sign language even if someone in their family is deaf.

Eventually I had to tell him that I had to go because I had other guests I had to tend to. But I told him and his family that if he wanted to talk to me again, just have one of the employees page me and I'd come find him. I got to see him once more, as he was leaving. He told me that was the best day he'd had in a long time, because someone took the time to talk to him in sign language.

It's funny. All I wanted to do was pick up trash. But I ended up making so many people happy. That turned out to be one of the best jobs I ever had. I guess sometimes God has different plans for us.

I thought about how many times I'd seen that happen in my own career, and others'. I've been put in an assignment I thought I'd hate and then loved it so much I didn't want to leave. I've seen people grudgingly accept roles working with people they didn't like, but ended up learning more from those people than anyone else.

I concluded there are a lot of reasons why that happens. In my case, my boss simply knew more than I did about the pros and cons of different jobs. After all, that's why she was the boss and I wasn't. I should have trusted her judgment more than I did.

In Kenny's case, I think his own depression blinded him to what he really needed and would be good at. Fortunately, the Dollywood managers could see through all that. When you have several people telling you you're wrong about something, it's a good sign that maybe you should listen.

But the other reason I think this happens, is the impressive human capacity for resiliency and a positive mental attitude. That I'm-going-to-make-the-best-of-this-crappy-situation outlook on life. Usually, when you adopt that attitude, whatever little thing you didn't think you'd like about the job will get swamped by the many things you find to love about it.

Then one day, after we'd been open about two weeks, it started raining really hard. I was at the Ranger Park, standing underneath a carport with a lot of other people to wait for the rain to stop. And I saw this woman walking up the hill wearing a yellow raincoat with a hood. She came up to where we were all standing and took her hood off. She was dressed kind of plain, wearing blue jeans and a baggy western shirt. It didn't look like she had any makeup on or fingernail polish or anything. And her hair was all smushed down because of the hood.

She saw my uniform, and walked right up to me. She said, "I want to thank you for being here. This is my first time to see this part of the park since it opened. And I think it's just great!" Then she asked me, "How do you like working here?"

I told her, "It's fantastic! I never dreamed I'd get to work here. But it's really been amazing."

Then she talked to some other employees standing there with me. And then she said, "Well, I've got to go get ready for a show. It was nice talking to all of you." And then she pulled her hood back up and walked back down the hill in the rain to where she came from.

About that time, my boss came driving over in a little golf cart. He jumped out and ran up to all of us and said, "What'd ya'll think? What'd yal'll think? Wasn't that awesome? You got to meet her!"

I didn't know what he was talking about, so I said, "Meet who?"

He said, "Seriously? That was Dolly Parton."

I said, "Nawwww. That wasn't Dolly Parton." But then I saw in the newspaper the next day that Dolly Parton was in town doing a show.

I thought that was pretty neat that she showed up like a regular person and walked through the rain just to meet us. And then she talked to us just like we were no different than her. It was just the way I wanted our disabled guests to feel, so I thought that was pretty cool.

~ ~

I'd been heavy most of my adult life. I mean, I was fat! I got up to 310 pounds at one point. I would just eat a whole bag of potato chips. When you're like that, you just don't care.

Back then I was working as a counselor at the Tennessee School for the Deaf in Knoxville. One day I remember I was walking down the hall in the dorms. And I could see the shadow of two little boys coming up behind me, just about waist high.

One of them was walking like this . . .

Kenny held his arms out to his side in big, round curves, and rocked back and forth like a waddling fat man.

I knew they were my kids. I just didn't know who yet, so I turned around real quick, and said, "What are you doin'?"

Then the boy who was waddling said, "You're fat! You're fat!" He was kind of a mean kid.

The other little boy just came up to me and hugged me. Well, hugged me what he could. I was pretty big. So I hugged him back, and then I moved him away. He started crying and saying, "I don't want you to die, I don't want you to die!"

I said, "Who told you I'm gonna die?"

The boys said, "The other counselors." They'd overheard them talking to each other, and they said I would probably have a heart attack if I didn't do something about my weight.

That really moved me.

I realized what a bad example I was setting for the kids, and we're talking about fifty-three boys.

I wasn't like that when I was young. I used to work out. I used to play sports in school. In high school, I played football and ran track. I ran the 440 and 880. I ran the relays where you pass the baton. And I did the hurdles. I loved running. And at Gallaudet, I did wrestling and even tried gymnastics for a while. I was in great shape! I guess being in school and around other guys keeps you motivated to stay in shape.

But I realized I was also miserable being so overweight. Just getting in the car, I couldn't fit behind the steering wheel! I had to move the seat back all the way just to squeeze in. But I'm not that tall, so then I'd have to move it up as far as I could just so I could reach the pedals. Then you turn the wheel and it's hard because your belly is right there getting in the way.

I started going to the gym. And it was working. I started losing weight. But, it was like a yo-yo. I would lose some weight, and gain it back. Lose weight. Gain it back. I got down to 270 pounds at one point. But I knew if I wanted it to really work, I needed a personal trainer.

But I didn't want one who was gonna treat me like everybody else, or like an old man. I wanted one who would treat me like me, so I asked God to send me the right person. Someone that would be more like a brother.

Well, that was the same day I was starting a new acting class at UTK. I was in class with my interpreters. It was a three-hour class. And you had to have two interpreters for long classes, so they could take turns. That way they don't get ternal syndrome, or whatever you call it, from all the signing.

"Carpel tunnel syndrome?"

That's it.

Anyway, my back was turned to the door. Then, all of a sudden, my interpreters and a couple of other girls in the class turned their heads and looked right past me to the door. And they all had that look on their face. It's that face that people make when they see someone they think is really good looking, like they were about to drool all over themselves.

Then one of my interpreters said to one of the other girls, "He's either married, or he's gay." I turned around, and there he was. This guy was just walking in late. His name was Matt. And he was very handsome, and muscular. He was built like a body builder and he dressed like a model. And the way he took off his scarf and his hat. It was like he knew all the girls were staring at him. I just thought, "Gross!"

Well, I must have said it out loud, because one of the girls said, "You're just jealous."

I said, "No, I'm not!" I don't like people like that who *know* they're that good looking.

We had a break in the middle of class, so I went outside to walk around. And I just felt the Lord talking to me. He was saying that Matt was gonna be my trainer. I just thought, "No way!" I went back to class. After class was over, I felt drawn again to go ask him to be my trainer. But I just said no.

We had that class two days a week. And for the next two weeks, I kept feeling moved to ask Matt to train me. But he would always leave class before I did, so I used that as an excuse to not ask him. Plus, I thought it would be weird for a guy to go up to another guy and ask him, "Hey, would you work out with me?" I'm old enough to be his daddy. It might just be creepy.

So I told the Lord I'd make a deal with Him. The next Tuesday, right before class, I told God that I would ask Matt to be my trainer, but *only* if Matt stayed after class, and it was just me and him in the room. Nobody else could be in the room. Just us two.

When class was over, I started packing up my bag. After a while I looked up, and there Matt was, still loading up his backpack. Just taking his time. Then I looked around and realized, there was nobody else in the room. Just us two. And I thought, "Why did I make a deal!? Now I have to do this! Now I'm gonna be embarrassed." You've really got to watch what you pray for. Because you just might get it.

I walked over to Matt. He saw me coming, and he said, "Man, you're funny. I just love your video." We'd been making videos for the acting class.

I said, "I appreciate that." Then I said, "I'm gonna ask you a weird question, so don't think I'm tryin' to come on to you or anything. But, can you train me? I really want to lose weight and get in shape."

He said, "Sure. That's what I do part-time anyway. I love to be a trainer. I'm working on that and physical therapy." Turns out he was also a nutritionist, and he liked to kickbox and wrestle. And I like those things, too. We became like brothers overnight.

Well, not long after that, Matt came over to my house. He opened my refrigerator and pantry and a got a trash can. Then he just started throwing away all the junk. All the potato chips and dip. Things like that. Some of it he took for himself, because Matt could eat like a pig. Like a pig and a horse and an elephant. And he'd still have a six pack. But most of it he threw away.

I started training with him, and doing kickboxing and eating smarter.

When I met Matt I weighed 298. Today, I weigh 214 pounds. And it's all because of Matt.

FOUR DAYS WITH KENNY TEDFORD

After four days of stories, and dinners together, and watching us play squishy ball in the backyard, it occurred to me that something magical was happening. Somehow, without even trying, Kenny had worked his way into the heart of my family. My two introverts were charmed by his very presence. My nine-year-old chatterbox was enthralled into a raptured silence by his stories. And Matthew had finally overcome his discomfort with house guests, which has since lead to even more courage and comfort meeting new people and making friends.

But most insightful was my wife's reaction to the whole visit. Her original apprehension started to disappear when she realized she and Kenny shared something very important to both of them, their Christian faith. Plus, not much will endear someone to a loving mother more than winning the affection of her children. But there was more, so much more as I would find out later when I asked her to reflect on the visit.

She said, "You remember that story he told us at dinner about his trainer, Matt? Matt said things to him like, 'Come on, fat boy, move it!' Matt wasn't coddling him. He was pushing him like he would anyone else and expecting just as much."

She felt like that story gave her license to treat Kenny just like anyone else, too, and that was such a relief. Because, the truth is, most of us don't have a clue how to treat people with disabilities. We either pretend we didn't notice the disability, or that it doesn't exist, or we go overboard in a showy display to accommodate every imagined difficulty. And if we're not doing either of those things, we just shy away and avoid the person entirely.

And since shying away and pretending his disabilities didn't exist weren't options for Lisa, she probably felt pressured for the showy display option. The story of Matt relieved her of that burden.

She also appreciated his self-deprecating humor. "He makes fun of himself all the time. That puts people immediately at ease. When you're uncomfortable because you're unfamiliar with someone's limitations, or perceived limitations, you're not sure how to interact with them. The fact that he's so open about and makes fun of his own challenges, it puts you at ease, because he's at ease."

Lastly, she realized something about herself that we we're all guilty of, imposing limitations on Kenny that he didn't have. She explained: "For example, I found it interesting that he drove here by himself. I didn't expect that. Not knowing what his limitations were with his deafness and all of his health problems, I imposed that limitation on him. And it wasn't one he had."

"Not that he's a child, but I think parents do that with our kids all the time. We're often surprised at what they can do because in our minds, they're just kids. I realized I was doing the same thing with Kenny."

Indeed, we all had. But, over the time he was here, his disabilities just seemed to fade away and we got to know him as a person. We got to know him as the sweet, charming, and funny man that he is.

Lisa had been worrying how she was going to make this man comfortable in our home, given all of his challenges. "But," she concluded, "Kenny lives with those challenges every day, so they're not a problem for him. They were just a problem for me. And if he doesn't have a problem with them, why should I? Once I realized that, getting over those preconceived notions turned out to be easier than I thought."

Chapter 14: Graduation

While I was studying theater, I realized that the two performers who'd been influencing me the most were Red Skelton and Marcel Marceau.

I remember watching the Red Skelton show with my family when I was growing up back in the 1960s. One scene I particularly remember from that show was when he had Marcel Marceau as a guest. Marcel Marceau was a mime. He did all his acting without saying a word. When Red Skelton introduced him to the television audience, he complimented him by saying, "You are marvelous!"

Marceau responded without words. He turned his head, and waved Skelton away. Then took his hand, reached behind his back, and handed Skelton a white carnation. Skelton took the flower, and bowed to Marceau to show that he appreciated it. All without saying a word.

I understood everything that was happening. The gestures, facial expressions, and body movements told the story. I learned that an entertainer could eat, drink, and even talk without making a sound. Every time I played with my dog, Susie, I pretended I was Red Skelton or Marcel Marceau. When she liked my performance, she would lick my cheek, or bark and wag her tail at me. If I was boring, she'd lie down and fall asleep.

I could tell if she was interested when she tilted her head. And I knew I was miming the right way if she would come and look in my hand for food when I pretended I had food in it.

Susie was my first audience.

So here it was, forty-seven years later, and I thought, "If it's possible to get my dog interested in my performances, imagine what I could do with a human audience!" Susie convinced me that having deafness was a gift. From that time on, I watched comedy shows, mime performances, movies with famous actors like Marlon Brando or Clint Eastwood, and particularly old, black-and-white movies with Charlie Chaplin. And that helped me do better in my theater classes at UTK.

Kenny was determined to finally get a college degree he'd tried and failed to earn at MSU and Gallaudet. And, perhaps without knowing it himself, he used the same three tools he used to learn to walk again after breaking his neck.

First, at fifty, he was no longer the lazy student he was in his twenties. He attacked his studies with vigor and diligence and seriousness.

Second, he didn't let pride get in the way of asking for help like he had done so often when hearing words he didn't understand. This time, he made sure he had interpreters in all his classes so he wouldn't miss a thing. Plus, he didn't hesitate to ask a friend or roommate to explain something in a textbook if he didn't understand the words.

And last, this time he found his inspiration not in a person, but in an idea. He knew he could help people with his stories, which he was doing one-on-one or in small groups. But imagine how many lives he could touch if he could speak to audiences of five hundred or a thousand at a time! And he'd become convinced the only way to do that was if he had a degree. "Who's going to want a nobody without a degree to speak to audiences like that?" he thought.

Getting his degree was his way to achieve the dream he'd had since the third grade: To be that stick figure man on the podium making the world a better place through his stories.

In August of 2008, at the age of fifty-four, Kenny Tedford received his Bachelor of Arts degree in Theater from the University of Tennessee at Knoxville.

Not long after I got my degree, a friend of mine named Libby Tipton told me about a Master's program in Storytelling at ETSU. That's East Tennessee State University in Johnson City. I loved storytelling, and that sounded like the perfect degree for me. I made an appointment to see the man in charge of the program, Dr. Sobol.

I went to Johnson City. When I got to his office, the door was closed, so I knocked on it and waited. Nothing happened, so I knocked again. Then I heard someone yell something that sounded like, "I said, 'Come in!'"

He sounded a little impatient. I went in real quick and said, "Hello, my name is Kenny."

"Oh, you're the deaf guy!"

"Yes."

"Oh, I'm so sorry. Can you understand me?"

"Yes, I can."

"Well, come in, come in. Have a seat." Then he cleared off some books from the chair on the other side of his desk. And we sat and had a nice chat. I kind of just rambled like I'm doing now, telling him about my life. Then he told me he could see me as a storyteller, and that I had a gift. But he said the master's program would take a lot of time and effort. Then he said, "Before you spend a lot of money and get involved, I want you to do something. There's a National Storytelling Conference going on in Gatlinburg. It just started today. There are world-famous storytellers performing there, and your friend Libby will be there, too. I want you to go there tomorrow and see if you like what you see. If you do, come back here Monday and we'll start the paperwork."

My ears perked up when I heard the name of the conference. At first, I thought it was a mistake. But I confirmed it several times. It would be at that very same conference, exactly four years later, that Kenny Tedford and I would meet! Except that time we would both be invited to attend not only as participants, but also as speakers.

What a small world, I thought. I couldn't wait to hear what role it played in Kenny's life before it brought him to me.

I drove to Gatlinburg the next morning and went straight to the convention center. I remember opening the door and going up the steps. I was nervous because there were so many people there and I didn't know any of them. Everyone was just standing around. I guess they were on a break. Little groups of people standing here and there.

Now, I've been to lots of conventions before. Usually it's a bunch of businessmen standing around. They might even say hi to you. But mostly they just listen to the speakers and take notes. And then you go to your room and that's it. But I could tell this place was exciting just when I walked through the door. And I hadn't even heard anyone speak yet.

I passed a man in a wheelchair wearing a gas mask. Well, it wasn't a gas mask. It was to help him breathe. He was really thin, and I assumed he had cancer or something. He didn't look very well. I saw him take the mask off when he wanted to talk to somebody, and then he'd put it back on.

There was a Native American couple who I found out later told stories while doing dances. There was a Mormon man there who told stories with little pieces of folded up paper. There was an Indian woman in her native clothing. Everybody was laughing and talking. It was like I walked into a fairy tale. Even now I get goose bumps just thinking about it.

Even then, I started to feel moved. Since I was eighteen, I've always asked God for guidance, to give me some kind of sign. And He was giving it to me. I felt at home here, and I'd just walked in the door!

I went up to the counter, and there were two ladies there. That's where they give out the name badges and a little folder. Sometimes at these things, you even get a coffee mug with the name of the event on it. And maybe the name badges would have little colored circles on them that let you get into different events, like the big ball.

I just walked up and said, "I'm looking for Libby."

The lady said, "Oh, are you deaf?"

I said, "Yes. That's why I need Libby."

"Oh, okay. She's interpreting a storytelling event right now. But I'll go get her."

She stood up and I said, "No, no, no. Don't do that. I can wait."

Both of the women looked at me funny, and some other people stopped to look, too. And then a man stuck his head out of an office door nearby. I guess I must have said it too loud. The lady said, "Oh, we don't mind."

So I said it even more firm. "Do. Not. Get. Libby. She'll kill me."

Then they started laughing. "Why would she kill you?"

I told them, "That woman is dangerous! Do you know who she is? My God, you do not go get Libby when she is interpreting for deaf people."

The snarky smile on Kenny's face told me that accusation was unconcealed sarcasm and these women knew it.

Well, that made them laugh even more. But then they turned around and started talking with their back to me, so I couldn't tell what they were saying. I thought maybe they were gonna call the police because of what I said, even though I was just teasing.

They kept talking with their backs to me, and even with the man in the office, back and forth. One lady started typing on her computer and printing things out and stuffing them in a folder. Then she handed me the folder. On the front of it was my full name, Kenneth Lee Tedford, Jr. Then she said, "This is your name tag," and she hung it around my neck. "You can attend anything here."

I just looked at her. I said, "Oh. Well, I saw the program, the cost of the workshops, the speeches, the breakfast. That's all like, three hundred bucks. I can't afford that."

"Oh, silly. We took care of that. You go enjoy yourself. There are people behind you in line I need to take care of." And she smiled at me.

I walked away looking at my name tag with tears in my eyes. I thought, "This is not happening." It was like a dream. But I knew there was a purpose to it. If I lived like Christ tells me to, there would be a purpose.

About thirty minutes later, Libby came out. She smiled and came up to me and said, "Come on. The next session is about to start. The storyteller is Doc McConnell!" Apparently, Doc was a famous storyteller. Everybody was excited to hear him talk.

We went in and walked all the way up to the front. She told me to sit on the front row.

Exactly where Kenny and I met, I thought with a smile.

And she went up on the stage right in front of me so she could do the sign language interpreting.

And the next thing I saw was behind me. It was the man in the wheel chair with the mask. Some ladies were pushing him up to the front row right next to me. I thought that was pretty cool that I would get to sit by him. I already liked him since he didn't let his sickness and his mask keep him from talking to people.

When they got to the front, the man stood up out of his chair and started walking, all by himself. But he didn't sit down by me. He kept waking past me, and up the stairs right onto the stage. That was Doc McConnell!

He sat down on a stool in front of the microphone, and took off his mask. Doc told the most amazing stories that day. The crowd laughed with him and cried with him. When he had his mask off, I watched him. When he put it on to breathe, I watched Libby. By the time he finished an hour later, I knew I was home.

A line of people went up to meet him and hug him, and some of them were crying. But, one of the neat things about being deaf and sitting on the front row is that I got to him first. I walked up and said, "Wow." Libby introduced us and he shook my hand. She told him I was gonna get a master's degree in storytelling.

He told me, "Good for you!"

I stayed the rest of that day and the whole next day. At the end, everybody stood in a huge circle holding hands and singing songs. People like me made new friends. Other people said goodbye to old friends.

On Monday, I went back to ETSU. As soon as Dr. Sobol saw me, he said, "I knew you'd be back." I filled out the paperwork, and started classes.

Doc passed away a week later. August 16, 2008. That was his last performance.

I added Doc McConnell to the list of people along with the old lady on the bus, the fat lady at 7-Eleven, teacher with the box of crayons, and the old man at McDonald's. One more stranger who passed through Kenny Tedford's life only for a moment, but made an enormous difference. One more stranger who helped make Kenny Tedford who he is today.

As part of my master's program, of course, I had to write and tell a lot of stories. Most of the stories I told then, and that I tell today, are true stories about me or what I've seen happen in my life. But some of them are fairy tales.

One time when I had to write a new story, I started thinking about the fairy tales I heard in the first grade the ones where

none of the characters ever had any disabilities. And how the
teacher told me that when I grew up, I could write stories with
any characters I wanted. You remember?

"*I do.*"

So I did!
I wrote my own version of *Cinderella*. Only in my version it
was called *Cinderella and the Hot Pink Wheelchair* because in my
version, Cinderella couldn't walk. So when her fairy godmother
turned her rags into a beautiful white dress, her old, rickety
wooden wheelchair turned into a fancy, hot pink wheelchair,
like one of those racing chairs you'd see in the Paralympics. With
Firestone tires! Then, when she turned the pumpkin into a glass
coach, it had a powered loading ramp for her wheelchair. And
when Cinderella got to the castle for the ball, the fairy
godmother turned the steps into a ramp so Cinderella could roll
right down into the ballroom, straight into the waiting arms of
Prince Charming!
Next, I wrote my own version of *Snow White and the
Handsome Prince*. Except, in my version, it was called *Snow White
and the Blind Prince*. And you can guess why.
My teacher was right. I could make my stories have any
characters I wanted. And they didn't all have to be perfect. They
could be like anyone.

*A half century had passed since he made that observation and
challenged himself to right that wrong. And he made good on it.*

Around that same time, I started doing a lot more
performances. I started acting in community theater. I did some
comedy routines. Spoke at storytelling festivals. I performed in
some movie shorts produced by other students. And I started
giving speeches for organizations and at conferences.

The one I was most proud of is one I called "The Magic Crayon." Of course, I told the Magic Crayon story from when I was a kid. But I also told them about growing up deaf and with brain damage, about my parents dying, wanting to grow up to be a storyteller, about labeling people, and how I got to where I am today.

The first time I gave that performance was at the Crumley House Brain Injury Rehabilitation Center in Limestone, Tennessee. I chose the Crumley House for my first performance because one of my main goals as a storyteller is to help people with disabilities. And that means helping the people who take care of them, too. And at the Crumley House, I knew there would not only be people there who were disabled, but also their parents, spouses, teachers, counselors, doctors, and nurses.

I wanted to tell my stories to anyone who is part of the lives of people with disabilities, so they could understand what life's like for them. I want those people to understand how easy it is to label disabled people and prevent that labeling from happening.

When I started that first performance, I wasn't sure it was working. There was a young man near the front, sitting backwards in his chair, facing the window. He didn't seem interested in anything I was saying.

Then, about ten minutes into the story, as he listened to other people laughing and shaking their wheelchairs and yelling out "Amen!", he turned around in his chair and started laughing. That was the highlight of the performance for me.

When it was over, one of the nurses asked me to come over to where she was standing next to a man in a wheelchair. The man was pushing with his arms with all his might, trying to stand up out of his chair. He tried a few times, and couldn't do it, so he fell back down in his chair. But then he sat up straight and smiled and started clapping. He looked at me and said, "I apologize for not being able to give you a standing ovation."

It really moved me. But all I could say was, "Thank you." It was a really humbling moment.

Then a lot of other people came up to me and told me they were inspired by my performance. It really made me feel like I had accomplished what I came to do. But then this one 85-year-old military veteran kind of summed it all up when he said, "You tell great stories for a retarded, deaf guy."

Kenny's face lit up as he let out three or four full belly laughs, and concluded:

That about says it all.

~ ~

Up until this point, every part of Kenny's life that I'd documented had happened before I met him. So while the events spanned six decades of time, to me they all had a similar sense of past-tenseness, historical events separated from me in space and time.

But there were two meaningful events that happened after we started our interviews. And that made them somehow more tangible and real.

One was in the Fall of 2013. Kenny had started working again at the School for the Deaf in Knoxville. He described it to me less than a week after it happened . . .

I was walking across campus with some of the teenage boys I counsel. All of a sudden, they started grabbing my arms. I said, "What are you grabbing me for?"

One of them said, "You're falling over."

"No, I'm not."

"Yes, you are!"

Then, one of them said, "Kenny, for the last three days, you've been walking like a drunk." Then he told me he wasn't gonna tell my boss that I was drinking on the job. He said, "We'll just keep it between us."

And that was pretty funny, because he knows I don't even drink.

Well, I had to go to the doctor's office that week anyway. I'd had another stent put in my heart recently, and he was supposed to check on it. While I was in there, he said, "I think something else is wrong. I notice that one of your eyes is open more than the other. And your behavior is a little odd. I'd like to ask you some questions." Then he started asking me questions like, "Are you seeing any spots?"

And I told him, "Yes, I have."

Then he said, "Are you losing your balance, or have you fallen in the last week?"

"Yes."

So he said, "You're goin' straight to the hospital. Now."

"No, I'm not. I've got work to do."

"Not anymore. You're either having a stroke, or you had a stroke, or you're bleeding in the brain."

So I went to the hospital, and they did an MRI. That's how the brain doctor found the stroke. It was in the lower back of my ce-RE-bell-EE-um. Or, cere-BEE-llum. I can't pronounce it. Anyway, the back, left part of my head.

I guess that's the part that controls balance. Because if I'm not careful when I walk, I look like I'm drunk. I kind of fall over to the left. But it also made my vision worse, too. So now it's tough for me to walk up and down stairs. I can't really tell where one step stops and the next one starts. I just see the wood, or whatever it's made out of.

The next time Kenny and I met, I paid close attention. I walked slower and let him hold my arm when we had to navigate stairs. Even the step off the curb after leaving a restaurant made him a little uneasy. He seemed older and more fragile than the man I remembered meeting just over a year earlier.

But the more time I spent with Kenny, and the more my affection for him grew, the more important it was for me to complete this project. Not for me, or even for the world, but for him.

What if another major heart attack or stroke cut his time short, and I hadn't finished his story? Would it be something I'd regret for the rest of my life? Would I find myself thinking, "I wish I'd just worked a little harder on that manuscript" or "If only I'd made it a bigger priority."? I wish . . . I wish . . . I wish . . . If only . . . If only . . . If only. Disappointing myself was both forgivable and forgettable. Disappointing Kenny was becoming unthinkable.

Each time we met, my commitment and motivation grew.

~ ~

The second post-interview event was when he found out in 2014 that his younger sister Mary Bess had cancer. . .

She was very sick, and she didn't have long to live. I didn't want to see my sister in that kind of a state. I hadn't seen her in seven years, and I just wanted to remember her as my little sister. All bubbly and sometimes quiet. Just my baby sister. She's a tough cookie. Always very independent. Wouldn't allow anyone to do anything for her. That was just Mary.

I got a postcard from my sister-in-law, who I haven't seen in twenty-seven years. With big, bold letters, she encouraged me to go see Mary. "PLEASE, GO SEE MARY BEFORE SHE DIES."

A dear friend named Jim, who I consider a spiritual advisor, and a friend, and a fellow storyteller, he told me I need to go see Mary. I need to get closure. I need to hear Mary say she loved me one last time.

So I went to Memphis, from Jonesborough, Tennessee. By the time I got to the hospital, she was already in and out of a coma. As

I went to look for her room, a nurse came around the desk and I told her I was looking for room 520.

She said, "Please tell me you're Kenny, you're Mary's big brother."

I said, "Yes, I'm Kenny."

And she grabbed my hand and pulled me away. She led me to room 520. She rushed me in and pointed me to my sister. She said, "Talk to her. Talk to her. You're all she's been talking about. Her big brother, Kenny. I know she'll fight to wake up if she hears your voice. Talk to her. She can hear you."

So I leaned over and kissed her on the forehead. And I said, "Mary, this is Kenny."

I looked over at the nurse and she said, "Keep talking. Keep talking. I know she'll wake up."

So I said it again, several times. "Mary. Mary. This is Kenny. I came to see you." I had already been holding her hand. I had it cupped in mine. Then, all of a sudden, her hand moved up and back down to the bed. Then her body raised up a little bit, and she started breathing heavier and heavier.

I turned to the nurse again because I was concerned and I didn't know what was going on. The nurse had tears running down her face. And she said, "Keep talking. Keep talking. She's fighting to wake up."

So I turned back to Mary, and I said, "Mary, it's Kenny. I came to see you." Then suddenly, her eyes opened up! And she looked at me with her sparkling, beautiful eyes. And she said, "Kenny! You came to see me!"

I said, "Yes, Mary, I came to see you."

I turned to the nurse again, and she was crying more now.

She said, "Oh, this is amazing. She woke up to see her big brother." And then she left the room.

I looked back at Mary, and she started squeezing my hand. And she said, "Kenny! You really came to see me."

"Yes, Mary. I came to see you."

Now Kenny was the one crying. Not in the story. But here in front of me.

And just like Mary would say, even as a baby girl, she said, "Why?"

I just laughed and laughed and then cried at the same time. But she just looked at me. Then she reached over for a Kleenex in a box beside the bed. And she handed it to me and said, "Stop it. Stop it . . . I'm not goin' nowhere."

The nurse came back in. And she still had tears on her face. She looked at me, and she had the most beautiful smile. And she said, "Now, tell her a story. She's been waiting to hear from you. Tell Mary stories."

So I did. I started to tell Mary stories about she and I when we were young. I told her stories about her and a dear friend, Sharon.

Mary started smiling and wobbling her head back and forth. Agreeing to the stories. I went on for about fifteen minutes. Stories about family and friends, only stories she would know. But mostly telling her how much I loved her. She mumbled several times, but I couldn't understand what she was saying. Then, finally, we both just looked at each other. It was peaceful, and amazing . . . the way she looked.

And then she looked at me, and smiled, and said, "I love you, Kenny."

I said, "I love you, too, Mary." Then she closed her eyes and went back to sleep.

It was so awesome that I had the chance to say goodbye. And to hear those words that Jim said I needed to hear: "I love you, Kenny."

Later that day, I got to see my other sister, Sandy. We had a good time talking, and sharing stories. When it was time to go, I followed Sandy out to her car. She turned around and told me she was proud of me. Then she hugged me. She put her arms around me and gave me a kiss on my cheek. And she said, "I love you, Kenny . . . I always have."

I said, "I love you too, Sandy." I would have cried, but I felt so peaceful. I felt like a new person. I'd grown so much from just hearing those words, "I love you, Kenny." First from Mary, and now from Sandy, both on the same day. And I got to tell them I loved them, too.

It turns out I had finally learned the lesson that I started to learn when I was eight years old. To not ever have to say, "I wish I had said . . . I wish . . . I wish . . . If only . . . If only . . . If only." I had gotten to tell both my sisters how much I loved them on that same day in Memphis.

And I'm so glad I did. Because that was the last time I ever spoke to either of my sisters again.

Mary died two days later. She never woke up after I spoke to her in the hospital. It was March 10, 2014.

Four months later, I got a text from my nephew, Ted, in Bartlett, Tennessee. He begged me to pray for his momma, Sandy. Said that she was very sick on Friday. Thursday she had gone in for just an office visit with the doctor about kidney stones. She was supposed to be home the same day. Later that night he texted me again and said they didn't think she would make it till morning.

I prayed that night, and the next morning I got another text from Ted. He said his mom had passed away in the night. It was July 5th. I was just in shock. But at the same time, I had peace, knowing that I had a final chance for them to tell me, "I love you, Kenny," and that I'd been able to tell them. Those words are powerful.

Kenny'd had the faraway stare for some time now. His voice weak and halting. Eyes red and glassy.

I always encourage everyone, no matter how shy they are. And particularly for men who are raised to never say that, because it's not masculine or it's not a man thing to do. That's crazy! I say "I love you" to everyone who's important to me. Not just members of my church or my family. But my friends.

We all need to hear those words every once in a while. It's not that hard.

Midmorning on the fourth day, our time had come to an end. It wouldn't be our last set of interviews. But it would be the last to happen in my home. As he was about to step into his car to leave, Kenny turned to me and said,

Do you know what my two favorite parts of this visit were?

"No," was all I said. But what I was thinking was how fascinated I was by the question and even more fascinated to hear the answer. It could have been so many things: being in a house full of people, being around children again, home-cooked meals, staying in a home he described as one he could never afford.

It was none of those.

One was when Matthew asked me to come upstairs and tell more stories.

Kenny's eyes lit up like a child on Christmas morning as he told me.

Oh, brother, that was the greatest thing ever! That's when I knew I was getting through to him.

As a storyteller, Kenny lived for that kind of feedback. Glowing reviews on feedback forms at the end of a speech are too impersonal and perfunctory. Even a standing ovation pales in comparison. Everyone knows all it takes is a handful of people to stand up and stretch their legs in the front row and the rest of the crowd will follow like lemmings. But a nervous, introverted, teenaged boy, taking a risk by walking uninvited into the bedroom of a half-naked deaf man to request an encore performance? Now, that's high praise.

"And the second thing?" I asked.

Watching you play with Ben in the backyard the day I got here.

"Really? Why's that?"

Because it showed how important it is to you to be a good father, and that reminded me of my daddy. I mean, you had a guest who'd just arrived in your home. You could have told Ben you'd play with him later, but right now you had to pay attention to me. Or, you could have told him that we had too much work to do, since I've only got three or four days here. But you didn't. That's his time to spend with you every day, and you gave it to him. It was like watching my daddy play with me.

Thank you.

I joined Lisa on the porch to wave goodbye. As he pulled away, I glanced at Lisa to see a look that told me we were thinking the same thing. I've interviewed hundreds of people for books, or articles, or podcasts, many of whom end up meeting my family.

Kenny wasn't just another one of them.

He was one of us now.

How remarkable a thing it was that had just happened. In the course of four days, Kenny had gone from professional colleague, to friend, and finally to family member. Certainly not something I expected to happen. But perhaps that's because it wasn't like any other four days you might spend with someone. In those four days, I'd witnessed most of a lifetime go by, six decades of Kenny Tedford's lifetime, in all its bittersweet detail.

Like I'd learned from his dinner with Sandy, the witch who became his angel: Once you get to know someone, really know them, it's hard not to like them. Or, in this case, even love them.

Whatever the explanation, the little restaurant box of crayons that was my family now had one more member, and felt more full of color than it ever had.

I wondered what beautiful pictures we'd make together next.

~~~

"I think we should tell people how things worked out at ETSU, don't you?"

Yeah, for sure.

I had four more heart surgeries during the two years I was working on my master's degree. But I kept going.

Then, in 2011, I got invited to be a featured storyteller at the St. Louis Storytelling Festival scheduled for early May of that year. It was a long way from Johnson City. But classes would be out by then. I'd miss one event I was supposed to attend. But I thought getting to speak in front of a big audience in St. Louis was more important, since that's the whole reason I was working on the degree in the first place.

Well, I went to St. Louis and gave my performance. I told them about growing up deaf and with brain damage. I told them some new funny stories I was working on. And I finished by telling them the Magic Crayon story. Only I didn't tell them it was about me.

At the end, I told them that little boy grew up and studied hard. And that his dream eventually came true. Even though he wasn't in town to get the diploma himself, that very morning at 11 o'clock, that little boy received his master's degree in storytelling. And today he is a professional storyteller, speaking in front of a huge audience.

And as I was telling them this, I pulled out that funny square hat they make you wear when you graduate. And I put it on. Then I reached up and picked up the tassel and moved it over to the other side of the hat. And I told them that it was a true story. And I knew it was true, because I was that little boy.

I thanked them and bowed, and the audience applauded. It was the proudest moment of my life.

It's hard to believe. It'd been a half a century since they laughed at me for thinking it, for thinking I could grow up to be that stick figure man behind the podium. But on that day, and on that stage, I had become a master storyteller.

Chapter 15: Your Own Box of Magic Crayons

What I Learned from Kenny

If you are someone with different abilities:

#1 <u>Believe in yourself</u>: The biggest barrier to your success isn't your disability. It's your attitude. Your success might come harder than for other people. And it might take you longer. But you can do it. Believe that you can succeed, and you can. Believe that you will fail, and you will.

#2 <u>Be the teacher</u>: Don't be offended when people violate all the advice in the section below about how to be around people like you. It's natural. Look at it as an opportunity to teach them. When they ask you questions, just answer them as directly and honestly as you can, even if the questions hurt: "What's it like to be in a wheelchair? Why do you talk funny? Is it true blind people hear better? You seem different, what's wrong with you?" Answer their questions. Then you can teach them how to ask it better if you think they should. Be a teacher, not a victim.

#3 <u>Share your stories</u>: You'll remember your own life better by telling your stories. More importantly, your stories will help other people navigate life when they face similar problems. And as Kenny found out, sometimes your story could even save a life.

#4 Find strength in your faith: One of the greatest benefits of spirituality is its ability to help people face seemingly insurmountable challenges. Regardless of what your religious background is, having faith in something bigger than yourself is a comfort worth investing in. When you put something else worthy at the center of your attention, everything else in life seems to fall into a better station.

#5 Know that you are loved: Many of the factors that most influence risk of suicide (lack of financial stability, social inclusion, or freedom of mobility) disproportionately affect people with disabilities. What Kenny found that most helped him deal with depression and thoughts of suicide was the reminder that he was loved by the family and friends around him. When you find yourself feeling depressed, and we all do, don't push away the people who love you. That's when you need them the most.

#6 Forgive others. Forgive yourself: Everyone gets treated badly now and then. But people with different abilities sometimes get taken advantage of more than others. Find it in your heart to forgive people. If you don't, the anger will eat at you like a cancer. And while you're at it, forgive yourself. Give yourself room to make mistakes by forgiving yourself for not being perfect.

#7 Lead by example: Treat other people with different abilities the way you want to be treated. This shows other people how.

#8 Turn bullies into friends: It's easy to not like people you don't know. But once you get to know them, even a little, it's pretty hard not to like them. Get to know your enemies. Besides, if they had a friend like you, maybe they wouldn't need to be a bully.

#9 Don't take yourself too seriously: When you laugh at yourself before anyone else does, they won't be laughing *at* you. They'll be laughing *with* you. Self-deprecating humor keeps you from feeling like a victim, and helps others relax and feel more comfortable in your presence.

#10 Be happy with what you have, instead of focusing on what you don't: You may not have your sight, or hearing, or legs that work like everyone else. But that doesn't mean you can't be happy and appreciative for what you do have. Even if all you have at the moment is a cup of coffee and a newspaper, focus on that. Make the best of even the worst situations and maybe they won't be the worst situations anymore.

#11 Dream big: Don't discount any idea because you think someone like you could never do it. If a cognitively impaired, deaf boy who couldn't speak until he was ten years old can become a master storyteller, you can do anything. Be inspired by those you love and admire to accomplish those big dreams.

#12 Every time you fail, try again: It takes an enormous amount of perseverance to succeed in life even when the deck is stacked in your favor. You'll need more. Once you've dreamed those big dreams, keep at them until you succeed.

#13 No matter what job you do along the way, work hard and do it with pride like your mom and dad were watching you: Every dollar you earn is worth just as much as a dollar earned anywhere else. How honestly you work to earn that money, and what you do with that money, will say everything that needs to be said about who you are as a person.

#14 Use your common sense, just like everyone else: Don't leave home with only 17 cents in your pocket. Balance your checkbook every month. When people offer to help you, let them. Listen to what your doctors and nurses tell you. And no matter what, never ever eat rotten tuna or spoiled mayonnaise.

#15 Say "I love you": Especially to the people you love, so later you won't find yourself saying "If only . . . If only . . . If only . . ." or "I wish . . . I wish . . . I wish . . ." You never know when you won't have another chance.

If you love someone with different abilities:

#1 Learn to speak their language: If your loved one is deaf, learn sign language. Blind? Learn Braille. It sounds obvious. But most people don't do it because it's hard. Learn it anyway.

#2 Walk a mile in their moccasins: Learn what their life experience is like. Rent a wheelchair for a day. Wear earplugs for a weekend. Wear a sleeping mask for an hour (supervised by a friend). Be creative. Learn to feel their pain, their fears, their thoughts. Cry with them. Laugh with them. And never stop loving them.

#3 Do not be ashamed of them: Don't hide them from family and friends because they're embarrassing to you. Show them off the same way you would other children or friends. They need to know you're proud to have them be part of your life.

#4 Don't impose limits on them so they don't impose on themselves: Assume they're just as capable as you are. If it's not a problem for them, it shouldn't be a problem for you.

#5 Let them struggle: That's how people learn. Resist the urge to swoop in and solve all their problems for them before they get a chance to try and fail. Be there. But be there as a safety net.

#6 Don't talk down to them: Speak to them in the same tone of voice you would with anyone else. The patronizing, sing-songy tone people often use when talking to infants or pets should be reserved for infants and pets. Everyone knows what you're doing. For the same reason, avoid pointing out how "special" or "brave" they are. They know what you mean. Just talk to them like you would anyone else.

#7 Recognize you have disabilities, too: Whether it's getting lost driving a car, struggling with 8th grade algebra, or something else, we all have different abilities and different disabilities. Sometimes your ability is someone else's disability. And sometimes it's the other way around. Kenny Tedford is perfectly comfortable speaking on a stage in front of hundreds of people. Can you say the same? Have some humility and compassion for other people's disabilities. That way maybe they'll have compassion for yours.

#8 Talk openly and plainly about taboo topics: Whether it's religions, sex, or politics, people who have less than perfect vision or hearing, or who are non-neurotypical may be less likely to follow the euphemisms or the other wink-and-a-nod subtleties used to discuss such matters. Just say what you mean.

#9 Don't introduce them with their disability: She isn't your "deaf friend." She's your friend. He isn't your "autistic brother." He's your brother. You don't need to warn anyone about their abilities. They'll find out soon enough on their own. Would you like to be introduced as someone's "fat sister" or "ugly brother?" Probably not. The qualifier isn't necessary. Drop it.

#10 Include them: Take them with you to the zoo, ball game, movies, or anywhere else you go with other people. Saying you left him with Grandma because "It's too crowded at the game; he wouldn't enjoy it," is really an excuse for your benefit, not his. Did you go running with them before the accident? Try pushing their wheelchair on your next run. Didn't invite your brother to the opera because he's deaf, and you didn't think he'd enjoy it? Ask anyway. Most would tell you, "Don't say 'no' for me. Let me do that. I might surprise you."

#11 Don't invalidate their feelings: "You're too funny to get depressed. . . You're not the kind of person to let your disability bother you . . . That's not like you." You might think saying things like that show you're being supportive. It denies their feelings. Maybe they're just telling you that their life is hard right now. Acknowledge that.

#12 Watch your language: Words can hurt. And social norms with language change over time. The words "retarded" and "handicapped" used to be common. Now they're considered demeaning. Keep up with what language is most respectful. Or, better yet, just ask what they prefer.

#13 Say "I love you" to the people you love: This is so you won't later find yourself saying "If only . . . If only . . . If only . . ." or "I wish . . . I wish . . . I wish . . ." You never know when you won't have another chance. (Yes, we wrote this one twice. It's that important.)